PICKING UP THE TAB

Picking Up the Tab:

The Life and Movies of Martin Ritt

Carlton Jackson

Bowling Green State University Popular Press
Bowling Green, OH 43403

Other books by Carlton Jackson:

Presidential Vetoes
The Great Lili
Zane Grey
J.I. Rodale: Apostle of Nonconformity
The Dreadful Month
Hounds of the Road
Who Will Take Our Children?
Hattie: The Life of Hattie McDaniel
A Social History of the Scotch-Irish

As co-author:

Foundations of Freedom
Challenge and Change
Two Centuries of Progress

As editor:

Zane Grey's *George Washington: Frontiersman*

Fiction:
Kentucky Outlaw Man:
A Novel Based on the Life of George Al Edwards

© 1994 by Bowling Green State University Popular Press

Library of Congress Catalog Card Number: 94-79194

ISBN: 0-87972-671-7 clothbound
       0-87972-672-5 paperback

Cover design by Dumm Art

This book is lovingly dedicated to my grandchildren:

Colleen, Megan, Katharine
Travis, Patrick, Austin

Acknowledgments

So many people help to write a book that it is impossible to say just who was the most significant. Basic good manners, however, dictate that some effort be made. First, no author would go very far without good libraries and librarians. One of the best in this country is the Margaret Herrick Library of the Academy of Motion Picture Arts and Sciences in Beverly Hills. I wish to pay tribute to the wonderful young people at Herrick Library who helped me with this project (and also a previous project, *The Life of Hattie McDaniel*): Val Almendarez, Laureen Asa-Dorian, Lisa Epstein, Steve Garland, Tony Grezman, Lisa Jackson, Lynn Kirste, Amy Lejman, Scott Miller, Naomi Selfman, and Elaine Thielstrom. If I omitted someone, please forgive me: thanks for your help.

In the course of writing a biography, especially one that deals with a Hollywood personality, one comes into contact with all sorts of egos. Therefore, I wish to thank all those Hollywood personalities (who are discussed in the text) for their aid through personal or telephone interviews or through letters. Mrs. Adele Ritt, at my invitation, read the entire script, and made numerous useful suggestions, as did my friend and colleague, Joe Millichap of WKU's English Department.

Local librarians play the most important part in faculty members' efforts to write anything. Therefore, I thank Susan Gore and her staff at the Interlibrary Loan Department at Western Kentucky University for their unfailing courtesy and willingness to help. The research committee at Western Kentucky University helped with funds, and I am, of course, appreciative. I would be remiss in my gratitude if I did not mention the help and support that have come to me over the years through Professor Richard Troutman, Chairman of the Department of History at Western Kentucky University. But, of course, as we all know, the departmental secretary, Liz Jensen, actually runs the department, and my gratitude to her knows no ends.

viii   Picking Up the Tab

Finally, I must thank my family, who has stood by me so many years: my children, Beverly, Daniel, Matthew, and Hilary; and the grandchildren, Colleen, Megan, Katharine; and Travis, Patrick, and Austin. And to Steve and to Grace. And, as always: Pat.

Western Kentucky University   Carlton Jackson

Contents

Preface

Martin Ritt was the greatest maker of social movies up to this point in American history. That is why—because I have been teaching U.S. social history now for over three decades—I wrote this biography. The themes he employed are right at the heart of the American experience. As my book quickly makes clear, I was much more interested in content in dealing with Martin Ritt than in method. Of course, method is important; it is the instrument by which one exhibits his beliefs and philosophies. I have maintained throughout my work, however, that Ritt's method was the cinema; his substance was themes of social injustice, individualism, the loner, the outsider, and the religious person who only wants to do well by his fellow man. These are the reasons I maintain that my biography of Martin Ritt is not just another Hollywood biography: Ritt rejected most of Hollywood's glamour image; and certainly his ego was not anywhere near the Hollywood average. He was common—if anyone who lives most of his life in the aura of Hollywood can be judged so—in his tastes and appetites. He eschewed most social functions, the lifeblood of Hollywood celebrities. His routine was to go to bed at 9 each night (except when *Monday Night Football* on ABC went beyond such time) and get up each morning at 5. He certainly was not one of the show-biz thousands who think they have to work all night and sleep all day. He was an American original, and I hope my book will show that characteristic.

With his movie career, Ritt started out with *Edge of the City*, a film about the horrors of racism. His second endeavor, *No Down Payment*, reflected the ready willingness of many Americans to go into hock for what they considered to be the American Dream. His third and subsequent films dealt also with the human condition; what it is that *humans* have to face in points of realistic life situations. No matter what political crisis is going on at the moment, the lives that most people live today are the same as they lived yesterday. It

1

was this theme that Martin Ritt so wanted to capture; it was this theme that he did capture.

Martin Ritt's life was so paradoxical. He was born a Jew in New York City, yet he delineated Christian lives in the American South. He loved the South, as only an outsider can. He came the closest of any movie director in the twentieth century to show what the historical and the contemporary South were and are really like. He approached the South—as indeed he approached all his other subjects—from a nonjudgmental view. He did not start out with either praise or condemnation, without first examining the facts—to know if there were any exceptions to the prevailing philosophies—or stereotypes. Like a good historian, he let his research lead him to his conclusions; he did not have the conclusions before he began the research. When I am discussing each of Martin Ritt movies, some readers may conclude that I get more into a *book* mode than a *film* mode. There is the risk that I tend to critique each movie as though it were still the book, novella, short story, or article from which the movie was adapted. There were some instances when Ritt made a film from a book that was quite a wide departure from the original script of the author. *The Sound and the Fury*, for example, comes to mind, as does *Hud* and *Stanley & Iris*. But it must be kept in mind that Ritt's forte was the cinema; whatever he adapted to suit the cinema had to meet the criteria he wished to pursue. Thus, no matter if he did depart from the material from which his material was taken, he remained faithful to the intent, whether that intent was manifested in a northern or a southern setting. Martin Ritt was faithful to the materials laid before him to such an extent that never before had any director been able to match him in this respect, nor, for that matter, afterwards.

What was it like to see Martin Ritt's films on the screen? There was actually very little violence: no car chases, no slasher killings, and no overt sex orgies. There was nothing of a panoramic nature that would attract people to a Martin Ritt movie. His motion pictures were filled with dialogue and personalities. With the exception, perhaps, of *The Great White Hope* and *The Molly Maguires*, there were no great panoramic crowd scenes in Martin Ritt movies. There was development, denouement, and conclusion, but there were no great dramatics.

That is why Martin Ritt comes off better on small-screen television than on wide cinematic expanses, and this, of course, explains why it is easier to analyze Ritt's films from the book perspective than the movie. It is certain that he read every novel from which he made a movie; but he trusted the screenplay in most instances more than he did the original creation.

In this biography of Martin Ritt, I have tried to present *why* he made the movies he did, and how. Motivation is everything. I hope I will attract an audience who appreciates, first of all, good films (*Hud, Sounder, The Spy Who Came In From the Cold, Murphy's Romance, Stanley & Iris*, and many more that were socially oriented), but also those readers who recognize that the truth can be sought after in many forms; in this instance, the form is cinema. First and foremost, Martin Ritt's quest was that of social justice. He used his films to achieve that realization. Throughout his long years of moviemaking, he was more right than wrong.

Chapter 1

◆ ◆ ◆

Genesis of a Filmmaker

In 1963, when Martin Ritt was shooting *Hud*, possibly his most remembered movie, he spent some time setting up the cattle slaughter scene.[1] One of his scriptwriters, Harriet Frank, Jr., recalled how he did it:

None of us knew the business end of a cow, I could tell you. I'll tell you how much he [Martin Ritt] knew about cattle. In *Hud* he was trying to arrange cattle as if they were actors for a scene. Trying to put them in the right positions, you see. He went up behind one huge cow and tried to push it, to move it where he wanted it, and it let go all over Marty. From his breast bone on down to his toes. You can imagine the sight he presented.[2]

For some time Ritt just stood still, unable to say or do anything. A Texas cowboy named Bob Hinkle,[3] strode up to him, and said in a slow, infuriating Texan drawl, "Hell, Marty, it's just grass and water."[4] When he finally could get his voice back, Ritt exploded, "Yeah, but it's still shit!"[5]

(Years later, Frank and her husband, Irving Ravetch, wrote this scene into the script for *Norma Rae*. When Norma Rae and the union organizer are out in a pasture, he slips on a pile of fresh cow manure. Norma Rae laughs and tells him, "It's only grass and water.")

The story illustrates how, at just about every making of a Martin Ritt film, there was at least one incident that lasted for years in the memories of the participants. When he was making *Norma Rae* in Opelika, Alabama, he amused and entertained not only his crew but the good citizens as well by suddenly starting to tap dance in the middle of a street.[6]

Ritt was amusing, cajoling, and demanding, and his actors and actresses loved him for it. They always knew

5

where he was coming from, and where they stood with him. From *Edge of the City*, his first movie, in 1957, to *Stanley & Iris*, his last, in 1989, Martin Ritt was, along with Frank Capra and Sidney Lumet, a distinctively non-auteur director, avoiding genre as much as possible. He moved easily from one subject to another in his filmmaking; he could capture the motifs of the "Western," the "Southern," and the "Eastern," with equal ease, and gained the reputation of being the foremost maker of social films in the United States. He believed the social approach the best way to make a statement about numerous things in America he deemed unjust and inequitable. As Charles J. Maland said about Capra, Ritt "came to see filmmaking . . . as a moral responsibility."[7]

He became notable, too, in filmmaking circles, for being an "Orson tamer," and a "Richard tamer." Orson Welles worked with Ritt on *The Long Hot Summer*, and Burton on *The Spy Who Came In From the Cold*. He met these two forceful personalities head-on; an act that built up the mystique of his Hollywood reputation.

Did his Jewish background have anything to do with the kinds of movies he made? Over the years, he himself said no. But he could not ignore his ethnicity any more than blacks could avoid their past when making films. Ritt knew his history. He knew of the persecutions of Jews over the centuries, just as blacks were aware of their downtrodden positions. Perhaps Ritt was subconsciously affected by a minority frame of mind. Maybe that is why he tried so hard in his movies to uplift and glorify the human spirit.

Martin Ritt's father, Morris, liked to put on airs as he frequently strolled through "Alphabet City" (Avenues A, B, and C in New York's Lower East Side) wearing a black coat with a velvet collar, a derby hat, and carrying a cane. Though he was not an aristocrat, he wanted his neighbors to think so because of his life's experiences.

Born in Berdichev, Russia, about 1884, he immigrated to the United States in 1909 but was not naturalized until several years later. He had worked as a second mate on the Hamburg Steamship Line, and in the process had learned German and two or three other languages, and had landed several times in American ports. Also he spent a few years in Switzerland working as a civil engineer. Thus, when he decided to settle permanently in New York, Morris Ritt thought of himself as more sophisticated and street smart than most of the other immigrants.

Morris opened an employment agency for newly arrived immigrants and became an important figure around the neighborhood of Avenue B and 10th Street. He could usually speak to the newcomers in their own languages, an ability that impressed everyone who met him.[8]

On 2 March 1914, however, he was not much interested in impressing his neighbors or counseling immigrants. He had not even kept up with local news for the past few days— a practice developed on his arrival in America. He paid scant attention to the fact that the worst storm in 12 years was hitting New York, cutting off power and turning on fire alarms all over the city,[9] or that his favorite team, the New York Yankees, had arrived in Houston, Texas, for spring training. He was on his way to the Lying-In Hospital on Second Avenue and 7th Street where his wife, Rose, was getting ready to deliver their first child.

Rose Lass (a name later changed by some of her kinsmen to Lewis) was born in 1892 in Bialystok, Poland,[10] (at that time occupied by Russia), and she immigrated to the United States as did her future husband, in 1909. She met Morris at a social function around 1911 and the two were married a year or so later.

Morris Ritt was somber and serious toward matters in life, but Rose Ritt turned out to be the opposite. A neighbor described her as a "tough cookie."[11] She smoked, drank, drove a car, and if the occasion called for it, "cussed like a man."[12] Once, according to local tradition, Rose accepted a ride through Central Park with an acquaintance. When he got "a little personal," Rose insisted that she heard a noise that must be a flat tire. When he got out to inspect, Rose slid across the seat, put the car in gear, and took off, leaving her would-be lover behind.[13] She also had the disconcerting habit of grabbing small boys' crotches and jokingly asking them if they had wet their pants.[14]

The child born on 2 March 1914—their first child—was a boy, and they named him Martin. Martin Ritt would go on to worldwide fame as an actor and film director.

After she had borne Morris Ritt another child, a daughter named Dorothy, Rose started her own career. She became an agent, with her office on 46th Street, for chorus girls. For many years Rose Ritt was well known in New York circles for her work with models, chorus girls, and would-be actresses.

For some time the family continued to live in the Lower East Side. They did not, as so many of their Jewish compatriots did, change their names once they got to America. In the early part of the twentieth century, Jews were stereotyped into certain businesses and occupations. They were "supposed" to go either into banking or the clothing business. Possibly, Morris did not change his name because it did not sound Jewish. It sounded German, and no one automatically assumed that Morris was from Russia and Rose from Poland.

Martin found himself in the middle of a highly ethnic neighborhood where, as the saying went, "it was Europe in the homes and America in the streets." When he got to school age, he went to Public School 64; in the afternoons when finished with regular schooling, he spent many hours at cheder, or Hebrew school. Going to and from cheder made Martin and his Jewish classmates open targets for other children, primarily the Italian.[15] He was in a fight almost every day. "I was a tough kid," he later said, "and probably drew upon that ethnic tension" when he started to make movies.

In time the family moved uptown to the Bronx and lived in an apartment at 1654 Monroe Street. Martin and Dorothy's best friends were Jerry and Selma Arnowitz, who lived in the same building. Very frequently the two, accompanied by Rose—but never Morris—visited the Arnowitzes and played cards with Jerry and Selma's Uncle Boris. While it was true that Morris and Rose shared the same apartment, it was equally evident that the two went their separate ways.[16]

While living in the Bronx, Martin attended the Rhodes preparatory school. There were only two areas that interested him at this time: one was sports (he had ambitions of becoming a coach), and the other was literature. Already, at an early age, he had taken on physical characteristics of stockiness and muscularity. Indeed, many of his friends referred to him as a "jock," which he took as a compliment. He would have been totally incredulous at this time of his life if someone had told him that one day he would become a famous movie director.

One setback for Martin came when Jerry and Selma moved away from the Bronx to Montclair, New Jersey. He and Dorothy, and sometimes Rose, visited the Arnowitzes, riding the train from the Bronx out to "the country," as urban New Yorkers at that time referred to New Jersey. They always brought candy, fruitcake, and other "goodies" with them. If it was wintertime, all the friends gathered around the big fireplace and played Martin's favorite game, charades. He liked charades because it involved acting. Everyone affectionately called him "Motel," pronounced "Muhtel."[17]

After some time at the Rhodes Academy, Martin enrolled in DeWitt Clinton High School. There he continued his interest in sports, playing on the varsity football team as a halfback, and taking up boxing, baseball, and basketball on the side. He also got an after-school job at a butcher's shop. As before at his schools, the only academic subject Martin seemed to care about was English and American literature. His teachers were impressed with his reading abilities. In fact, he was a gifted reader; for all of his life he read everything he could find—from Chaucer to comic books.

Another blow came to Martin when he was about 14 years old. Apparently, his mother, Rose, had one affair too many, and Morris decided to divorce her.[18] Morris forced Martin to testify against his mother in the ensuing court proceedings, a distasteful act for the young boy. He had never been close to his father, and this incident only caused the estrangement to widen.

Just before Martin was graduated from DeWitt Clinton, Morris died, still in his forties, possibly of a heart attack. With his passing, Rose and her two children were left on their own with the family finances; they inherited nothing from Morris. With the Depression bearing down in full swing in 1932, the family's purse strings were not in the greatest shape. They were so bad, in fact, that Martin feared he might have to postpone one of his newfound desires: that of going to college somewhere. He wanted to realize his ambition of becoming a coach and, at the same time, find some good books to read.

He rejected the idea of going to a big university: he was afraid of getting lost in it, and also he feared that he would get hurt in a "big-time" football game.[19] He sent out numerous applications for both admittance to an institution of higher education and for an athletic scholarship. The school which finally came closest to matching Martin Ritt's ambitions in 1932 was tiny Elon College, near Burlington, North Carolina.

Elon at that time was in an athletic conference called the "Little Six." The other schools, besides Elon, which played in this conference, were Guilford, High Point College, Lenoir-Rhyne, Catawba, and Atlantic Christian (now known as Barton College).[20] From time to time, Elon played such giants in football as Duke University and North Carolina State but mostly for "warm-up" purposes before the season began.

It seems clear that Martin went to Elon primarily for economic reasons. Over the door at the Administration Building was this sign:

THIS COLLEGE IS OPERATING UNDER BANKRUPTCY LAWS

In his freshman year he could not play football and it seems evident that he was not on any kind of athletic scholarship. Later in life, Martin varied his accounts of whether or not he attended Elon under a scholarship. He told a reporter from the *Daily Times* of Burlington, North Carolina, in 1966, that "I did not get an athletic scholarship at Elon, though I did play football there...."[21] But then, he told Jack Hirshberg in a private interview in September 1969: "Yes, I won an athletic scholarship for football at a school, Elon, in North Carolina. I wanted to play football."[22]

It is probable that Martin went to Elon the first year as a regular tuition-paying student. And, indeed, the tuition at Elon was lower than any school in the East he had contacted. Then in his second year, he received a modicum of support for his services to the athletic department in general and the football team in particular.

Regardless of his circumstances, Martin was a popular student at Elon. The team for which he aspired to play and then did play, was called "The Fighting Christians of Elon College." Since Martin was an American second generation Jew he certainly did receive a lot of ribbing from team and classmates. He took it all in stride.

Martin also surprised many of his colleagues by his religion—or perhaps more accurately—by his lack of it. He always credited his studies at cheder in New York for teaching him a system of ethics and morality. But religion, he said, was never really an important part of his life. Both Morris and Rose emphasized secular learning over religious activities. Nevertheless, he was bar mitzvahed, but religion and his Jewishness never controlled his life and career.[23]

At Elon College every Friday—possibly showing its strong commitment to Protestantism—there was ham on the dining table, where the entire student body ate. Martin, unfazed, usually called out to one of his mates, "Pass the turkey, please,"[24] and then ate the ham with gusto. (In later years, Paul Newman always sent him a ham at Christmas. There was no religious connotation to the gift; Newman had found a Virginia ham he liked, and was sharing it with his friends.[25]) In those days of economic privation, there were also many rabbits served on the dining tables of Elon and many another college, especially in the South, and euphemistically called "turkey."

Ritt amused his Elon classmates by sometimes tap dancing during the dinner hour. He also continued his love of charades which, in a way, was his substitute for acting. He was not consciously seeking a career in acting at the time, but he might as well have been. He said later that at Elon he studied nothing in particular and his big ambition was just to get through school "with the least amount of trouble."[26]

At Elon, Ritt's top professors were Leon Edgar Smith and A.L. Hook, and that was because they both taught literature and rhetoric. He made high scores in all of his classes, but American, English, and the German language and German literature were his best subjects. His least successful pursuits were economics and business law, where he consistently scored in the 80s. He was apparently a neater person as a freshman than sophomore. In his first year at Elon he received three and one-half demerits for "room neatness," but this number grew to a whopping ten during his sophomore year. Also, in one of his classes he learned the art of debating and concluded that it was close to acting, or the law. He acted in a few plays for the drama department at Elon, sometimes going "on the road" down to Chapel Hill for performances at the University of North Carolina.

He was a member of Sigma Phi Beta at Elon, and was initiated into this fraternity not once, but twice. On the first occasion he had to get names off all the tombstones in the surrounding cemeteries. Second, he and a friend, Charles Holmes, were blindfolded and then dumped way out in the countryside. As luck would have it, they found a nearby farmer on the way to Burlington. Martin and Charles beat their fraternity brothers back to town.[27]

Ritt wore straight-legged knickers, a la Sam Snead, at Elon, as did most of his colleagues. Sometimes he wore the knickers and his white athletic socks for well over a week at a time. He was not alone in this endeavor as his college mates also tried to stretch a depression dollar as far as it would go.

When he finally did get to play football, he found it disappointing. He became a halfback for "The Fighting Christians" but mostly as a second-stringer. He did make some starts, but not frequently. Moreover, the football team had fallen on hard times in 1932-33 and lost most of its games in the "Little Six" conference and with other teams. Duke defeated Elon 45 to 0, Emory and Henry shut out Elon 12 to 0. Elon finally made some points against Roanoke but still lost 19-7, while Randolph-Macon soon held them score-less again with a victory of 20-0. Elon won against Langley Field 7-6, lost to High Point 6-0, defeated the Newport News Apprentices 19-6 and then lost to Lenoir-Rhyne 12-7, and Guilford 26-7.

His photograph in an Elon athletic brochure was captioned: "Martin Ritt hails from New York. He is also a sophomore and a halfback. Ritt is full of vigor and is out to make good." At the end of the school year in 1934, however, Ritt decided to quit. He was second-string on a team that lost most of its games, he did not get enough financial support, and by now he had decided he wanted to be a lawyer. In May 1934 he packed his bags and said goodbye to his friends at Elon College.

In a way, however, Ritt never said goodbye to Elon College, for while there he formed a life-long affection for the South, coming to love the quiet, easy-going ways of the vast rural areas. A keen observer of Southern society while at Elon, he noted, among other things, the meek and humble ways in which black people acted in the presence of whites, and thought it wrong. He was mindful of the degradations heaped upon the South, both black and white, by economic and social backwardness. He learned that drama—as he frequently put it years later—is caused by change and conflict, and believed that the South fit that description better than any other part of the country. Thus, it may well be said that the Elon College experience gave Ritt much of his subject matter when he did begin to make films.

When Ritt left Elon, he enrolled in St. John's University in Jamaica, N.Y., to study law. "I didn't have to spend too much time there to know that law wasn't for me," he said, adding emphatically, "to hell with that. It was a waste of time."[28]

The most immediate reason for Ritt's leaving St. John's was that in the summer of 1935 he took a theater tour of the "Borscht Circuit" in various upstate areas. He went primarily out of curiosity and because his athletic background enabled him to develop a physical fitness program for the players. At the Hotel Waldemere, in New York's Catskill Mountains, a director offered him the part of Crown in *Porgy and Bess*. He played the role—without singing—in blackface. He exuberantly reported to friends that he had been "very effective" in that part,[29] and he exclaimed that he liked the sound of applauding people.

His part as Crown caused Ritt to think seriously about a career in show business. One of his mother's brothers, Abe Lewis, had been a street dancer back in Poland. Shortly after arriving in America, Abe's "gypsy" dancing had been good enough to get him into New York's Palace Theatre. Also, Ritt recapitulated his experiences of acting in student plays at Elon and of visiting the agency of his mother, Rose, on 46th Street. He concluded that while there was not much that was literary or intellectual in his family background, there was at least a modicum of show business,[30] causing him to emote: "I realized I could only be happy in the theater."

Soon after *Porgy and Bess*, he became a part of President Franklin Roosevelt's New Deal agency, the Works Progress Administration, gaining employment at the Federal Theater Project, directed by Holger Cahill, whose job was to subsidize playwrights and performances. Ritt became, as he said, a "WPA proselyte." He added, "my politics were always liberal. It was a product of my being a minority. . . . I said whatever I felt. The WPA allowed me to have that attitude."[31]

The WPA Theater Project made no effort to control the content of the scripts or performances it sponsored. Some of America's greatest authors and playwrights got their start through this federally funded program. John Cheever, Richard Wright, and Conrad Aiken were just three of dozens who received government support.

While the Administration did not try to control the scripts, some members of Congress voiced objections that in certain instances there was too much criticism of the government and the "American Way of Life." Congressman Martin Dies of Texas was upset by some of the material coming out of the Theater Project, and so he formed a committee to keep an eye on the writers and performers. The Dies Committee was, in part, the inspiration for the creation, after the war, of the House Un-American Activities Committee (HUAC), which terrorized so many creative people, including Martin Ritt, for practicing freedom of thought. The mere fact that Ritt's name was connected with the Federal Theater Project later would lead to dire circumstances.

Ritt worked mostly with the Theater of Action on 27th Street. His first performance for ToA—which did not bode well for future scrutiny by government agencies—was in the May Day parade of 1935.[32] Later in that same year Ritt played professional football as a halfback for the City Island Slickers, earning $15.00 a game.

Many of the participants in ToA lived together in a big house in the Village. Ritt did not join them; he commuted each day from the Bronx. One of ToA's biggest projects was to go out on trucks into the city and give skits that dealt with the social problems of the day. They appeared frequently in union halls to give messages to workers that were basically socialist in orientation.[33]

Ritt gave this description of his first days at the Theater of Action:

I was as strange to them as they were to me—I was totally unpolitical. I was an athlete. They couldn't assume I could read a book or do anything like that. . . . One of the worst guys in that regard was Nick Ray, most snobbish. . . . I said something to him and he replied rudely, and [impulsively] I said if you say that once more you're gonna go out on your ass, and that ended the conversation. I was rough in those days. I was very free with my hands. Playing cards backstage once with Howard da Silva, and we had a fight.[34]

These lines certainly were foreshadowings of a future Martin Ritt on the scene in Hollywood.

At ToA, Ritt came under the influence of a director he called "Gadget," the nickname for Elia Kazan. One could see a future Martin Ritt in the way Martin in 1935 described "Gadg."

"Of all the directors I've ever seen work, he was the greatest seducer: he made you feel you were great . . . and got the best out of you. . . . He was a director who'd take an actor aside and put his arm around him . . . He understood, and made very quick and bright perceptions about people."[35] Much the same was said many times about Martin Ritt in the years ahead.

In Theater of Action, Martin had small roles in such plays as *Crime*, and *Plant in the Sun*. His affiliation from 1935 to about 1937 with ToA brought him to the attention of other acting groups in the city, and opened a few doors for him.

One was the Glasgow Theatre, where he auditioned for and won a part in William Saroyan's play *The Time of Your Life*. His role called for him to dance, and by now Martin had become an able street dancer. After several rehearsals Martin walked into the theatre one day and saw up on the stage "a young Irish kid"[36] doing a fabulous dance. The producers had decided that they wanted the kind of dance in the play that would "stop the show." Thus, they fired Ritt and replaced him with Gene Kelly.[37] (Ritt and Kelly were the closest of friends for half a century. Every week, almost without fail, Ritt visited Kelly's home in Beverly Hills, where they and their colleagues watched *Monday Night Football*.[38])

The widest and most important door opened for Ritt because of his ToA experiences was entry into the famed Group Theatre, prominent in New York from 1931 to about 1940. There were several founders of this acting company, but the principal one seems to have been Harold Clurman. It patterned itself after the Moscow Art Theatre, which toured New York in the late 1920s. One of the Group's primary beliefs was "There will never be a Utopia, but we ought never to quit fighting for one."[39]

A major feature of the Group Theatre was its ensemble approach to acting. There were no stars; indeed, everyone was listed alphabetically, and there were no solo curtain calls.[40] When the company went on the road, its members traveled and lived collectively. In the mid to late thirties some of the Group turned to the Communist Party as an answer to the social problems besetting depression-ridden America.[41] Others began actively to support the forces—one was the Abraham Lincoln Brigade—fighting against General Francisco Franco in Spain.

Martin Ritt's association with the WPA, the ToA, and then, to cap it off, the Group Theatre, definitely fore-shadowed troubles ahead with the "Red-hunting" committees of the 1950s. In the thirties, though, Ritt thought nothing of what might lie ahead. He reveled in the company of such talented and dedicated people.

The most significant person for Ritt in the Group Theatre was Elia Kazan. He sent Ritt to Southhampton to "push scenery" for $20.00 a week. An important by-product of this assignment was that he could attend Kazan's teaching and directing school without paying tuition. Though Ritt and Kazan became estranged in the years ahead, they were close friends in the late thirties.

After some time working in the theaters on Long Island, Ritt was brought back to Manhattan in 1937 to work in a Group Theatre production of Clifford Odets's *Golden Boy*, performed at the Belasco Theater. Again, as with the "Borscht Circuit" a few years before, it was Ritt's athletic ability rather than his acting, that got him the job. He knew how to box a punching bag. (He had grown up near the Lower East Side home of Rocky Graziano and sparred with him occasionally, and had boxed at DeWitt Clinton and sporadically at Elon and St. John's.)

His assignment was to shape up Luther Adler for one of the principal roles in *Golden Boy*. (John Garfield was the other principal.) "I took Luther to the gym to try to get him into shape—I took him to the Old Pioneer Athletic Club. He walked in; the stench was so incredible! He'd never been around jock straps and sweat shirts."[42]

During *Golden Boy*'s performance, Martin's job was to beat tattoos—since he was the only member of the ensemble who knew how to do it—on the punching bag, and give sound effects during the ring scenes. Later, Ritt liked to tell his friends that his first play for the Group Theatre was a "real hit."[43] For his services, he received $25.00 a week for rehearsals (minimum equity) and $65.00 for each performance.

Because of his punching abilities, he was promoted to assistant stage manager for the productions of *Golden Boy*. Also, in later performances he got a small role in the play. "I had exactly two lines. Remember the guy who runs in to announce that Joe has won his fight by a knockout? That was me."[44]

(Another actor who got a job in *Golden Boy* was Karl Malden. He reported in November 1937 to the stage door and was told to wait in the "green room." "I walked into the 'green room' and there was this other fellow there," who turned out to be Martin Ritt. Both auditioned for *Golden Boy* and both went on to gain parts in the play, and to become assistant stage managers.[45] During the next year, 1938, Martin and Karl again were in the same play, Irwin Shaw's *Little People*. Also, they went together to Lake Grove on Long Island to work for the Group Theatre's summer camp. Ritt's association with Malden, like that with Gene Kelly, was a long and friendly one.)

Soon after Martin began work with the Group Theatre he made the acquaintance of Harold Clurman, its principal founder. Clurman told an assemblage of players: "This is the eighth year of the Group Theatre, the greatest acting company on the face of the earth."[46] Incredulously, Martin looked around to see if either Clurman or anybody else were smiling at this claim. "No one was smiling, so I guess he meant it and I guess they believed it. I paid careful attention."[47] (Years later, in 1979, Ritt told Jack Garfein that "as long as I work I will send a thousand dollars a year to the Harold Clurman Theater in New York."[48])

Ritt's career was greatly influenced by the Group Theatre. Perhaps the ensemble method of acting led him away from the auteur theory of directing. Perhaps, too, this artistic collectivism helped to keep him from winning an Academy Award or of ever having the big hit that always eluded him. Given a choice, however, between the way he did things and how things might have turned out if he had been more a conformist, he most assuredly would have chosen his own way.

For the rest of his life he held on to the Group-inspired belief that culture could transform politics. A small number of people—by setting examples—could affect a country's politics; individualism was of utmost importance. Politics was too often in the hands of selfish interest groups, and could in many instances thwart what was clearly in the public's best interest. Of the Group—one of the examples of how culture could transform politics—he exclaimed: "I never met a body of people who were so devoted, who cared, who were socially oriented, and were deeply humanistic. Never before or since have I met such a body of people. The Group Theatre turned out directors or teachers, not actors."[49]

For the next year or so after *Golden Boy* Ritt worked around the Group Theatre in one capacity or another. In addition to *Gentle People*, he acted in *Two on an Island*,[50] (a Playwrights Company production). His physical appearance, however, limited the kind and number of roles he could play on the stage. He stood five feet ten inches tall and generally weighed 200 pounds more or less, with an accent on "more." He had a dark complexion, and his black hair was always shortly cropped. He usually wore horn-rimmed glasses over his dark eyes. Increasingly, Ritt began to look for ways other than acting to express his theatrical drives. He moved scenery, served as a drama coach for various plays, and thought increasingly about directing.

On 25 September 1940, Martin Ritt married Adele Wolfe, also known as Adele Jerome, a dancer of some note. She had been married to Menachem ("Manny") Wolfe for five years, from 1933 to 1938.

Martin met Adele at a meeting of one of the numerous radical clubs in New York which she frequented. He went to some of these meetings as much out of curiosity as anything else, but he did find confirmation for many of his developing ideas about social structures. Adele was once a member of the Young Communist League, among other organizations, as well as a John Reed Unit. She was an organizer for the National Committee for the Arts, Sciences, and Professionals, an organization that was ultimately added to the U.S. Attorney General's list as a front for Communist activities.

Martin was always liberal in his politics, and by 1939-40, he definitely sought to ennoble those people he considered the down and outers. His experiences at Elon College showed him the plight of black people in much of the United States, and his daily observance of the unemployed standing in food lines in New York led him to believe that the U.S. government was not doing as much as it could to alleviate the situation. The Group Theatre helped him to become socialist in outlook; whether he ever belonged to the Communist Party or not is problematic. Adele reported, "I don't know if he ever actually signed a card or not. He was around these meetings, but not as an organizational person."[51] Later, during the 1950s, Adele was investigated by the authorities as much as or more than Martin Ritt himself.

His political leanings did not keep him from being drafted into the armed services during World War II. He was inducted into the Army Air Force on 13 April 1943 and served until he was honorably discharged as a corporal on 3 January 1946. His first major assignment was in Champaign, Illinois, where he studied weather patterns. He was just about to be transferred to India, to report weather to American Armed Forces operating in Asia, when a talent scout found him and thought he was suitable for a play the army planned to sponsor. He was therefore assigned to Special Services, lived in a special barracks along with other stagebound GIs, and "played a lot of gin rummy." The play which kept him from going to India was George Cukor's *Winged Victory*. (Ironically, his old friend, Karl Malden, also got a part in *Winged Victory*, and the two played in the same scene for the next two years. They were crew members in the "naming of the ship" scene.[52]) In Ritt's opinion, *Winged Victory* was a "lollipop patriotic story which wasn't up to Cukor's skills."

More satisfying for Ritt than *Winged Victory* was the opportunity to direct Sidney Howard's play about the struggle against yellow fever, called *Yellow Jack*. He chose his own rehearsal times, backdrops, and players. Phil Barnett, Whit Bissel, Alfred Ryder, George Petrie, George Reeves, Grant Richards, and John Forsythe, were the principal actors in Martin Ritt's production of *Yellow Jack*. It played, primarily to military audiences, all the way from the District of Columbia to the Actor's Lab in Los Angeles. *Variety* said that Ritt's direction "built tempo and emotion right through to the end, displaying master showmanship."[53] Such notices did not hurt him at all a few years later when he returned to the New York theatrical scene.

He said of *Yellow Jack*: "I had always wanted to direct . . . I [had] played prize fighters, cab drivers, whatever—you name it . . . and I wasn't going to settle for [those roles]. I knew the only way out was either to write or direct. . . . I had a chance to do this play [*Yellow Jack*] that I had always admired very much. I loved the play, and I organized a cast."[54]

Discharged from the army in 1946, Martin was not completely unknown in New York stage circles. His only directorial credit was *Yellow Jack*, but some people remembered his past affilations with the Theater of Action and, above all, the Group Theatre. There was a new mood of liberalism throughout the movie and theatrical worlds in the immediate postwar period, and Martin's past acknowledgment of socialist politics made him known to many producers and theater owners. Moreover, the revolutionary world of television was just around the corner. Ritt optimistically reckoned his chances at making a living in show business to be extraordinarily good.

By 1946 he had acquired two interests that became life-long habits. One was horse racing. He loved to go to the races, not necessarily to bet—at least for the first few races— but to study the horses, and thus be in a position to make an educated bet once he did begin to wager. He told a friend to go around to the stalls before a race, and if any horse "has been shitting," don't bet on him because that means he is too nervous. In time, he became an expert handicapper, and owner of several fine race horses.

Another "vice" was playing poker. By all accounts, he was the fiercest poker player ever to hit New York and subsequently California. He raised capitalism to new standards as he bluffed and poker-faced his way through one game after another. He took the game seriously, even with his friends. There was to be no "repayment" of bets after each game with Martin Ritt.

Also by the late forties, Martin had picked up a great deal of jargon that seems to go with theatrical people. If he liked a script or play, it was—taking a cue from the garment district—"full cloth." If he did not like something, it was "not his dish," or "not his cup of tea." These latter statements were kisses of death (at least to Ritt; some of these projects were later performed by other directors) to would-be plays and movies, and their authors knew that Ritt had spoken definitively and absolutely.

Despite his massive frame, he became quite a dancer. He had tap-danced as early as his Elon days, but now in the forties he became adept at all kinds, including the waltz, jitterbug, and various Latin-American dances. To a considerable extent, one could credit Adele with developing Martin's grace on the dance floor. She said, "when you looked at Martin Ritt he was like a big bull or something; and then when he started dancing he was like an elf."[55] Reporters remarked on how awkward and ponderous Martin appeared to be out in public. One writer even said, "If Ritt were an animal he would be a rhinocerous, if a weapon he would be a tank, and if an artifact a truck tire."[56] Yet, when he got on the dance floor—especially with Adele—he was capable of "astonishingly speedy and graceful deportment."[57] By 1946 Martin was a married man, a veteran, an actor of some remembrance, and one credit of directing behind him. He had become a man of the world, having seen enough of life to know that social injustice was widespread. It was obvious to him that one way of correcting inequities was through the medium of art as expressed in the theater, and later in the movies. He had a sense of ethics and morality infused into him by his experiences at cheder. He made up his mind that any play or movie he might direct, whether historical in subject matter or contemporary, would make a statement about the human condition. He was unswerving and uncompromising in this ambition, and he told his friends that to maintain his own ideals and philosophies in a world that might disagree with him, he was willing to "pick up the tab." That challenge was tested at length in the years ahead.

Chapter 2

◆ ◆ ◆

Plays and Problems

Imagine a small Tennessee town where God, his son, and the devil, all appear at the same time. The first two work to solve community problems while the third is up to his mischief as usual. God is personified in Mr. Peebles and the devil is Mr. Hooker.[1]

Martin Ritt's first play after discharge from the army— for the Liebling-Wood Production Company—was staged at New York's Music Box, and it starred Howard Smith as Mr. Peebles and Rhys Williams as Mr. Hooker. Ritt was attracted to the play because its philosophical statement touched upon one of his life-long interests: the relationship and interplay between good and evil in this world. He received $2,500 for directing it.

Mr. Peebles and Mr. Hooker was one of many plays with strong theological themes that Ritt staged, though a self-acknowledged agnostic. ("I don't have much use for religion," he was fond of saying.) Later, in his movie career, he made several pictures that were not at all considered in poor taste by the religious establishment. Much of Ritt's social commitment corresponded to the oft-stated but rarely realized objective of churches to achieve social justice for all classes of men. Ritt did in his plays and movies what religion idealistically said it was doing in its churches.

Late in 1946 Ritt directed *The Big People* (at the Lyric Theatre in Bridgeport, Connecticut; and the Falmouth Playhouse in Conamessett, Massachusetts) for $2,000, and then, early in 1947, returned to his first directorial achievement, Sidney Howard's *Yellow Jack*, which he had directed in the army. The play dramatized the fight against yellow fever. Several characters in the play, following the lead of Dr. Carlos Finlay, inject themselves with the disease and prove that it is caused by mosquitoes.[2] Once this procedure had been followed, medical science was on the way to a cure for this dreaded malady. Starring Raymond Greenleaf and Alfred Ryder, *Yellow Jack* was well received, and ran off Broadway for an entire season. One reviewer said: ". . . [M]ost of the performance is a clear, stimulating narrative of one of the great moments in the battle for human living."[3]

Ritt also staged Dorothy Heywood's *Set My People Free*, (at the Hudson in New York) starring Canada Lee, a "marvelous" play, he thought, about black people and their struggles against injustice. In mid-1947 he signed an agreement with Production Management to direct Dorothy Gardner's *Eastward to Eden*, a play about Emily Dickinson and her futile search for true love, perhaps a foreshadowing of the feminine films Ritt made thirty years later, in the 1970s.

His last play before going primarily into television was *The Man*, a melodrama, written by Mel Dinelli, and starring Dorothy Gish, Don Hammer, and Peggy Ann Garner. Performed at the Fulton Theatre, this Martin Ritt production deals with a widow who hires a handyman, Howard Wilton, to keep things repaired at her rooming house. She takes a motherly interest in him, but he is a psychotic criminal, who finally kills her. Though the play ran for about seven months, reviewer Brooks Atkinson summed up many people's feelings when he wrote that "*The Man* was well done, but it was depressing and not something that could be casually enjoyed."[4] One had to think about it. Later, Ritt injected some kind of pensive necessity into almost every film he made and, though they were entertaining, they were not "casually enjoyable." This fact might partially explain why he never won an Oscar for best director.

As the 1940s drew to a close Martin Ritt had become someone to be reckoned with in New York theater. His services were sought because he was already gaining the reputation that, while being a stern taskmaster, he was an "actor's director." When he accepted a play and then considered who he wanted to perform in it, he got everyone together with scripts around a big table and had readings. Then he carried out many rehearsals, and here he gave performers so much individual attention that some of them learned that when Ritt stopped a scene, even before he could say anything, the actor would remark, "Yes, I know what you mean."[5]

It was highly predictable that Ritt would be in on the ground floor of much that happened in the late forties and early fifties in the new medium of television. A letter from "Sam" of the Cecil Presbrey Advertising Agency in early 1950 exclaimed, "There is no doubt in my mind that . . . you are headed for a distinguished television career."

He first produced and directed *The Fight Game*, a 12-and-a-half-minute documentary for Intercity Television, followed by *They Came Out Fighting*. He soon became involved with the Columbia Broadcasting Corporation, directing weekly programs on *Teller of Tales*, and *Climax*. For some time, Ritt and his long time friend Yul Brynner jointly directed and acted in *Starlight Theatre* for CBS from a studio on Ninth Avenue. Ritt and Brynner alternated their roles: one week Brynner directed and Ritt acted and the next week Brynner acted and Ritt directed. At the beginning of each week, said cameraman Hamilton Morgan years later, Ritt stalked into the studio and told everybody what a "lousy" job Brynner had done the preceding week. Then a while later Brynner walked in and pronounced his "negative" judgments on Ritt's performances of the prior week.[6] Their bantering was, of course, all in fun: they liked and respected each other immensely.

Possibly the best known of Ritt's affiliations with CBS was his directing and acting on the very popular series, *Danger*. Here, as with *Starlight Theatre*, he frequently collaborated with Yul Brynner. In reference to *Danger*, he recalled years later that "the early days of television were very good and very formative because you cut on the air. You did everything under pressure."[7] He noted also that a number of people who would go on to become movie directors were nurtured by live TV and that early television was the only time in its history that had the excitement of the first days and weeks of radio.[8]

Since acting and directing on early television were extemporaneous, some problems periodically developed. Once when Ritt acted in a *Danger* program, he played a bank teller being robbed by two men. When told to walk over and open a safe, Ritt saw the cable jam on one of the two cameras behind the robbers. "I knew if I went over there [to the safe] there would be no film." He solved the problem by improvising. "I said, 'fellows, that safe is empty. I know a safe that's got a lot of money back here, but if I give it to you, will you let me off the hook?'" By this time everyone sensed something wrong. Martin said to the robbers, "Just move out of the way," enabling a back-up camera to follow him to the other side of the stage. "Afterwards," he explained, "the director thanked me. If I had moved, he would have been dead. The show would have been over. We would have had nothing but God knows what. Those were very exciting days."[9]

The emphasis in *Danger* was upon one or two basic roles without "junking up" the program with action and plot. A viewer's interest could be sustained in a twenty-five minute program only by allowing him to know a strong personality in the script, and to care about him. Apparently this strategy worked, as a fan wrote to Ritt that in one of his *Danger* performances, he "created a character of real flesh and blood . . . [who] . . . could also have been maudlin, or hammed all over the place."[10] Another letter spoke of Ritt's "poignant and powerful" performances.[11]

In addition to *Teller of Tales, Climax, Starlight Theatre,* and *Danger*, Ritt also guest directed from time to time. For example, he did *No Time for Comedy* for the Playwrights' Repertory Television Theatre, aired on the American Broadcasting Company on 12 December 1951, earning $1,000 for his services. For NBC in early 1952, he signed a contract to direct *The Aldrich Family*, sponsored by the Campbell Soup Company. These were supposed to run for nineteen consecutive weeks, but for unforeseen reasons, they did not. And therein lies a story.

The newsletter *Counterattack* had been formed in May, 1947, by a group of former FBI men.[12] The first listing of Martin Ritt in *Counterattack* was on 23 May 1952, in an article entitled, "How Many Liver Pills Will Answang, Conway, and Ritt sell?" In 1947, *Counterattack* alleged, Ritt helped several Communist Party locals of the Retail, Wholesale and Department Store unions stage their annual show. And in 1951, he was billed as "a lecturer at the Communist Party's . . . school run by People's Drama." And just "this week," lamented *Counterattack*, Ritt had been featured in a role on *City Hospital*, sponsored by Carter Little Liver Pills, and run on alternate Tuesdays by CBS-TV.[13]

After he had directed a dozen or so plays off Broadway and acted in some 150 both on stage and television, Ritt went to work at CBS one day to direct another *Danger*, and, without warning, found that he had been fired. "One day I was working," he put it colorfully, "and the next day I was out on my ass."[14] Apparently, the most immediate reason for his dismissal from CBS was that *Counterattack* had criticized the *Danger* series as being "appropriately named." Sponsored by the Block Drug Company, manufacturers of Ammident Toothpaste, Omega Oil, and Minipoo Shampoo, *Danger* had several "suspect" people working for it, including Martin Ritt, who, in 1951, had sponsored the Waldorf "Peace" Conference, and "helped Communist-controlled unions put on propaganda shows."[15]

He had become a victim of the television blacklist that affected so many theater people in the early 1950s. He was to pay a price for his leftist political and social leanings but, as always, he told friends, he was willing to "pick up the tab" to hold on to his beliefs and principles.

The House Un-American Activities Committee was, as noted previously, an offshoot of the Dies Committee that had operated against the Federal Theatre Project back in the 1930s. In the immediate post World War II era, theaters and movies were in the vanguard of liberal reform movements: both had the capabilities of pointing out unpleasant truths about the United States. For example, as Martin Ritt often asked, why were so many people—the blacks in the South and the factory workers in the North, among others—deprived of governmental compassion and benevolence? Why were thousands without any medical care, either from the medical profession itself or the government, because they did not have enough money? Why were the capitalists and other wealthy people allowed to gain political power only because of their economic situation? These and a dozen other "whys" presented themselves just after World War II and begged for answers. Those—including Martin Ritt—who sought to give the answers were frequently the targets of mean-spirited bureaucratic agencies.

Of course, there were plenty of people in the United States to gainsay Martin Ritt and his fellow leftists. "We have it better in this country than anywhere in the world," was a statement frequently heard. Those who disagreed should simply "go somewhere else to live," such as the Soviet Union. There was, it seems, enough dogmatism to go around.

Trouble ahead for Martin Ritt had been easily foreshadowed by a June 1950 publication by the American Business Consultants, entitled *Red Channels*, a book sponsored by *Counterattack*, and listing numerous entertainment people and organizations who were, in some way, affiliated with the Communist Party. The purpose of *Red Channels* was to "show how Communists have been able to carry out their plan of infiltration of the radio and television industry." Also, it wanted to show "the extent to which many prominent actors and artists have been inveigled to lend their names . . . to organizations espousing communist causes."[16] The publication admitted that many of the people listed were not necessarily "sympathizers" of communism, but may have been duped into lending their names innocently to the "cause."[17]

Ritt was not mentioned in this 1950 publication, but many of his close, long-time friends were. Luther Adler, of the Group Theatre, was reported as a member of the Abraham Lincoln Brigade, and many other "Communist Front" organizations.[18] Stella Adler, also of the Group Theatre, was a "New York League of Women Shoppers" member, as well as the American Committee for Protection of the Foreign Born.[19] Ritt's lifetime friend Walter Bernstein was listed in this *Red Channels* report as being involved in the Scientific and Cultural Conference for World Peace, Civil Rights Congress, and the 1947 May Day Parade in New York.[20] Other of Ritt's friends included in the *Red Channels* report were Morris Carnovsky, Lee J. Cobb, Howard da Silva, John Garfield, Arthur Miller, Earl Robinson, Pete Seeger, Irwin Shaw, and Orson Welles.[21] With this kind of lineup, Ritt did not have a chance. The wonder is that the Communist-hunters waited so long to list him.

Did Martin Ritt ever join the Communist Party? He gave different answers to that question in the years ahead. He told Rex Reed of the New York *Sunday News* that "I didn't think it was any more sinful than joining the priesthood or being any other kind of evangelist. It had to do with beliefs for what could save the world."[22]

He said later, however, "I was never accused of being a Red. I was never named. I was never subpoenaed. It was simply guilt by association. It was known that a lot of my friends leaned toward the left. . . . I had a humanistic bias. . . ."[23] He added that "I was never aligned with the Communist Party in any organized way. I was just for people working and performing politicized material."[24]

His wife, Adele, remembered that Martin "was not a joiner." He was around various leftist meetings in New York, "because his friends were there." Everybody in his and her circle, Adele pointed out, was greatly concerned about unemployment during the Depression and the lack of medical insurance. "Anybody with any sense of morality, ethics, or humanity," she said, "was involved, and the place where most of the action was taking place was the Communist Party. I don't know if he [Martin] ever signed a card or not, but he was around these meetings, but not as an organizational person."[25] Whether or not he ever joined is actually not the most significant matter in regard to Martin Ritt and the Communist Party. The *perception* is the important thing; he certainly was *perceived* as Communist by hundreds of people.

The Federal Bureau of Investigation charged that Ritt had at least been connected with a number of organizations determined by the Attorney General's office to be Communist fronts. One was the National Council of American-Soviet Friendship, and another was the Cultural and Scientific Conference for World Peace. An FBI report out of Los Angeles in December 1964 stated that a report of 1954 had indicated that "Martin Ritt had been a member of a Communist Party Cell in New York in late 1946 or early 1947."[26] (Even as late as Christmas 1964, the FBI was still keeping tabs on Martin Ritt. A report from their Los Angeles branch indicated that he was leaving for a six month pleasure trip abroad, visiting England—to shoot *The Spy Who Came In From the Cold*—Ireland, France, Spain, Italy, The Netherlands, and Belgium. The FBI report never made it clear why it was interested in 1964 in Ritt's travels.[27])

It is undeniable that Martin Ritt was around many leftist groups and that he knew several Communists, particularly in his early career. His affiliation with the Federal Writing Project under the Works Progress Administration, his work with the Theater of Action, and then, above all, his joining the Group Theatre, made him a marked

man in reference to the loyalty question. He was a liberal
who believed in raising his voice against what he deemed to
be injustices toward thousands of underprivileged citizens.
But in the milieu of the late forties and early fifties dissent
was not easily tolerated. The Cold War had begun, our
atomic secrets had been purloined by the Russians, and we
were "losing" China to the Red armies led by Mao Tse-tung.
For anyone even to hint that some foreign countries might be
solving their domestic problems better than we, was simply
not acceptable. Therefore, one could argue that the work of
the Un-American Activities Committee was as much to
create conformity to the "American Way of Life"—whatever
that was—as to oust Communism from among us. Adele Ritt
pointed out that "we keep forgetting that the Communist
Party was not illegal in the United States."[28]

Martin Ritt's past affiliation with the Communist Party,
however, was not the immediate reason for his blacklisting.
He was accused by a Syracuse, New York, grocer of giving
funds to Communist China in its fight against the armies of
Chiang Kai-shek.[29] He never confirmed or denied whether he
helped the Communist Chinese. *Red Channels* listed a group
called "American Friends of the Chinese People," to which
many of Ritt's friends and associates belonged. It is also true
that he was interested in later years in filming some of
Edgar Snow's work, particularly *Red Star Over China*.

Was there actually a "blacklist" of television personalities in the early 1950s? There were always plenty of
people around to say no. In fact, some of the networks came
in for their own share of being accused of Communist
affiliations. FBI Director J. Edgar Hoover frequently referred
to CBS as the "Communist Broadcasting Corporation."[30] Why,
then, would CBS fire Martin Ritt for espousing the same
causes it did?

Of course, the whole matter of HUAC and the "blacklist"
lent itself to enormous chunks of hyperbole. No one seemed
wise enough to ask why CBS, a private capitalist organization, would *want* to be Communist. Neither, apparently,
was anyone interested in the difference between social
criticism and communism. Thus, it was easy for people with
a certain mental bent to identify whomever they wished as a
"Communist collaborator." HUAC, in some instances, forced
people to testify about their former Communist affiliations.

As soon as they did, many of these witnesses were immediately fired from their jobs. HUAC's report to the 82nd Congress, 3 January 1953, unctuously said: "Instances have come to this committee's attention where several of these witnesses have been forced from gainful employment after testifying. . . . This action on the part of present or prospective employers seems grossly unfair to the committee."[31]

Red Channels and other red hunting publications had an effect, because the matter of how performers and directors were hired became a leading issue. Typical of this dialogue was Vincent W. Hartnett's article, "Rascalry on the Air Waves," which appeared in July 1950 in *Catholic World*. Hartnett, a former naval intelligence officer, said, "By hiring scores of Communist and pro-Communist producers, directors, writers, actors, and technicians, many of our largest corporations have indirectly but effectively helped subsidize Stalinism in this country. This defies adequate understanding, when one considers that if Stalinism took over, big business would promptly and violently cease to exist."[32]

He mentioned the Wildroot Company, which sponsored *The Adventures of Sam Spade*, while its creator, Dashiell Hammett, belonged to at least ten Communist fronts. *The Goldbergs* was sponsored by General Foods, and the series' star, Gertrude Berg, in the past had been a Communist Fronter. Television Theatre, sponsored by the Ford Motor Company, had staged television plays with Frederic March, Judy Holliday, and Marsha Hunt, all with past or present Communist affiliations. The biggest "subsidizer" of communism, however, said Hartnett, was Proctor & Gamble, which spent at least $20 million each year for its TV shows. "One would think," Hartnett wrote, "that a corporation with such a huge investment in the American capitalist system would be ultra-cautious about the 'talent' it hired at fancy prices."[33]

Attitudes such as those expressed by Hartnett were easily acceptable in the America of 1950 and 1951. This was the era of the "Hollywood Ten," when some writers and directors went to jail for refusing to tell HUAC whether or not they had ever been members of the Communist Party. Public opinion was sensitive and touchy on the issue of communism; not only was it not sympathetic to the Hollywood dissenters,[34] it greatly facilitated Senator Joseph McCarthy's new round of red hunting in the early fifties.

Thus, big businesses followed the conservative lead of public opinion in determining what players and directors they would support. It did not take them long to conclude that they could not jeopardize their sales—"The need to make money superseded everything else"[35]—by having "reds" working for them. Pressure from the corporations, who, so it was reported, worked out their own "gray lists" of unacceptable performers, led to these dismissals.[36]

Ritt said that his reinstatement to television would have been fairly simple: "I kept getting offers to do TV, always with the proviso that I do something I felt was indecent and inhuman. They wanted me to take an ad in the trade papers and deny I ever knew some of the people I knew—not deny that I knew them, but say that I didn't know what they represented, that they were indecent people and they had led me astray.[37] Ritt described those from HUAC who were asking the questions: "They were people not accustomed to power—and suddenly they had power. They were trying to break the will of all of us who resisted the implications of McCarthyism."[38]

At times HUAC hinted that Ritt would not even have to name anyone; just admit that he had been misled: "You know, for a guy who wasn't working to be called in and told, 'Listen, I've got a job here for you. Twelve-fifty, fifteen hundred dollars a week. You don't have to name anyone. All you have to do is say you were misled.' And to have to say 'no' again and again—well, that's how I lived during what could have been some pretty good years."[39]

Although it is true that Martin Ritt's television career was ended by the blacklist, he was still active in New York theater. He played in Clifford Odets's *The Flowering Peach*, for example, during the early fifties (in Baltimore while Odets visited New York), as well as directed Robert Kintner's, *The Turning Point*, and a bit later, Perry Burgess's *Who Walk Alone*. Also, he went into teaching at a school that collaborated with Robert Lewis at the Actors Studio in New York. Cloris Leachman remembered that he joined her group at Actors Studio "weaving across the floor" as a body work coach beat out a rhythm on tom-toms. "He was the lightest one on his feet. He was like the rhinoceros or whatever in

Fantasia by Disney. He was a wonderful dancer."[40] He began teaching as a replacement for Curt Conway for a couple of weeks. Joanne Woodward recalled that Ritt got the job "because he couldn't work in television anymore because of the blacklist," and that she was "entranced by him as a teacher."[41] He taught in the style that Elia Kazan and Robert Lewis had instructed him: in a "naturalistic," character-driven way; they, in turn, had been affected by Lee Strasberg's methods. Ritt's early students included Eli Wallach, Anne Jackson, E.G. Marshall, Maureen Stapleton, and Steve Hiller. Where the Group Theatre turned out good directors, Ritt said, the Actors Studio developed "some damn good actors."[42]

(That Ritt was a success as an acting teacher was attested to in 1957 just when his movie career was starting, and he had moved to California. Conway wanted him to be a guest director or lecturer for four weeks out of every year. Ritt replied that 40 of his creative weeks during the next year would be taken up with Cinemascope, so he could not possibly return to New York to direct or lecture. "However," he told Conway, "along with the other maladjusted Hebrews and itinerant *goyim*, I would be happy to be of whatever help I can."[43])

Ritt also spent a great deal of time at the racetrack during his five-year period on the blacklist. He became one of New York's most capable handicappers, and he honed his poker playing skills into what one person called a "computer type proficiency." He arose early—a life long habit of his— and frequently went to one of New York's many all-night movie houses and whiled away the morning. Sometimes, however, he joined his friend Herbert Rubensohn at RIPS, a public tennis complex at Sutton Place.[44] There, Rubensohn taught him many fine points that made him an excellent tennis player.

Then as soon as the racetracks opened, he would be there. (Years later, Ritt and his good friend Walter Matthau became known as the "Odds Couple"; Ritt being the best and Matthau being the worst.)[45] While Martin directed plays, taught acting at Actors Studio, watched movies, bet on horses, and played tennis and poker, Adele sold advertisements for the telephone company, earning $130 a week. The two were neither poor nor unhappy during this period; it was only that they were forced to do things that they would not otherwise have done if Martin's television career had not been shortened. Another blacklisted writer, Ritt's good friend Walter Bernstein, slept on the Ritts' couch while he was waiting to be reinstated to the creative world. (As is well known, many writers hired "fronts" to present their material to the television networks, and this enabled them to sustain themselves and their families. Years later, Ritt directed *The Front*, a dark comedy about the blacklist period, starring Woody Allen.)

Though Ritt was saddened and angered, and sometimes artistically frustrated, at finding himself and many of his friends blacklisted, he was never bitter about it. He had done what his own proclaimed principles had taught him to do, and he was, as he said, "picking up the tab."

"They wanted me to turn my friends in," he said. "A rat does that, and has to live with it the rest of his life."[46] This statement undoubtedly haunted him for the remainder of his life, for his mentor and one of his best friends, Elia Kazan, began to name names for the House Un-American Activities Committee. Ritt never lost his theatrical respect for Kazan, or "Gadg," as he was affectionately called throughout New York cultural circles. But his personal feelings toward him changed immensely. "Oh, Kazan and I still talked, but it was never the same. His behavior didn't help our relationship."[47]

Though other of his friends and acquaintances such as Clifford Odets began fully to cooperate with HUAC, Kazan's testimony hurt Ritt the most. "That relationship [with Kazan] and that event [Kazan's testimony] in his life probably had one of the most devastating effects on him. . . . He and Elia Kazan were like brothers. . . . They were inseparable. . . . When Kazan . . . turned and named names . . ." it hurt Martin Ritt.[48] "It's too bad we fell apart," Kazan reported of Ritt. "I never stopped being fond of him."[49]

Why did Kazan turn against many of his friends from the old Group Theatre days? To keep his job is the most frequent answer to that question. However, Kazan himself (or more accurately, his wife, Molly, whom he credits in his autobiography) wrote "Where I Stand," first as an advertisement for *The New York Times*, (12 April 1952) and then as a reprint in July 1952 in *Reader's Digest*. "I believe that the American people can solve this problem wisely only if they have all the facts about Communism. I believe that any American who is in possession of such facts has the obligation to make them known, either to the public or to the appropriate Government agency. . . . The facts I have are 16 years out of date, but they supply a small piece of background to the graver picture of Communism today. . . . Why did I not tell this story sooner? I was held back, primarily, by concern for the reputations and employment of people who may, like myself, have left the Party many years ago."[50]

One friend told Kazan: "Name the names for Chrissakes. Who the hell are you going to jail for?"[51] Kazan remembered the "arrogance" of the Party's "literary police" at the Group Theatre, and claimed that a party meeting was held every Tuesday night in Joe Bromberg's dressing room.[52] "Was I a leftist?" he asked. "Had I ever been? Did I really want to change the social system I was living under? Apparently, that was what I'd stood for at one time. But what shit! Everything I had of value I'd gained under that system."[53]

Film authority Kenneth Hey brought up another possible reason for Kazan's testimony. When planning *On The Waterfront*, Columbia's president, Harry Cohn, depended on the advice of Roy Brewer in reference to the labor problems depicted by the movie. Brewer, who headed the conservative Motion Picture Alliance for the Preservation of American Ideals, suggested that the labor agitators in the movie be equated with Communists.[54] Kazan and others protested this move, but when the movie did appear, it made it clear that mobster control was "analogous to Communist party control over the individual."[55] The insinuation here is that Kazan capitulated, in part, to save his movie. Whether he did or not is like asking Martin Ritt if he ever joined the Communist Party. Again, the most significant thing about the matter is perception.

Kazan's naming of names—even some that had already been named—in Martin Ritt's opinion, did little good because, as Kazan himself had said, they dealt with people who generally had ceased to be Communists. Ritt frequently pointed out his love for the Group Theatre and for the people in it, and he believed their reputations and careers should not be jeopardized in 1951 and 1952 for something they did even before World War II started, and which, by now, many had generally repudiated. He possessed loyalty of friendship, but Kazan's decision to cooperate with HUAC brought it right to the point of breaking.

Still another unpleasant outcropping of Ritt's black-listing, largely unknown to him at the time, was a close and thorough surveillance by the FBI and other government agencies. Both he and Adele—perhaps one should say, especially Adele—came in for some very close official scrutiny. (In 1978 Adele and Martin requested their files from the FBI through the Freedom of Information Act. Though the report gave them most of what they wanted to know, names of the informants against them were blacked out. Not to have done so, said the FBI, would have been "an invasion of privacy."[56])

On 6 November 1951, the FBI office in Charlotte, North Carolina, reviewed Ritt's records from Elon College and interviewed people to acquire "all available background information" on him.[57] The FBI knew that Martin had visited Israel from 1 July to 3 August 1947, and that he planned a trip to England in February 1952 in connection with some television programs he wanted to peddle in that country. In reference to this proposed trip, the FBI asked the State Department to inform it if the Ritts applied for passports.[58] The State Department later told the FBI that Adele had not finished all the questions on the application form dealing with past Communist activities.[59] After the trip to England, the Ritts went to Austria, in April 1952. Apparently, the FBI knew exactly which hotel (the Moser) they stayed at in Klagenfurt, and subsequently knew their address in Italy (Via di Villa Bonelli). Back in the United States at various addresses in New York the couple were apparently put under surveillance from 7:30 to 10:30 a.m. and from 3 to 6 p.m. each day.[60] Adele discovered only later that she had "been followed on a one-to-one basis."[61]

On 10 October 1953 Ritt departed New York on BOAC Flight 510, headed for London. He did not book return passage. The FBI knew about it, and requested both the Bureau of Customs and the State Department to inform the agency when Ritt returned.[62] His visit to Europe was viewed with suspicion by the government agents "because of Ritt's reputation, the cost of the trip, and the vague statements that Ritt made . . . concerning the purpose of the trip."[63] Ritt was described in this and other reports as being "one of those in the theater whose political views were questionable,"[64] and therefore subject to scrutiny.

Further information on Ritt dug up by the FBI and its informers was that Adele and Martin planned in early 1952 to throw a party "wherein Negro actors and white television producers were to be invited with the ultimate end of selling the producers the idea of utilizing the Negro talent in television plays."[65] Just why this information was "vital" enough to warrant a report from the FBI was never made clear.

One might ask in these matters, how could Martin—if he was not a Communist—set himself apart from his wife, Adele? Both of these individuals—Martin and Adele—were fiercely independent, always giving each other their space. Given their personalities, it was entirely possible for Adele to belong to many clubs without Martin's likewise joining—and, of course, vice versa. Just because one of the couple followed a certain pattern did not necessarily mean that the other would as well.

The period of the blacklist only confirmed for Martin Ritt what he had long believed: Americans were much more conformist than they liked to think. He did not suffer sadness, particularly, because of the blacklist; it was more like anger than any other emotion. If he had not been committed before to producing and directing plays that depicted the social conditions of his characters, he certainly was after the experience of the blacklist. In one way or another, everyone of his plays and films after the early to mid fifties had to do with how Americans thought about the leading social issues of their day.

Despite his inability to work for television, Martin Ritt was a busy man during the 1950s. He traveled, taught, bet on races, played tennis and poker, and directed plays. One playwright he came to know and admire was Arthur Miller, one of the entries in *Red Channels*. Ritt said years later that he "worked around" Miller's *Death of a Salesman*. On opening night, one couple walked out on the play. The husband, obviously a salesman, turned to his wife and said, "I always told you that New England territory was no good."[66]

In 1954, when Ritt was acting in Odets's *The Flowering Peach*, he telephoned Miller and said that producer Robert Whitehead would let him have his theater each Sunday evening for a one-act play, using *Peach*'s cast.[67] In a few days Miller came up with an autobiographical scene in a warehouse where he had worked in the 1930s, called *A Memory of Two Mondays*. "I gave it to Marty who asked me to read it for him. . . . This was the sort of thing he was looking for but it wasn't long enough for a full evening and could I think of something to go with it?"[68]

Miller continued: "In a couple of weeks I wrote another story I had known for quite a while, 'A View from the Bridge.' It came quite fast and I remember meeting Marty a day after he'd read it and was glad to see him trying to hold down his excitement. He was a sensitive, square-built, poetic roughneck who seemed to have been suckled on Broadway cardgames—I recall him saying his mother was a professional gambler. He used to play with Lee Cobb in the latter's dressing room during the Salesman run and said he was the worst poker player he'd ever met."[69]

A View from the Bridge had an "improvisational feeling," and Miller wrote it "for actors to play not for critics to tear apart."[70] Star actors of that time came primarily from the theater rather than film or television, so they had no problem with the stage. Jack Warden was signed to play Marco in *View*.

Finding someone to play Eddie Carbone was more difficult than casting Marco. Lee Cobb's name was mentioned. "But there was hesitation because Lee . . . had informed before the Un-American Committee and Marty had been an old friend of his from the Group days and was contemptuous of him for his lack of principle."[71]

Still, Miller believed that if Cobb were not considered for the role, it would be "blacklisting" for moral reasons. As Miller explained: "Marty had to grit his teeth but he agreed to make the offer, and Lee's agent replied—unbelievable as it seemed then and now—that Lee could nct play in a play of mine lest he bring down the wrath of the American Legion on his head and ruin his movie career! His refreshingly open opportunism sent both of us reeling around the office with laughter."[72]

Ritt told Miller about a young unknown actor he had recently met named James Dean. Miller concluded that Dean was a part-timer "who was trying to look proletarian." He gave this description of Dean's "testing" for *View*: "Marty was kind of giggling at his childish behavior and kept inviting him to come through the doorway and have a chair which he reluctantly agreed to do. He was doing us a favor even by showing up. I don't recall more than a couple of moody grunts coming out of Dean, but he did seem to have a kind of insane inner unity, despite his obviously imitative Brando-like resonances at the time. In general I thought he was putting on an act but a good one. In any case he was far too young for Eddie. . . . Marty kept chuckling about his charming childishness after he left."[73]

Van Heflin got the part of Eddie Carbone in *View*, "a fine actor in the wrong part. . . . He couldn't really mouth the dialogue . . . so he ended up 'acting.' The same went for most of the others who, as Marty knew, had no visceral connection for the piece."[74] Miller summed up Ritt's direction of *A View from the Bridge*:

It was Marty's first Broadway directing job and while I thought . . . that the production was inauthentic I couldn't blame him; I suppose it was doomed once it was decided to make it into a 'Broadway show,' something to which the play nor Marty had the slightest connection. The whole thing seemed stilted and unfree, without any 'play' in it. But Marty hadn't the clout as yet to resist this . . . drift into some kind of 46th Street 'classicism' . . . .[75]

But the "46th Street 'classicism'" led to other things.

A View from the Bridge may not have been successful according to Broadway standards, but it did open an important door for Martin Ritt. Producer David Susskind, showing his disdain for the blacklist, asked Ritt to direct a movie written for television. From Robert Alan Aurthur's play, *A Man Is Ten Feet Tall*, came the movie *Edge of the City*.

Martin Ritt showed the influence that television had on him in his directorial debut. He centered the movie around three characters, a practice he had used successfully on the *Danger* series.

Starring John Cassavetes and Sidney Poitier, *Edge of the City* gives a stark portrayal of racism in the big city, and by extension, the entire country. Axel North, actually Nordman, (Cassavetes) is a drifter "killing his mother" by telephoning her from around the country and listening only to her bewildered voice as she tries to get him to speak to her. As it turns out, North is an army deserter and does not want his family to know his whereabouts. Earlier in his life Axel had "killed" his brother, Andy, in a wreck that left Axel with merely a bump on his head. The only words Axel and his father had spoken to each other since the accident were "Good Morning," "Good Night," and "Go to hell."

In New York Axel gets a job as a dock worker, only to be extorted by Charley Malik (Jack Warden) for a quarter an hour. (After Malik learns Nordman's true identity, the price goes up to half a dollar an hour). Axel's best friend is Tommy Tyler (Poitier) and the bond between them grows rapidly. Tyler takes it upon himself to protect Axel from Malik. Axel confides his deserter role to Tommy; he changed his name, he says, to North, because "these days it pays to be 110 percent American." He cannot turn himself in to the authorities because he would get at least twenty years in prison, and then it would be too late to prove himself to anyone: "a guy's gotta do something before somebody can love him."

After much foreshadowing and build-up, a terrible grapple-hook fight occurs between Tommy and Malik, and Tommy is killed. Axel decides, after considerable soul-searching, to reveal the truth about the fight to the authorities, even though it means that his true identity will be discovered. After choking Malik into unconsciousness, Axel telephones his mother. Much to his surprise, Axel's father takes the telephone and tells his son: "You're all we got. We want you to come home."

Thus, reconciliation and redemption became two leading themes of *Edge of the City*. Also in this, his first movie, Ritt established two more themes that permeated many of his future films: that of the outsider,[76] and troubled racial relations.

Ruby Dee played Lucy, Tommy's wife, in *Edge of the City*. She remembered the scene where Axel comes to tell her that Tommy has been killed: "I'd wanted to do it before lunch because such scenes are easier on an empty stomach. We broke, however, before the big scene and lacking the will power, I suppose, lunch loomed more importantly than imagined sorrow in the great beyond of another hour. . . . Lamenting to Marty how I had sinned, he stilled the exuberant after-lunch crew. . . . He understood. He gifted me with the necessity of time. He taught me how to woo the moment's delicate truth though trapped in cement. How to thread the needle blindfolded. It was a lesson that lives with me today."[77]

Edge of the City was a low budget film, costing only $450,000[78] to shoot—mostly in a railroad yard in New York City. Though it received critical acclaim (the *Sunday Times* of London said it was "splendidly directed" by Ritt),[79] *Edge of the City* was not a box-office success, setting up a pattern followed in so many of Ritt's films in the future. For one thing, the movie did not play in the South,[80] and many cinema managers in other parts of America declined it also because of its depiction of friendship between a white man and a black man.

One unfortunate outcome of *Edge of the City* was that it threatened the friendship between Ritt and Kermit Bloomgarden, the producer of Miller's *A View from the Bridge*. Apparently, Bloomgarden planned to take *View* on the road, with Jack Warden continuing in the role of Marco. He wrote testily to Ritt: "You know how difficult it has been to get anybody with a name to play this part for the tour . . . but now, thanks to you, you have eliminated that possibility. . . ."[81] Ritt replied just as testily: "I find the oversimplification of your letter simply fantastic. . . . If Jack was so important to you why didn't you sign him before this or certainly why didn't you make a move at him after I told you our thinking . . . [about signing him for *Edge of the City*]. . . . I can't imagine what is in your mind to make you write me such a letter."[82] Things did not improve. Bloomgarden retorted: "Assuming that you knew nothing about my plans, when you told me about your getting involved with Jack and I told you I planned to send Jack out on tour you, not me, should have backed out of the picture. I believe this to be true on any ethical or moral ground."[83] There the argument stopped, for Ritt did not respond to Bloomgarden's letter.

Edge of the City proved to be Ritt's entree into Hollywood. Buddy Adler, head of production at Twentieth Century Fox, invited Ritt to Hollywood to direct a movie based on John McPartland's novel, *No Down Payment*. It deals with four couples in the immediate post World War II era living beyond their means in a California subdivision called Sunrise Hills.

Jeffrey Hunter (Dave) and Patricia Owens (Jean), Pat Hingle (Herman) and Barbara Rush (Betty), Tony Randall

(Jerry) and Sheree North (Isabel), and Cameron Mitchell (Troy) and Joanne Woodward (Leola) make up the cast of this sociologically significant movie dealing with middle-class morality and social climbing. Dave is a brilliant electronics engineer with a flirtatious wife; Herman is a store manager with doubts about his wife's religious inclinations; Jerry is a used-car salesman always looking for the big deal, and drinking far too much for his wife's comfort; and Troy is a brooding emigre from Tennessee who runs a service station, with ambitions of becoming Sunrise Hills's police chief, constantly at odds with his wife who wants to be a mother even though she gave their first child away because he was born out of wedlock.

Several themes develop out of *No Down Payment*. One is racial exclusivity, as Sunrise Hills bars for some time a Japanese-American from moving into their midst. Another is social promiscuity as each couple tries to outdo the others in backyard cook-outs, cocktail parties, and getting ahead faster than any of the others. Certainly another thematic development is sex, as the movie constantly foreshadows events that occur from Troy's lust for Dave's wife, Jean. And, perhaps the most important theme of all is that the American Dream comes with a hefty price tag.

The movie's denouement occurs when Dave is away in San Francisco and Troy has discovered that he cannot be the police chief because he lacks a college degree. In a drunken rage he orders Leola from the house and a few minutes later sees Jean through a window across the courtyard. He staggers over to her house and rapes her.

The next morning Dave confronts Troy, who unrepentantly shouts at Dave: "You can't hold a woman forever just by using brains." Then Troy continues to work on his car, but in his agitation he hits the jack and the car falls on him. Dave retrieves him, but too late: Troy is dead. The final scene of *No Down Payment* ends with everyone (except Leola, who was leaving) attending church. Again, this was one of many movies that Ritt, despite his agnosticism, made with the church as central to many of the events. Reviewer Colin Young quoted one person as saying that religious people should see the film—despite the rape—"because it opens and closes with church-going scenes."[84]

It was widely acknowledged that Joanne Woodward "stole the picture."[85] In some degree, this opinion might have issued because of Ritt's way of directing. First, Miss Woodward stated, Ritt insisted on having rehearsals—not generally common at that time in Hollywood—during the shooting of *No Down Payment*, but he did allow his performers to improvise from time to time. Of most importance, however, Ritt allowed Woodward to start a scene or improvise into a scene before rolling the camera—a practice that "absolutely mesmerized" the cameraman. According to Woodward, "It was like starting a scene off-stage and coming in with something. Of course, they [Hollywood people] were not accustomed to that at all. It was fascinating, and in *No Down Payment* Tony Randall, Cameron Mitchell, and myself were the only ones that had done anything like this previously."[86]

Jerry Wald produced *No Down Payment* and he "rode herd" on it probably more than Martin Ritt would have liked. For one thing, he did not think Miss Woodward's hair was quite right for several of her scenes. He wrote, condescendingly, to Helen Turpin that "while I realize she is playing a character from the South, it is important that we make sure she looks good at all times."[87] There were a few problems, too, with the language of the movie. Even though it had a rape scene, a few "hells" and "damns" had to be eliminated that were deemed unessential to moving the story forward.[88] Wald reported to Ritt that he hoped *No Down Payment* had the qualities of entertainment and enlightenment. If so, it would reach a point of universality and be long remembered. It should be clear in the movie that the rape made Dave and Jean's marriage stronger than it ever had been before. This realization, plus the church scenes at the beginning and end of the picture, should, he believed, produce a very positive cinematic experience for America's moviegoers.[89] *No Down Payment* was popular enough to recover Fox's investment but, as with *Edge of the City*, it was not particularly successful at the box office. Perhaps life styles were changing too fast in the America of the late fifties and on into the sixties for the movie to stay pertinent over a lengthy period of time.

No Down Payment started a new round of blacklist problems for Martin Ritt. Several prominent right-wing Hollywood personalities objected to his presence in California. His direction of plays by Arthur Miller, they said, dictated against his taking up the profession of movie work. His association with the Group Theatre did not endear him, either, to certain members of the Hollywood community. Apparently, his greatest detractors at this time were Adolph Menjou, Ward Bond, and above everyone else, John Wayne. Ritt liked Wayne personally and at one time even talked about offering him a movie part;[90] politically, however, the two were light years apart.

By this time, 1957, many movie and TV companies had their own "little FBI cubbyholes."[91] Spiros Skouras, head of Twentieth Century Fox, wanted to see Ritt's dossier to examine the complaints made against him by some of the Hollywood community. As soon as it was publicly known that he would direct *No Down Payment*, Ritt was subpoenaed by HUAC. The committee tried to serve the subpoena on him in New York, but he was in Hollywood. HUAC's not knowing the exact whereabouts of Ritt probably accounted for the fact that he was never personally called before it.[92]

Skouras requested Ritt to come to New York and voluntarily appear before HUAC and clear his name once and for all. Again, as Ritt had in the past, he refused. "I haven't done anything I have to clear myself for," he told Skouras. "I have nothing to say to this committee. . . . I've lived this long without doing anything I'm ashamed of and I'm just not going to capitulate."[93] If Skouras could not accept Ritt's explanation, Martin informed him, "I've worked for three days. Pay me."[94] Finally, Skouras saw the futility of the whole thing and pronounced the continuing criticisms against Ritt as "a lot of shit,"[95] and said "O.K., you go back to Hollywood, and you better make good pictures."[96] This incident between Ritt and Skouras strengthened Ritt's position in the movie industry, because now he no longer had to fear being fired either for making an unacceptable movie or for things that related to his past.

In the years ahead Martin Ritt denounced communism on numerous occasions. He felt that it was too regimented and created a too brutal system of government for many peoples around the world—all to the detriment of the individualism he so cherished. But he did always remain a Socialist—a person "who was not blacklisted for nothing."[97] "Anger drew him to the left," said one of his admirers, because of social injustices he saw in his own country, but "love kept him there."[98] Despite his denunciation of communism when he got older—into his fifties and sixties—Ritt continued to be angry at dishonesty and anything that degraded people; he continued to rage at the exploitation of helpless people, a condition just as true in the United States in varying degrees as in any country in the world.[99] He was, indeed, a "man of the left,"[100] a humanist, someone "who cared"[101] about the human condition. His movies in the years ahead certainly did delineate his philosophies of value and life.

From 1946 to 1957 Martin Ritt went from a career of directing plays in New York and elsewhere to being a Hollywood director of movies. The blacklist period of his life confirmed the social shaping he had earlier received in his experiences in the South at Elon College and in the Depression of the 1930s. He remained angry at the blacklist, but it was a kind of anger that lent itself more to *correcting* social injustices than simply *lamenting* them. He therefore used his skills as a movie director and actor to correct, to make a statement, about the world in which he lived. For the next 33 years, from 1957 to his death in 1990, Martin Ritt perfected his craft.

Chapter 3

◆ ◆ ◆

Pre-Hud

Edge of the City almost cast Martin Ritt into a new genre of filmmaking. Even while he directed *No Down Payment*, he began to receive letters from friends and admirers in New York about developing the "Eastern." These would be films dealing in a "realistic manner with everyday people facing adult, contemporary situations,"[1] with the vast majority being set in New York. Recent achievements such as *Marty, On the Waterfront, Twelve Angry Men*, and *Edge of the City* had caused critics and trade papers to talk about a "new American realism."[2]

Ritt was invited to a symposium in New York to discuss the "Eastern." Attending the gathering would be the men "who write, direct, or are involved in one way or another in the creation of these new films."[3] The symposium's chairman, Gideon Bachmann, editor of *Cinemages*, told Ritt in an invitation to attend that "you have things to say that need saying."[4]

While agreeing with the philosophy behind the "Eastern," Ritt did not attend the symposium. He said it was because he was in the "middle of another film";[5] yet, it certainly would have been within his character to keep from becoming identified with any one particular film genre. He did not believe in auteur theories, either in early life or at the end of his career.

He relished all the attention he was now getting because of *Edge of the City* and *No Down Payment*. Not the least of this attention came in proposals from around the country that he film this play and script or that novel and documentary. Among others, he considered *The Sea Shell*,[6] *Sun at Midnight*,[7] *The Lost Streetcar*,[8] and *The Greatest Ride in Town*.[9] Apparently, Ritt was involved in some of the early negotiations leading to the epic movie *Spartacus*. His old

47

friend Yul Brynner said that Ritt's summary of the gladiators in *Spartacus* "is exactly what we all tried to accomplish."[10] He thought he and "Marty" should have a meeting and go through "the whole thing" and "arrive at our own conclusions."[11] Apparently, at least to Brynner, the obstacle in filming *Spartacus* was Kirk Douglas, who had imposed himself on the movie. "I have no faith and no liking for Kirk Douglas's acting and at this point for his box office value," Brynner wrote. And then he added: "Frankly, it makes me quite sick to give an inch in this [to Douglas] and everything inside me rebels against it."[12] In addition to receiving ideas for movies and negotiating for those already in progress, Ritt was also besieged with pleas for help from various individuals. One person, wanting a part in a Ritt movie, exclaimed that he was about to lose his home. "If you can possibly do something—well, what can I say?"[13] Ritt always sympathized with those who came to him for help, and he answered almost every letter he received. He never did, however, let anyone take him on a guilt trip. Invariably, he advised them to get a good education, and then come back to see him.

The movie which kept Ritt from attending the "Eastern" symposium was *The Long Hot Summer*. His love of the South, instilled in large part by his days at Elon College in North Carolina, was probably greater than any "Eastern" genre of movie making. He told a reporter, "I like the pace of the rural south and southwest, the work of it, the fair shake of it. The people [in the South] are tough and funny."[14] He abhorred southern racism, and all other racisms as well. But it was not only white against black that propelled the South; it was also class against class. Perhaps it was these different levels of human confrontation that caused Ritt to speak frequently of the "profound South."[15]

Ritt's adhesiveness to the South was fortified by the novels of William Faulkner. Well before he went to Elon, Ritt was a consummate reader, ranging in his tastes all the way from comic books to philosophical tomes. He became increasingly certain in his early film directing career that he would put some of Faulkner's work on the screen.

Though the theme for *The Long Hot Summer* was a composite of several Faulkner works, its main inspiration was *The Hamlet*, set in the steamy environs of Frenchman's

Bend, an isolated Mississippi hill town. (One critic, however, charged that the filmmakers' free adaptation of *The Hamlet* turned "Faulkner's anti-capitalist black comedy into a Horatio Alger bedtime story.")[16]

The Long Hot Summer revolves around a drifter (beginning the "outsider" theme for which Ritt became known in his movies), Ben Quick (Paul Newman), who is widely suspected of being an arsonist. Everywhere he goes, it seems, somebody's barn burns to the ground. He becomes involved with the Varner family, the patriarch of which, Will Varner (Orson Welles), is the most powerful man in the hamlet. He is not able to intimidate Ben Quick as he is everyone else who comes into his presence. "You're no better than a crook," Varner told Quick. "You're no better than a con man," Quick shot back.[17]

Varner becomes enamored of Ben Quick, even giving him a part of the estate to work, much to the chagrin of Varner's son, Jody (Anthony Franciosa). Varner wants Jody and his wife Eula (Lee Remick) to give him an heir, and he also does his best to avoid marriage to Minnie Littlejohn (Angela Lansbury).

The Long Hot Summer deals overwhelmingly with the theme of white classes in the South, and family relationships. The black stereotypical theme does not occur except perhaps when a young black boy is shown eating a watermelon. Antistereotypically, blacks mix with whites at a horse auction. The movie is a testament to Ritt's belief that the South was propelled not *just* by racial relations, but as well by class and family conflicts within a white socioeconomic setting.

As the relation grows between Varner and Quick, Jody becomes increasingly estranged, wanting respect from his father. He asks Varner, "Am I your son?" Varner replies, "You was born to me." The movie's climax occurs when an outraged Jody locks Varner into a barn and sets fire to it. While the barn is in flames, however, Jody has a change of heart. He releases his father, causing Varner to exclaim, "Hell fire and damnation! I've got a son again!"

Naturally, the townspeople accuse Ben Quick of the fire and they gather, apparently, to string him up. Clara (Joanne Woodward) rescues him in her car, and Varner tells the good citizens that he (Varner) accidentally set the fire while carelessly smoking a cigar. Then the truth comes out about Ben Quick: his father was the arsonist. Ben, however, has not seen his father since he was ten years old; yet he suffers for his father's wrongdoings. Suffering for the sins of the fathers, of course, is a longstanding theme in Southern literature and movies. The movie ends with Varner and Minnie and Ben and Clara planning marriage, and a new-found relationship between Jody and Eula and Jody and his father.

Some critics scored the ending as "nursery story—all lived happily ever after," and stated that *The Long Hot Summer*—which cost $4 million to make[18]—was merely another "victim of the studio system."[19] The film reminded the respected reviewer Bosley Crowther, of *The New York Times*, of "an afternoon storm making up above the still trees and sun-cracked buildings of a quiet southern town on a hot day. That look and feel reflect the sexual and emotional tensions among the characters, but the storm never comes."[20]

The Long Hot Summer was notable because, among other things, this was the first time Paul Newman played in a Martin Ritt movie, beginning a relationship between the two that lasted for the next 30 years. *The Long Hot Summer* was scripted by Irving Ravetch and Harriet Frank, Jr.—a husband-wife script writing team—starting a friendship and collaboration with Martin Ritt for many scripts in the future (*Hud, Norma Rae*, et al.).

The shooting of the movie also caused Hollywood watchers to speculate how it would all come out as Ritt, a gruff, swearing, opinionated director, and Welles, also a director of note, and with a volatile personality of his own, faced off against each other. Welles biographer Frank Brady wrote:

Almost immediately there was friction between the two men. "Two weeks after we started you could bet we wouldn't finish the film," Ritt has recalled. Orson observed: "There was a note of suspicion. I did not know what kind of monkeyshines I would have to put up with and the cast did not know what kind of caprices they would have to put up with with me." Battles over camera angles, costume details, interpretation of lines, and body movement raged, but somehow the two men managed to get through the film.[21]

Lee Remick remembered that she was somewhat intimidated by Orson Welles on the set of *The Long Hot Summer* "because I was so young." The film, shot in Baton Rouge, Louisiana, was, Miss Remick said, "at the wrong time of year. It was rainy and miserable." Why was Welles so intimidating? "He was just there: the size of him, the wit, his rapier tongue. He spared no one. He didn't care what you thought, and he was an icon. We were all in awe of him."[22]

The only person on the set who was not intimidated by "Citizen Welles" was Ritt himself. Remick recalled of Ritt, "He was wonderful. I loved him. He was like a big teddy bear."[23]

Joanne Woodward said that Welles himself was intimidated, at least "a bit," by all of the "method" actors in *The Long Hot Summer* and a "method" director.[24] He had not come up from the Group or Actors Studio. For Ritt to direct Welles, Woodward said, "was a very brave thing, although I think he admired Orson.[25] There was so much there" with Welles, said Woodward, "that I kept thinking: why doesn't he just take off that silly nose and be there in the part?"[26] Once, after trying to work in a scene with Paul Newman and Anthony Franciosa, Welles turned to Ritt and said, "I feel as if I am trying to ride a bicycle in a barrel of molasses."[27]

Throughout the Hollywood community Ritt (though he made no immediate remarks about it) became known as the "Orson tamer." Years later, Ritt told a reporter for the Toronto *Daily Star* that in shooting *The Long Hot Summer*, "we had to wait around a few days until the sun was just right."[28] Welles became restive and upset sitting around:

So when it's finally time [to shoot the scene] I find him just sitting and reading a Spanish language newspaper. He's not prepared for the scene. I'm pretty mad so I tell everyone, that's it. Let's strike the setup. We'll shoot something else. That night Welles calls me and says, "Marty, why'd you do that? You humiliated me in front of everyone." I humiliated you? What the hell do you think you did to me? Then I told him the facts of life. We got along fine afterward.[29]

In a more immediate setting, however, Orson Welles was not quite as contrite as Ritt's 1965 statement would indicate. Welles wrote Ritt an involved letter soon after *The Long Hot Summer* was shot. He had given an interview to *Life*

magazine: "I knew better than to open my fat kisser. . . .
Every instinct and all the sad experience of more than a
quarter of a century cried out to me to shut my trap."[30] The
"usual blandishments" of the press department, however,
caused Welles to grant the interview. He even let the
reporter into his house and "plied him with costly liquor and
eloquent praise of Martin Ritt." But the reporter "needled
away" on the subject of "the method," undoubtedly hoping to
catch Welles in "some indiscretion." The only quote the
reporter could pry out of Welles, however, dealt with the
"monkeyshine" statement.[31] All of this caused Welles to say to
Ritt:

I don't ask you to reply to this at all, and certainly I don't need to
be told that the same cunning process of selection was applied to
your remarks on the subject of myself. But I would like you please
to lend whatever attention you can spare to some partial undoing
of the impressions that I gave you such a rough time; that only a
nice combination of tact and guts managed to restrain a
temperamental kibitzer (me) from blowing up the whole picture in
everybody's face.[32]

Welles said that "the sour truth" was that producers
frequently hesitated to name him as director of their pictures
because they feared he would "challenge their function, or
interfere with it; and other directors are reluctant to direct a
director."[33] Welles, in an enormous gush of ego, complimented
Ritt, (who refused to give immediate interviews about his
relations with Welles), by saying that of those who had
directed him, "only the very best, or, at least the kindest,
have resisted the temptation to pose before visiting
newspapermen in the interesting role of 'Orson Tamer.' "[34] He
was glad to note, he said, that Ritt was "patently free" of the
"need for such ego-bolstering devices."[35]
    Welles's ego continued unchecked as he wrote to Ritt, "I
. . . put it to you that the legend of my celebrated ferocity
(only to be harnessed by the unique skill and saintly
forebearance of whatever director is the last to give out an
interview on the subject) is sustained at some considerable
cost professionally to myself."[36] He spoke of the "last job,"
that is, *The Long Hot Summer.* "Such fitful moments of
misery as we may have shared had to do, not with my criti-

cisms of you, but of myself."[37] He spoke of the "twenty odd
days" when he "languished" in "solitary confinement." Then
he emoted:

The days lengthened into weeks; I grew cross-eyed from watching
the slow dissolution of an infinity of rubber profiles; I was almost
simmering away in a tin trailer whose geographical position in the
drab backwaters of the Louisiana bayou country seemed to have
faded from the memory of those who first set me adrift. One good
outburst at the end of such a stretch in solitary is the just due of
any forgotten actor. . . . The point of all this is, that, in a dwin-
dling market, a reputation for being the Maria Callas of Character
Men has grown beyond my professional means.[38]

Welles closed his letter by asking Ritt to do what he (Welles)
had not: "If you have any merry anecdotes in your repertoire
in which I'm represented as snapping and snarling under
your clever whip, I ask you to withhold such yarns from
general distribution until I get another job and can afford to
enjoy a jolly good laugh on the whole subject."[39] Throughout
much of Ritt's career, he scorned egos and social life. Perhaps
his early connection with Orson Welles had something to do
with creating that philosophy.

Characteristically, Welles did not furnish his mailing
address to Ritt in this letter, so it took some time for Ritt's
secretaries to find it, in Rome. Ritt thought Welles's letter a
"little intense and sober."[40] Ritt had, he said, spoken of
Welles only in ways that were complimentary. "In addition to
having considerable respect for your talent, I grew quite fond
of you during the making of the picture [*The Long Hot
Summer*]."[41] The film had opened to good reviews and Ritt
thought Welles would be pleased by the reactions to his
performance.[42] Ritt confirmed what several critics said about
The Long Hot Summer when he wrote: "I feel the film itself
has a certain weakness toward the end which makes it seem
oversimplified and naive. But on the whole, it's good lusty
fun and occasionally quite saucy and even momentarily
touching."[43] Ritt closed his letter to Welles by saying that "I
hope we can work together soon again, Orson. This in itself
should dispel any childish rumors."[44] Orson Welles never
made another movie—Ritt disliked the phrase "motion
picture"[45]—with Martin Ritt.

Though *The Long Hot Summer* received a Screen Directors Guild nomination for a best-director Oscar, the movie did not fare well at the box office. In fact, it perpetuated a condition that had already set in for Martin Ritt. He made "think" movies, which always gained him attention but never "the prize." He was described on the set as "anyone other than the director. He is short, stocky, bullnecked, blackbrowed. . . . He looks tough and he is tough."[46]

By 1958 Martin Ritt was a "known" in Hollywood and the world of movies, but he was not yet universally admired, as he would be in later years. He attracted attention by wearing jumpsuits—a few years later he would have 35 of them—one especially outfitted for him to wear with a bow-tie for formal occasions.[47] He told a reporter that the jumpsuits were "a small amusement of my life."[48] Some reports gave deeply psychological reasons why Martin Ritt favored the jumpsuit. It was "leveling," said some, from top to bottom. Ritt himself gave the best explanation, especially since he was in and out of weight-loss programs: "the jumpsuit is comfortable."

Of great moment in Martin's and Adele's lives was that in 1957 they became parents. Their daughter, Martina Sue Ritt, was born 24 November 1957, and their son, Michael, a couple of years later. Both children were adopted.

In later years, both Tina and Mike frequently accompanied their father on location sets. Ultimately, Tina became an assistant to the director, and was given screen credit in many of Ritt's films. Mike was a talented carpenter and often made background props for his father's films. He worked in carpentry, for example, on *Sounder* and *Conrack*. Both Martin and Adele always took pride in their two children.

Directly after *The Long Hot Summer* Jonathan Productions of Los Angeles contacted Ritt for two more pictures. One was an "Eastern," and the second was yet another adaptation of a William Faulkner work. At this early stage of his movie directing career, Martin Ritt had the best of two worlds. He could make the "Eastern" with ease, for that was his background, and he could make the "Southern" with comfort, for that was his love.

The "Eastern" had a working title of "The Flower Maker," and, produced by Carlo Ponti and Marcello Girosi and scripted by Joseph Stefano, this Paramount production was titled in its final version, *The Black Orchid*. The movie deals with Rose Bianco, the widow (Sophia Loren) of a middle-class gangster and the amorous advances toward her of a businessman, widower Frank Valenti, (Anthony Quinn) and the objections of both their children to their proposed marriage.

The Black Orchid, on the whole, is a study of human conflicts, and how they are ultimately resolved. The resolution comes with a device that Ritt had used before: religious faith and the church. When Frank expresses his intense wish to marry Rose, he says, "When you want something so bad you don't care what happens, is it because God wants it that way?" His companion replies, "The Devil works that way, too." Frank tries to get Rose to go to church with him and "pray together" that the conflicts of their children would be worked out. Rose replies, "I need more than church right now." Frank and his future son-in-law, Noble (Mark Richman) go to church and pray. While there, Rose's son, Ralphie (Jimmie Baird), who has escaped from a work farm, shows up. In the meantime, Rose goes over to Frank's house and confronts his daughter, Mary (Ina Balin), and, after a stormy session, Mary has a change of heart, and becomes friendly with her future stepmother. These reconciliations (Ralphie's appearance and Mary's capitulation) are the situations for which Frank Valenti earnestly prays. The movie definitely gives the idea that prayer is the catalyst behind the happy ending. *The Black Orchid* was not the first of Ritt's movies in which religion and the church play such an important role. Nor was it the last.

As with Ritt's immediately previous movie, *The Long Hot Summer*, *The Black Orchid* was faulted by critics for going through some 90 minutes of "soap-opera" conflict, and then resolving everything in the remaining six minutes. One reviewer said that all of the problems were resolved by "five minutes' talk, a cup of coffee, and a lesson in frying sausages."[49] The *Hollywood Reporter*'s review, however, was quite favorable: "*The Black Orchid*, like *Marty*, is a rich and warm story of Italian . . . life in America. . . . It has all the combinations of humor and sound psychology that Hollywood usually has to seek in a published novel. Martin Ritt's direction is sensitive and buoyant."[50]

The Hollywood Reporter's reference to *Marty* raised some questions about the movie that swept the Oscars in 1959. For years the rumor persisted that Paddy Chayevsky wrote *Marty* with Martin Ritt in mind. Ritt said in 1976 that he had always heard the rumor, "but I can't substantiate it."[51] Another publication, *Saturday Review*, stated that *Marty* was written with the intention of offering Ritt the title role,[52] first because he typified the character of "Marty," second because in 1959 he was known as much for his acting as his directing, and third because he had had some of the same experiences—coming as he did from the Lower East Side—as the movies' main character (for example, Ritt worked for a short time in his youth in a butcher's shop).[53]

Certainly Ritt was not bothered in 1959 about *Marty*; he was apparently thoroughly intrigued by working with Sophia Loren and Anthony Quinn. He said that Paramount took something of a chance with Loren because in the old Hollywood production line, producers would have been obsessed with her physical charms and beauty and never given her an opportunity to show her talents at acting.[54] In the movie, Sophia Loren wears black, but "you couldn't hide her equipment even if you were foolish enough to want to do so. With her, the black wardrobe merely adds to her beauty and appeal."[55] (Corroborating Ritt's statement was a reviewer who said Loren was not "what you'd call a quite convincing representative of the immigrant school."[56]) The only problem between Loren and Ritt in *The Black Orchid* was that Ritt did not speak Italian. During the preproduction rehearsals he had trouble getting her to understand what he wanted, particularly when it came to "inner emotion."[57] The two finally worked out a system: "When I'd start to explain, she'd circle a finger violently while pointing at her heart and all I had to do was nod affirmatively. She's good in any language, even sign language."[58] One letter writer attributed Loren's "fulfillment" as an actress directly to Ritt: "At least Sophia's lucky . . . her most unusual talents found a master . . . [in *The Black Orchid*]."[59]

Ritt was pleased also to be working with Quinn, who had a "buccaneer" reputation in Hollywood. Yet *The Black Orchid* required no "macho" imaging, and Quinn "presented no problems."[60] He played the role "with great tenderness and gentleness without the . . . physical force seen in some of his earlier performances."[61]

If Ritt was fascinated with Loren and Quinn, it is true that at least Quinn was thoroughly enamored of Martin Ritt: "I found Martin Ritt a very direct, not-complicated (at least to the obvious eye) director, but [he] had a wonderful way of directing."[62] Quinn remembered one scene (probably when Frank proposed to Rose), when Ritt took him to one side and said:

Tony, that was a wonderful scene you just did, but I would like for you to cut it in half, and I said "Oh yes," and I understood what he meant, to underplay it by half. So I went back, and I did the scene with Sophia, and I undercut down to half. Then he said, "Oh, that was wonderful, wonderful," and took me over to the side and he said "Please cut THAT in half." So I said, "My God, where would I be, down the cellar?" So I again went into the scene and cut that down in half. Then I thought "My God, I don't even know if I'll be heard." Then he came to me and he said, "Tony, just take one more chance, and cut what you just did, to another half." So suddenly, I was practically whispering, and I had to find means to communicate with her by almost mumbling, and I must say it was one of the best scenes I ever did. So he taught me a lot about cutting down, in acting.[63]

Years after *The Black Orchid*, Ritt was complimentary of Quinn's acting abilities. "Well, Tony is a daring actor," he said, "and he's wonderful and easy to direct, but I did have some fights with him." Quinn, however, recollected, "Now I don't know what fights he was talking about, because I never had a fight with Marty Ritt . . . but I guess he considered that telling me to cut down in half, a fight."[64]

On completing *The Black Orchid* Ritt took up his other movie activity for 1958, an adaptation of William Faulkner's *The Sound and the Fury*. Like *The Long Hot Summer* before it, *The Sound and the Fury* deals more with white familial and class relationships than with white-black confrontations. There are more racial stereotypes here than in *The Long Hot Summer*. Dilsey (Ethel Waters) is the household "Mammy"; though she does the cooking and the cleaning up, it is also clear that she bosses around the younger members of the family, both black and white. She fills the role of the historic "Mammy" in southern literature and filmmaking. There is a young black boy in the movie whose job it is to watch after Ben (Jack Warden), who cannot care for himself.

As in some of Ritt's previous movies, *The Sound and the Fury* deals with punishment for wrongdoings long after the perpetrator has become contrite. Again, based loosely on Faulkner (in the novel Jason was the villain; in the movie, the hero),[65] Quentin Compson's (Joanne Woodward) mother, Caddie (Margaret Leighton), deserts her the day she was born, forcing the girl to grow up under the iron hand of Jason (Yul Brynner). Ultimately the mother repents and wants to form a new association with Quentin, a development that Jason swears to prevent. After a time of "sound and fury," Caddie once again leaves.

When Quentin becomes involved with a carnival worker (Stuart Whitman), and then convinced that he is only out to get her money, Quentin develops a new respect for Jason, but at the same time confirms that she will not be "a left over person in this world."

Ritt's *The Sound and the Fury* is about the inevitability of consequences for various behavior. Quentin's mother set the pattern for her life when she left, and no matter how hard she subsequently tries, she cannot evade or change the lifestyle that she had undertaken for herself. There is a deterministic aspect to the lives of the blacks in the movie— one of menial, although benevolent, subservience to the wishes of the white household. And for young Ben, there can be no improvement in whatever life ahead he has. Thus, resignation, inevitability, degeneracy, and determinism, and even a hint of incest, are the themes for most of the roles in *The Sound and the Fury*. The time in which the movie is shot, the late 1950s, was apparently an age of "happy endings," even if such "happy endings" meant forced situations and conversations. The viewer of the film is left wondering what the future relationship is going to be between Quentin and Jason. A strong feeling is given that the relationship will not be negative.

This was the third movie Joanne Woodward had made for Martin Ritt, and she wondered why he did it.[66] She saw nothing "socially conscious" about the film; it was, she thought, absurd in some places. "I mean, suddenly there is Yul Brynner in a wig playing my uncle; I don't really know why Marty did that film."[67]

Nor were literary purists happy with the film, because it was markedly different from the book. Berry Reece wrote in

the *Jackson Daily News* that *Sound and Fury* "is entertaining but it ain't Faulkner, you'all."⁶⁸ Archer Winsten in
the *New York Post* scored the movie for symbolizing
"Hollywood's most deeply held doctrine, namely that men and
women who fight most fiercely must eventually love each
other the most."⁶⁹

Other reviews, however, were not so negative. *The New
York World Telegram and Sun,* said that *The Sound and the
Fury* "assembled some of the most powerful performances of
recent days under the discerning direction of Martin Ritt."⁷⁰
The New York *Daily News* claimed that "Martin Ritt . . . has
made a picture that gets under your skin and will stay in
your mind long after you have left the theatre. He has a
wonderful gift of presenting a dramatic scene so it will hit
you right in the heart; his humorous touches are brilliant
without being obvious."⁷¹ *Time* called Ritt's direction "sure
and vigorous,"⁷² *Variety* said Ritt's "staging reflects genuine
feeling," and that his "story points are made via strong
suggestions rather than any crude, graphic illustration,"⁷³
and Jackson, Mississippi, mayor Allen C. Thompson officially
proclaimed the week of March 1 as "The Sound and Fury
Week."⁷⁴

The Sound and The Fury was Martin Ritt's fifth movie.
He had become secure enough in his profession by 1960 to
express some thoughts and opinions about acting, directing,
and Hollywood in general. Already he had begun to tell
interviewers that "everybody forgets there were great
directors before there were film schools."⁷⁵ While not particularly denigrating all the film schools that sprang up after
World War II, he did believe that if one had any talent, one
could start right at the top in directing. "One doesn't really
have to have a degree to paint a picture, write a novel or
direct a movie. But a general cultural background is
helpful."⁷⁶

Directing, he said, was like writing a novel. "You got to
do something first,"⁷⁷ and he recommended acting above all
other activities (writing, editing, photographing, etc.) that
had to do with the motion picture process. Should one act
and direct according to Lee Strasberg's principles? Ritt gave
an athletic example as an answer. "It's like if you're coaching
football and you're working for John McKay at Southern Cal
or Tom Prothro at UCLA. Then you get a job coaching at

Iowa. You take some of what you learned and you add to it your own impulses, your own inclinations, your own talent."[78] So, with Ritt, one started with Strasberg and then made his own personal improvisations.

The social film, by 1960, had already become his forte. A social film was any production, either entertainment or documentary, which made a comment about something in our society. "No first class work lacks social impact."[79] An artist, he believed, should be the person most concerned about educational and social conditions in the community, because he was in a position to do something about them. Ironically, however, the first purpose of a social film was to entertain, not convert or even enlighten. Without the entertainment aspect of films, their social ramifications would be lost entirely. Ritt was to experience this phenomenon many times in his film career. Social films were intended for audiences whose emotional and intellectual maturity was above the 12- and 13-year-old-level. "A mature public is entitled to mature motion picture entertainment."[80]

Also by the early sixties, Ritt had come to terms with critics of his films. He expressed years later what he felt early on: "I don't conjecture too much about the insights of critics, be they philosophical or artistic. Critics have their own hangups as I'm sure I do, and they function from those hangups, prejudices, and occasional valid insights."[81] Ritt had had mixed reviews for his movies so far; occasionally, he was angered by them, but he did relish the directorial reputation that he had attained and the general acknowledgment of it by film reviewers around the country. Regardless of the reviews his cinematic works received, he had vowed by the early sixties that "unless I have an irresistible offer, I have decided to turn my broad back on the broadway stage and the youngster television and confine my activities to motion pictures."[82] In the theater or live television it was the performance of the moment that counted. In movies one had the leisure to cut scenes, performers, dialogue—in short, a motion picture director was not driven to impulsive behavior in the way stage managers and live TV directors were. Thus, the motion picture set became the place where Martin Ritt resolved to spend the rest of his career and life.

There was not a little irony, however, in the fact that Ritt's film directly after *The Sound and the Fury* did not live up to the personal standards he had set for himself. It was the only film he ever made that he said he was ashamed of, that he did "for the money." The film, which he always omitted from his credits, was *Jovanka e le Altre*, or in English, *Five Branded Women*; its setting is World War II Yugoslavia.

Silvana Mangano, Barbara bel Geddes, Jeanne Moreau, Vera Miles, and Carla Gravino are accused of too much camaraderie with occupying German forces. (Ritt offered a part in this movie to Lee Remick, but she turned it down because she did not want to have her head shaved.)[83] In retaliation, the villagers shave their heads and run them off. The women join the Yugoslav resistance movement, and are "made into savages," sacrificing everything for the cause. The movie ends with a German regiment advancing against two Yugoslavs left behind by their unit. While waiting, the couple speculate about the future of the world: "There will never be peace for people; the world will never change." The other responds: "We have to believe that the world will change; we must." During this conversation, the Germans advance, and the viewer knows that the two freedom fighters will not survive their onslaught.

Five Branded Women, produced by Dino De Laurentiis, was shot in northern Italy, around the Turin area. Ritt received $175,000 for directing it, plus transportation and expenses. Years later he told a reporter that if he had had enough money in 1960 he would have bought up all the copies of the film.[84] The film "just about wrecked me. I became ill. It was a terrible mistake."[85] One should never make a film, he argued, simply for the money—unless, that is, one were making a porno movie.[86] He chose his previous movies, he said, because they "moved him emotionally."[87] *Five Branded Women* had not, and he suffered as a result.

Most reviewers agreed with Ritt's assessment of *Five Branded Women*. It was a "disappointment" to one reviewer, and a "shoddy piece of work" to another.[88] One wrote, "If most of his [Ritt's] previous pieces had developed well and then ended badly, this one . . . just stayed indifferent all the way."[89]

Some observers, however, did not agree with Ritt and the reviewers. *Life* correspondent Dora Jane Hamblin wrote a complimentary letter to Ritt about *Five Branded Women*. It was the best war film she had seen in ages, she claimed, with an honest presentation of an "unpretty" theme.[90] "The extraordinary thing to me is that after two hours of it I didn't get depressed—I felt haunted."[91]

Variety faulted Ritt for the ending; as with his previous movies, it was "contrived."[92] One "moment of truth" tried to "erase the dissensions" of the previous 99, and it just would not work.[93] On the whole, however, *Variety* was complimentary: "The film's strength lies in Ritt's direction. If his story bogs down he is sure to follow with a storm of action. The movie is gripping in tone and adventurous in concept."[94]

Ritt took the blame personally for the failure of *Five Branded Women*.[95] He did not lash out at actors and actresses or producers. If he "picked up the tab" for negative things that happened to him when he had done little or no wrong, he was willing to do the same when he felt he had erred. His protestations, however, were not particularly well grounded. One wonders if he was simply anticipating reviewers' remarks when he spoke about the movie. If it had been as bad as he said he thought it was, his career would have ended right there. Yet, his greatest days lay ahead of him.

And he gave every indication of great days ahead when he involved himself in *Paris Blues*, a "minor classic," according to one critic.[96] Paul Newman and Sidney Poitier are two expatriate jazz men living in Paris, making the rounds of the city's nightspots with their musical talents. Two lady tourists, Joanne Woodward and Diahann Carroll, come to town and, of course, love affairs quickly blossom. The movie's plot deals with Newman and Woodward and Poitier and Carroll planning to return stateside and get married. Carroll keeps telling Poitier about the racial problems in the United States and Poitier insists that he does not want any part of them. Finally, however, he does return with Carroll. Newman, however, is an aspiring songwriter as well as performer and at the end of it all, he decides to stay in Paris. The movie's most poignant moment comes in the Gare St. Lazare when Woodward tells Newman: "You'll come to realize that you never had anybody so right for you as I was. . . ."

Even more important than the plot is the music of *Paris Blues*. Generally, Ritt's movies subdued music, used primarily to push thematic developments.[97] But in this film, the music supersedes plot. Compositions by Duke Ellington, wonderfully performed by Louis "Satchmo" Armstrong, rivets not only the audiences in Parisian bistros but in cinemas around the world as well. The music ranges from the soft and slow "Mood Indigo," played by Paul Newman, to the rowdy trumpet duet by Newman and Armstrong. In this scene Armstrong turns his horn on the members of the group, "mesmerizing them into joining him," and builds to a climax "that goes right into orbit."[98]

Newman took two months of lessons for his part in *Paris Blues*, becoming good enough, Ritt said, to "get himself a $100 a week job in a night club."[99] For the musical scenes, Ritt gathered native audiences together. In the Armstrong-Newman duet, the audiences were real Parisians. During the filming of that scene, which took eight days, Ritt said that he noticed a couple "who didn't look just right." He exclaimed, rather innocently, "Honest to God, they turned out to be men dressed as women. Good looking women. They're in some of the crowd scenes, but you'll never be able to spot them. I think we had every kook in St. Germain-des-Pres in that scene."[100]

Also of great significance in this movie is Paris itself. It serves as a backdrop for the long walks that Carroll and Poitier and Newman and Woodward take, particularly in the wee hours of the morning after the two men have finished their musical performances. Ritt was surprised on arriving in France from sunny California to note how much it was overcast and rainy. He immediately dubbed the city "Gray Paree." There was no "bloody sun," he said. "Then I thought, the hell with it. Let's shoot gray. Paris is gray most of the time anyway."[101]

The combination of a semblance of a plot, entrancing jazz music, and the city of Paris combined to create a well-received movie. *Variety* tended to give Paris the credit for the movie's success, speaking of "fascinating Parisian byways and bistros." Ritt, said the magazine, got "some rich, atmospheric sensations of Paris as he shows the two young couples in love, romance heightened by the glamorous city, sensations expanded and loosened by its freedom and vitality."[102] All things considered, *Paris Blues* was Ritt's best movie in the pre-*Hud* period. Critics liked this movie so much that they even complimented its ending, a situation that had rarely happened in Ritt's previous movies. The ending was consistent with the action and dialogue of the movie, not contrived or tacked on as in *The Sound and Fury, The Black Orchid,* and *Five Branded Women.* Whatever Ritt was, he was a survivor in possibly the most difficult place in the world to survive: Hollywood.

One success should beget another, but things do not work that way in the creative arts. No matter that the writer, artist, or performer might well know all the formulas to success; it is still quirks of fortune sometimes that one work is deemed "good" while another is scorned as "bad." Though not trampled as much as *Five Branded Women* Ritt's film immediately following *Paris Blues* put him back into the negative category in the repertoires of movie reviewers. The film was *Adventures of a Young Man* which, for English audiences, Ritt lengthened to *Hemingway's Adventures of a Young Man* (1962).

A collage of Hemingway's Nick Adams stories, the film starts out in the Michigan woods in 1916, with the theme—if there is one—that it takes a person's lifetime to know the simplest things. When Nick breaks up with Carolyn, the first thing he wants to do is get drunk; but then, "when I know enough, I'll write a book." Nick takes off, heading in the general direction of New York. The only really interesting person he meets along the way is "The Battler," masterfully played by Paul Newman. "The Battler" is an ex-boxer whose brain cannot stand one more blow.

Again on his way to New York, Nick almost has a change of heart about leaving Michigan. In fact, he stops at a railroad station to send a telegram to his father requesting return money. While waiting, the telegraph agent tells a story about another young man many years before in Nick's situation, who had intended to leave home, but was held up because of a snow storm. The agent ends his story with the statement "I wonder how it would have been if that snow hadn't fallen." After that, nothing can turn Nick back.

For some time Nick works with Billy Campbell (Dan Dailey) an advertiser for burlesque shows, and then finally makes it to New York. When he applies for work at a newspaper he is told to go home and get some experience. After a while at peeling oysters for a living, Nick goes to an Italian fund-raiser and winds up enlisting in the Italian

Ambulance Corps. He falls in love with a nurse in Italy, only to see her become a casualty in the fighting, dying in his arms. (The sequences of World War I were shot near Verona, Italy. Jerry Wald, the producer—who had also produced *No Down Payment*—kept sending international telegrams to Ritt. Either Ritt was too preoccupied or he did not want to be given any orders from such a distance, because he kept stuffing the telegrams into his hat. "After a while," said Eli Wallach, one of the players, "Marty's hat was bulging."[103])

When Nick comes home he finds that his beloved father has committed suicide and that he cannot get along with his domineering mother, Helen (Jessica Tandy). He has a limp from a wound in the war, and though just barely 20, he feels that "I'm an old man." He finally screams out to Helen, "The distance between you and me grows fifty miles each day." After his wartime experiences, there is no way he can live the quiet, peaceful life in Sidess, Michigan, as his mother wants him to. He leaves, once again traveling to New York. And this time, the viewer knows that Nick will find a job as a journalist. Perhaps this realization is one reason why *Hemingway's Adventures of a Young Man* won the Hollywood Foreign Press Award for best picture of 1962.

Reviewers faulted the movie because it had no theme. Its title, however, was *Adventures of a Young Man*, which certainly did imply that it would be a series of vignettes. What more is a person's life in reality? Rarely can one find a life with an early theme that stays constant throughout. Philosophy, religion, politics, and social outlook change many times for many people; therefore, what a person is at 20 is no particular sign of what he will be at 60. Perhaps the search for "theme" can be overdrawn.

One reporter believed that A.E. Hotchner's script of the movie was "indifferent," although Ritt's directing did "wonders with the unpromising material."[104] He said, "There is something offensively naive" about the notion "that a writer must roam around 'collecting' experiences as an artist collects souvenirs."[105] Yet, in reality, this is exactly what does and must happen. "Write about what you know," is the dictum of more than one fiction teacher.

It may well have been that Ritt by now, 1962, was wearying of the foreign setting, after the second movie in a row abroad. He had already begun stating that he wanted to make "American" movies, a sentiment that grew in the years ahead. By this time he had let it be known that he had no respect for the Communist Party, though he never lost his zeal for social justice—as would be indicated many times in future movies. It must have been that he wanted a setting closer to Hollywood, something that would be "uniquely" American. He later found such an instrument in *Hud*.

Between 1957, when *Edge of the City* was filmed, and 1962, the year of *Adventures of a Young Man*, Ritt had matured as a film director. In only five years he had become a man respected in his profession and looked up to by dozens of performers as the kind of director they wanted when they made their next movie. He had become fastidious in his ways. He insisted on dinner at six each night; even on the rare occasions when he went to social functions, he would leave if dinner was not served promptly at six. He went to bed each night at nine and woke by five the next morning. He lived for the movies that were available for him to make. He loved to play tennis and poker, go to the horse races as much as possible, and tramp in the mountains in the Los Angeles area. He loved sports, but did not particularly have a favorite team. He loved the symmetry and poetry of football and baseball, and could recognize them when others could not. Perhaps that is why, on weekends, he got into the practice of watching one ball game on television and listening to another on radio.[106]

As might be expected, numerous scripts came in for his consideration, and he and Adele read them. Ted Sherdeman sent in *The Last Frontier*, and thought it would be a natural for Paul Newman and his "associates."[107] Martin Baum forwarded *Trolley Car*, to which Ritt responded, "I keep thinking that there is a terrific need in this country for a modest budgeted comedy picture. . . . It seems that Hollywood has not been able to reach the funny bone of the great American public."[108] Interestingly enough, he said he wanted Buddy Hackett to play the role if he were to film *Trolley Car*, rather than the suggested Peter Sellers.[109] Ritt was in on some of the early negotiations for the filming of William Bradford Huie's novel, *The Americanization of Emily*. He steered clear of the argument that *Emily* was "Un-American."

If he had not had his mind on other things, he probably would have sided with Huie in the matter of *Emily*. He would have agreed with Huie's assessment that it "is not subversive or unpatriotic to depict an American admiral playing bridge in London before D-Day or drinking whiskey or eating steak or bathing with palmolive soap or enjoying the company of a beautiful woman."[110]

Ritt was too involved at the time with *Paris Blues* and *Adventures of a Young Man*. Even when these two assignments ended, he found that his interests lay other than with *Emily*. He knew it would become a good movie (which it did) but he had other things to consider. Not the least of those was the filming of one of Larry McMurtry's novels, *Horseman Pass By*. Set in Claude, Texas, the final title of the film was *Hud*, the name of the central character. It was to change Martin Ritt's life considerably, and to become one of America's notable films. Just as Ritt had not predicted the reception to *Adventures of a Young Man*, he certainly did not, either, with *Hud*. He had thought the first would be happily accepted and the second not. Just the reverse was true, showing again that no matter how much one thinks he knows the formula for success, there are always the twists and turns to make one a liar.

Chapter 4

◆ ◆ ◆

Memorable Outsiders:
From Hud to Leamas

In the 1960s some movies began to emphasize life's reality that good people are not always rewarded nor bad people always punished. Also the theme that "violence is violence" developed, whether good or bad people commit it. In no small way, these thematic developments owed their existence to *Hud*, a movie directed in 1963 by Martin Ritt.

Hud was the first of a three-picture deal Ritt and Paul Newman made with Paramount for their newly formed independent film company, Salem Productions. Such a business association between a director and an actor was rare; perhaps it was the first time in film history that such a liaison had occurred. Though Salem Productions did not last very long, it did release some notable films during its lifetime.

Both Ritt and Newman came to believe that the old adage that filmmakers should "send their messages by Western Union" was outmoded. While a film should, first and foremost, entertain its viewers, by the same token it ought to make them think and reflect upon the issues of their own day and time.

One such vehicle came to Ritt and Newman in the form of Larry McMurtry's first novel, *Horseman Pass By*. Irving Ravetch and Harriet Frank, Jr., (who had scripted *The Long Hot Summer* and *The Sound and the Fury*) believed there was a great part for Paul Newman in any movie that might be made from McMurtry's novel. There was a secondary character in it named Hud, who, along with several other people, poked cows and lived in the bunkhouse on his own father's ranch. Hud was a person given over completely to his appetites. He drank, smoked, cursed, and caroused to his heart's content. Ravetch and Frank wanted to revise *Horseman Pass By* to show the despicable nature of someone who lived entirely without a sense of responsibility. The result of their work was to form one of the great ironies in film history of the 1960s.[1]

As with previous movies, Ritt kept the cast small. In *Paris Blues*, for example, the quartet of Newman, Poitier, Woodward, and Carroll push the action and dialogue forward. In *Hud* Newman (Hud), Melvyn Douglas (Homer), Patricia Neal (Alma) and Brandon de Wilde (Lon) form the nucleus that propels the story.

The movie, set in Claude, Texas, was shot during the summer and fall of 1962. *Hud* got Ritt back on his native soil, after *Paris Blues* and *Adventures of a Young Man*, and it deals with the "outsider" theme that he admired so much. Ritt's outsiders are generally excluded from the society in which they live, causing their individuality and hostility to grow.[2] Many times, however, his outsiders relent (Ben Quick in *The Long Hot Summer*, for example) and join the society that scorns them. Certainly, this is not to be so with *Hud*. Hud is an outsider when the movie starts and, if anything, is more so at the movie's end.

The movie deals with the relationship between Hud and Homer Bannon. The son and the father are deeply estranged from each other because of an event that the movie never makes quite clear. It is, however, apparent that Homer had favored his older son, Lon's father, who had died. Hud is self-centered to the point that he cares for few other people. "You don't look out for yourself," he says, "the only helping hand you'll ever get is when they lower the box."[3] He believes that the world is "so full of crap a man's going to get into it sooner or later whether he's careful or not."[4] Thus, Hud adopts a free-wheeling lifestyle. He likes to drive his pink Cadillac convertible down the dirt roads of Texas at 80 miles an hour; and he also likes to have amorous affairs with other men's wives. He tells Lon, his teenaged nephew, "get all the good you can out of seventeen, 'cause it sure wears out in one hell of a hurry."

Homer regards Hud as an unprincipled man: "You don't care about people Hud. . . . You live just for yourself, and that makes you not fit to live with." Despite Hud's overtures to take over the cattle-ranching operations, Homer, a widower, retains control of his large rambling house set in the middle of the stark Texas wilderness. Hud keeps calling Homer "old man," intimating more than once that Homer should retire and turn everything over to Hud. It finally gets to the point that Hud thinks about starting proceedings to have Homer declared *non compos mentis.*

The housekeeper, Alma (who, in McMurtry's novel was black), keeps things together, at least for a time, pacifying the three men in the house with her great cooking. She pets the teenaged Lon and continually puts off Hud's sexual advances. Apparently, Alma has had a troubled past, leaving her home, and living with the Bannons, where she has a semblance of peace and content. On the whole, she considers Hud's advances to be innocent until one night, in a drunken rage, he tries to rape her. She leaves the household soon afterward. Definitely not remorseful, Hud smiles at her as she boards the bus, and tells her, "I'll remember you as the one who got away."

Certainly the most horrible thing that happens in the film is when the Bannon herd comes down with anthrax. After the hateful news is confirmed, Homer knows that the herd will have to be destroyed. Hud, on the other hand, wants to sell the herd quickly without telling any potential buyer about its affliction. When Homer reminds Hud of the legal aspects of the matter, Hud responds, "I always say the law is meant to be interpreted in a lenient manner. Sometimes I lean to one side of it and sometimes to the other."

In respect to the herd, Hud does not have his way. Plans are made to slaughter every cow on the Bannon ranch, including two prized Texas longhorn steers, which Homer personally shoots. All the others are lined up at a huge trench and methodically shot by neighbors, and officials from the state department of health. Ritt was later surprised to hear that some people thought he shot the scene this way because he was Jewish; that he wanted to "exploit the mass feelings of the horror and revulsion associated with the concentration camps."[5] This scene was not the only thing about the reaction to *Hud* that came to astonish him.

Hud was shot in black and white, and this seemed to elevate its dramatic propensities. James Wong Howe was the principal cinematographer, and he made stark contrasts between clear and cloudy skies and barren wasteland and lush countryside. As in *Paris Blues*, the scenery in *Hud* becomes a part of the thematic development itself. Also, as in his past pictures, Ritt used the camera in *Hud* to help tell the story. "I don't want anything to interfere with the story I'm trying to tell. I don't even like to use the zoom unless it's the only way I can get into a scene."[6]

Howe and Ritt fashioned the camera angles for the cattle slaughter in a way that the viewer does not see any animal "die" (the movie's crew was careful to abide by Texas animal laws). Yet, the viewer is still left "with an indelible impression of the slaughter's horrific efficiency."[7]

After the slaughter Homer goes downhill fast. He dies, presumably of a heart attack, but it is clear that his sorrow over the destruction of his beloved herd is too much. His death symbolizes the end of the pioneer west; as one author put it, "Hud brought seventy years of doubt about the cowboy hero to final disillusion."[8]

At Homer's funeral in a rural chapel, the minister tells Lon that Homer is "now in a better place." The boy replies, "I don't think so. Not unless dirt is a better place than air." This reply would have hurt Homer, for it is more in Hud's spirit than the grandfather's. Both Hud and Homer had fought for the upper hand in shaping young Lon's life and system of judgment. It seems that Hud has won.

After the funeral and back at the ranch, however, Lon packs his bags with the intention of leaving and finding his own way in the world. Still mocking, Hud tries to get Lon to stay, promising him a major interest in the ranch. All of his pleading is to no avail, and the movie closes with Hud standing alone in the doorway of the home, which is now entirely his. There is still the smirk on his face; he is not repentant for the troubles he has caused Homer. In fact, the viewer definitely gets the idea that Hud is rather pleased with the turn of events. One critic said that Hud is now the "master of the house, strong, alone, shut in, shut out, lusting for life, solaced by the bottle, arrogant to the end."[9]

Reviewers, on the whole, were quite positive in their reportage on *Hud*. More than one of them congratulated Ritt for getting away from the contrived endings of some of his previous movies. He remained strongly realistic in *Hud*, they said, right to the very end of the movie.[10] They complimented him, too, for bringing together four performers, all of whom had been trained in different ways. Ritt had to make them all understand what he meant, "and still not violate their own feelings about where they came from."[11]

Bosley Crowther, a frequent critic of Ritt for "naive and unbalanced" endings, was impressed by *Hud*. Ritt, he said, "has caught the whole raw-boned atmosphere of a land. . . . He has people who behave and talk so truly that it is hard to shake them out of your mind."[12] Another reviewer, Archer Winsten, who had often been critical of Ritt, said that Ritt "has done well by the flat, panhandle country, the dusty desolation of a lonely ranch-house, and the small, paved cleanliness of a little town." He still had to inject a negative note: "The picture [is] not conclusive in a satisfying way."[13] Pauline Kael, also a frequent critic of Ritt, believed that Homer's telling Hud "You never gave a damn" actually "tells us nothing, and it is just this gap [of *why*] that, had it been filled, might have made 'Hud' a great picture instead of a good one."[14] Justin Gilbert of the *New York Mirror* lavished profuse praise on Ritt: "The major credit for this incredibly arresting, earnest and commanding drama, full of reckless passions and moral persuasions, belongs to Martin Ritt."[15]

"What Ritt has done," exclaimed the *Saturday Review* "is first rate film making. He has drawn memorable perform-ances from his small, skilled cast."[16] Not the least of Ritt's accomplishments in *Hud* was that he used Paul Newman's "considerable personal magnetism first to cover, then to reveal the shallow egocentric, callous nature of Hud,"[17] and The *Sunday Express* in London believed that Hud exemplified a "contemporary attitude of cynical amorality."[18] In addition to these plaudits, *The Southern Jewish Weekly* believed that *Hud* unmasked "the shallowness of the western stereotype" by showing that Western themes and people were not always the great romantic epics and heroes that much of the rest of the country sometimes thought.[19] All of these favorable reviews, plus dozens of press, radio, and television interviews were heady stuff. Ritt was delighted and somewhat astonished at *Hud*'s reception.[20]

Ritt was nominated for the best director Oscar for *Hud*, only to lose out to Tony Richardson for *Tom Jones*. The movie did win the Cleveland, Ohio, critics' award as best picture, and the Hollywood Foreign Press again named him best director. (He had won this prize before, with *Hemingway's Adventures of a Young Man.)*

Patricia Neal won the Oscar for best actress for her portrayal of Alma in *Hud*. When she was first offered the part, she asked the Ravetches, "Do you think it's big enough?" On the night of the Academy Awards, she sent them a telegram: "It's big enough."[21]

Certainly, one thing that Ritt, the Ravetches, Newman, and Neal did not anticipate about *Hud* was the reaction to it of the country's youth. The makers of the movie wanted to show how Hud is smart-alecky, cocky, and disrespectful—in short, to show what a jerk he is. Also, they believed Homer would come across as the long-suffering, maligned father whose lot in life should have been better than it was. Lon, the nephew, was to be seen as impressionable, a person who will ultimately adhere to his grandfather's way of life. (Whether he did or not is impossible to say. At the movie's end, he simply leaves.)

The young people around the United States practically turned *Hud* into a cult movie. Far from being a "jerk," Hud is correct in his activities and opinions. Homer is the *real* jerk because he does not realize that he represents a lifestyle that, if it has not already passed, is at least going away very quickly. Lon is a "schmuck" who seesaws between his affections for his Uncle Hud and his Grandfather Homer.

Why did such an unexpected reaction occur? How did such an antihero as Hud become so glorified by so much of American youth? Ritt himself said philosophically that Faust has generally been a better literary character than God,[22] but admitted that if he had been as smart as he thought he was, he would have known that "this son of a bitch" I hated (Hud) would be loved by America's youth.[23] He should have known, he said, that Haight-Ashbury was "just around the corner," helping to herald a generation that resisted authoritarian figures such as they deemed Homer to be.

One of the closing sentences in *Hud* should also have cued Ritt to moods ahead. As Lon and Hud argue at the ranch house after Homer's death, Lon recalls that Hud had refused to be drafted in World War II. In the Vietnam War, which escalated wildly the year after *Hud* was released, this message of refusing to fight for a cause in which you do not believe was very powerful. It would be crediting the movie too much to say that it spawned a generation of anti-authoritarians who were prone to evade the draft. *Hud*, however, played its part in creating this national ethos.

Paul Newman explained the phenomenon in colorful tones: "We fucked up. We laughed about this."[24] Hud, Newman said, was given all the

external graces; he was good with women, he did all those macho things, he wore his pants right, he was a womanizer. But we thought that the fact that he was basically rotten at the core would be the distinguishable feature. What we didn't realize was that all of the other things overwhelmed that single flaw and he came away a folk hero. Yes, they [audiences] couldn't stand the old man, but they loved Hud. We just made a mistake. We thought people would turn away from him. He betrayed his neighbors . . . he would betray anybody, but he apparently was a part of the American Dream.[25]

Perhaps *Hud* comforted those with ideas that "art imitates life." Ritt, however, did not consciously go about making a movie that reflected the moods and opinions of millions of young Americans. He was as surprised at *Hud*'s reception as anyone else. Perhaps *Hud* is additional evidence that the creative process is unpredictable. Even its creators cannot say what the outcome of their efforts will be.

For years after the event, Paul Newman was "Hud" in the minds of cinemagoers. Martin Ritt was known primarily as *Hud*'s director, with reporters and critics tending to ignore his earlier works. He had simply wanted to make a movie about an insensitive person; he wound up creating a legend.

Only a director flexing his *Hud* muscles would have been as audacious as Ritt in his next project—again starring Paul Newman, although at first he turned it down. Ritt had long been interested in the classic Japanese story *Rashomon*, and he decided to film it. His doing so brought more complaints than plaudits, showing again that one success (*Hud*) does not automatically lead to another.

In 1951 the noted Japanese filmmaker Akira Kurosawa brought *Rashomon* to the United States. Playwright and screenwriter Michael Kanin was so impressed with it that he and his wife, Fay, wrote a play based on it that had a successful run on Broadway. The movie script of *Rashomon* floated around Hollywood for some time before it found a taker. Martin Ritt was the man to do it, and he retitled this ancient classic *The Outrage*. (Two working titles for the movie were *The Rape* and *Judgment in the Sun*.)

Rashomon concerns the nature of truth, and how to get at it. In the ancient saga, the Broadway play, and both Japanese and American versions of the movie, there are differing accounts of a rape and murder. Several explanations are set up for the outrage, only to be discredited in the end.

Kanin at first wanted to set *The Outrage* in the Middle East because it had the "ambience" of the original. Ritt changed Kanin's mind about the locale; he argued for the American West, because "it's the nearest thing to myth we have."[26] He found an area around Tucson, Arizona, "filled with symbolic overtones,"[27] and he knew this was the place to make the movie. (Much of the movie was also shot on top of Chatsworth Mountain, north of Los Angeles.)

The movie starts out at a dilapidated train station in the middle of a heavy rainstorm. (Actually, this scene was shot from a sound stage, because the film crew could not wait for rain in arid Arizona.) A preacher (William Shatner) waits for a train, to leave forever the uncontrollable violence he finds at Silver Gulch. A con man (Edward G. Robinson) is also waiting, and is very much surprised to learn that he is in the company of a minister. "A preacher?" he asks loudly. "Can't be. You woke me up. You usually put me to sleep." The entire movie is shot in a series of flashbacks from the train station as the minister and a prospector (Howard da Silva) tell the story. There are even flashbacks within flashbacks as the movie progresses, a factor that might have set heavily with some critics.

There has been a murder in Silver Gulch, to which the con man responds: "Just one? A slow day around here." It happens that a retired Confederate officer (Laurence Harvey) and his bride (Claire Bloom, who had also played this role on stage) are making their way through the desert when they are accosted by Juan Carrasco (Paul Newman). To carry out his wicked design, he entices the officer to look at a jeweled dagger. The naive officer follows Carrasco to a glade where Carrasco quickly subdues him, ties him to a tree, and rapes his wife.

In one version of the tale, Carrasco leaves and the wife unties the officer, who is infuriated with her for allowing Carrasco to despoil her, saying she had "enjoyed" the event. She is so befuddled with her husband's attack on her that she faints. When she wakes up, she finds that her husband has been stabbed to death. In another version, the wife wants to run off with Carrasco and she urges him to kill her husband. Still another version has it that Carrasco himself frees the officer and invites him to fight. The officer will not fight for the honor of his wife; in fact, he refers to her as "poor white trash." One other version has it that, after the officer is freed by Carrasco, the wife runs off from both of them, to which the officer states, "We're better off without her." This version, told by an old Indian (Paul Fix) who secretly watches the proceedings, explains that the officer accidentally falls on the jeweled dagger, and kills himself. As he staggers around after the event, the officer exclaims loudly in an exaggerated Southern accent: "Ah triyupped!" One reviewer said that this was the funniest line Harvey "has ever delivered in movies."[28]

The film ends back at the train station where the three men suddenly find an abandoned baby, a turn in the movie that caused some critics to argue that Ritt had returned to his previous practice of contrived endings. The baby is apparently used to symbolize new beginnings and to cause otherwise base men to rise to points of nobility. One of the trio at the train station, for example, takes all the money that had been left in the baby's basket. "You're a coyote!" another says. "What's the difference between me and the parents who dumped him?" the man rationalizes. Finally, however, the man—who already has a house full of children—takes the baby with him to provide it with a home.

As with *Hud*, James Wong Howe shot *The Outrage* for Ritt. He wanted to use the sun as much as possible in the film and shoot the scenes primarily using back light. He had to use infrared film to turn Paul Newman's blue eyes into black for the role of a Mexican bandit. In one scene, when someone tries to pull the knife out of Harvey's breast, Howe wanted to shoot up past the actor and move the camera into the mist. He built a special platform for this scene because he did not have enough time to dig a hole to handle the equipment. "It's been estimated that it costs the studio about

$100 a minute to shoot a movie," he said, so a platform here was economical as well as artistically satisfying.[29]

Everything the photographer does in a movie, Howe said, should be to advance the plot and action. He praised Ritt for being fairly easy to work with, and for taking on such a subject as *The Outrage*: "If we don't have people like Marty Ritt to make pictures like this, what are we going to do? How are we going to advance the art of motion pictures?"[30] Ritt perhaps gave the best explanation for *The Outrage* a few years later when he told a reporter, "If it's in, it's out with me."[31]

The film's writer, Frank Santillo, echoed Howe's opinion of Ritt. "The minute I walked in with the script under my arm, Marty looked at me, grinned, and said, 'It's a weird one, isn't it?' "[32] Santillo was impressed by Ritt's ability to cut while the film was still being shot. "It was as if he intuitively knew all along how the final film was going to look."[33] Both Santillo and Ritt credited Ritt's ability here with his earlier work in live television. Santillo said further that Ritt, when editing, "locks the film a reel at a time, and he would not go on to the next reel until that one reel was completed. There is no such thing as a rough-cut stage with him. A rough-cut reel, but not a picture."[34]

The music for *The Outrage* was composed by Alex North. He was pleased overall with the film, but he thought the comic sequence could have been eliminated. "Music," North said, "if it is done correctly, can add an entirely new dimension to film. It can embellish, enhance, and solidify an emotional mood that dialogue, or effects, or silences, cannot quite capture."[35] North, who also scored Ritt's earlier film, *The Long Hot Summer,* came up with a suggestion for 35 minutes of music for *The Outrage*. Ritt ultimately allowed eight.[36] North always thought there should have been more music in the film; it would have helped it, in his opinion. Ritt's experience with the Broadway stage was probably one reason why he did not want too much music in his movies.[37]

Many film reviewers simply ignored *The Outrage*, and this probably angered Ritt more than any unfavorable notices he might have received. A good critic, he believed, could teach something to everyone involved in a film, all the way from cameraman to director. He admitted that he did not know whether a creative person is the best judge of his work, and he quoted D.H. Lawrence: "Never trust the artist. Trust the tale. The proper function of the critic is to save the tale from the artist who created it."[38] But if the critic acted as though the film had never been made there could be no corroboration, positive or otherwise, between artist and reviewer.

Typical of the negative reviews was the one in *America*, which said that the kindest thing to be noted about *The Outrage* was that "it lost something in translation."[39] Another critic gave the opinion that "while Newman seems to find the role of Juan Carrasco rather hard going, he, Claire Bloom and Laurence Harvey all have their moments—though moments they remain."[40] Though the film had some "heavyweights," it failed to "establish the action in any really tangible setting."[41] Archer Winsten, always a tough reviewer, said of *The Outrage*, "This Martin Ritt production . . . must be pretty close to the end of the line, for the strain is beginning to show in exaggerated performances, at last reaching a frenzy that is almost slapstick comedy."[42]

Nonetheless, there were some positive reviews. Philip T. Hartung, writing for *The Commonweal*, strained to say something good about it. He was a long-time fan of the original story and of the film made from it by Kurosawa. "I found myself preferring 'Rashomon' with all the mystery and beauty of its eighth-century costumes and sets. But then I realized that American audiences who did not understand the Japanese language relied on English subtitles which did not translate everything. Perhaps if 'The Outrage' had not been so talky, I would have liked it more."[43] He did close his review, however, on a positive note, by asserting that "'The Outrage' was an absorbing, adult film, the kind that Hollywood makes too seldom."[44]

Newsweek said that Ritt was neither "too clear" nor "too fuzzy" in *The Outrage*. Speaking of the various versions of the rape and murder, the reviewer noted, "It is important that we not understand anyone too clearly, lest we miss the point of all of them."[45] According to A.H. Weiler of *The New York Times*, by filming the Japanese classic, Ritt "almost belligerently invited comparisons."[46] Ritt and his crew dissected various aspects of human frailty and "truth" to "create a brisk and challenging drama far removed from the norm in film fare."[47]

"Far removed from the norm of film fare" fairly well summed up *The Outrage* for cinema audiences and movie reviewers alike. First, Ritt undertook to refilm a classic that everybody who knew about movies considered to be near perfect to begin with. Therefore, it was audacity, belligerence, and ego—so it was commonly assumed—that caused Ritt to "meddle" with great art. Second, *The Outrage* was too philosophical for the pragmatic tastes of most moviegoers, and, indeed, most critics. Here was the "pensive necessity" built into a Ritt film to a greater degree, perhaps, than in any of his earlier works. We want to be entertained at the movies; we do not want to think about "truth," although with Vietnam, the Cold War, religious fundamentalism, and the like, in 1964, there were enough "truths," certainly, to go around. The big difference between *Hud* and *The Outrage* was the constancy of character. *Hud* begins in a certain way in the movie and ends the same. In *The Outrage* no one knows what the truth of the matter is. "Truth is relative" is one of the movie's major themes, but its relativity has to be arrived at by people after much more study and attention than 95 minutes of cinematic exposure. *The Outrage* is a film for thought, pensiveness, and philosophical musings. In its own way, it teaches us not to jump to conclusions in our lives, and not to judge too harshly those things which we do not understand. Also in its own way, the film is a great American classic which deserves much more positive attention than it has ever received.[48]

Martin Ritt was nothing if not a generalist. He felt at ease going from one subject to another, scorning, time after time, the so-called auteur theory of filmmaking, by which a filmmaker put his own special "stamp" on a film. (For example, Alfred Hitchcock was widely regarded as both a popular and an "auteurist" director.) Ritt never allowed the screen credits to say "A Martin Ritt Film," believing, as his friend Sidney Lumet stated, that "when I go out shooting, I'm dependent on the weather, the sun, and 120 people around me knowing their work. And I don't want to settle into a particular style, because to me the style is determined by the material itself."[49] Over the years Ritt developed a "powerful disrespect" for "auteurist" reviewers like Roger Greenspun and Vincent Canby, both of *The New York Times*. "Do you know who they think is a great director?" Ritt yelled one time at an interviewer. "Jerry Lewis! I've got to think they're total idiots."[50]

Ritt had to be moved by a script. It had to make him laugh or cry or both, or make him angry. If a script did not affect him personally, he would have nothing to do with it. Then, once he had committed himself to a script, he generally allowed its thematic development to dictate the kind of directing he would give it. His being a generalist was one reason why Ritt never won too many prizes. He was not identified with any one particular school of filmmaking.

His nonspecialization caused more scripts to come his way than would otherwise have been the case. He was interested for a time in a script called "The Menorah Men," a story about historically great art thefts,[51] but finally declined doing it because of other commitments. "The Peddlar," "Moonlight in Any Language," "A Trip to Czardis," "A Man Around the House," "The Hero Suit," "The Land That Touches Mine," "Gaily Gaily," "Virgin Full of Grace,"—all these, and more, were scripts that arrived for his consideration.

David O. Selznick spent several weeks trying to get Ritt and Newman interested in filming John Hersey's *The Wall*, even offering the script to them on a delayed payment basis.[52] Selznick lauded Hersey's novel by saying, "I have scarcely ever read a property which requires so little invention in the way of plot and story line."[53] Billy Rose forwarded "The Immoralist" to Ritt, a script based on a novel by Andre Gide.[54] Brendan Gill of *The New Yorker* sent Paul Brodeur's short story, "The Spoiler," to Ritt. He found it "damn good," but with some material that upset him. Children were involved in a tragedy, and he explained, "I am a father late in life and just the notion of a mishap drives me up the wall. To spend a year of my life with this subject matter would be next to impossible."[55]

One correspondent suggested that Ritt do a movie of the *Autobiography of Malcolm X*. For some time it appeared that Ritt would film Stephen Linakis's *In the Spring the War Ended*, about deserters in Europe during World War II.

Ritt received dozens of requests from hobbyists who were collecting autographs or material on old movies. "Since a long time," said one fan, "it is my wish to have your name in my collection of autographs of the most famous directors of the present time."[56] Another fan wrote in for "any old script" of a movie Ritt had made. Ritt sent him a copy of *Hud*. Numerous students in film schools wanted to work for Ritt on the sets for free, which generally could not be done because of union rules.

In addition to all these activities, Ritt very frequently conducted screen tests for aspiring actors and actresses. In most instances, he had to tell them to get more schooling and training, and then come back to see him. He also received and wrote letters about horse racing, long a passion of his. By now he owned some horses, and very frequently went to see them race. He also got in as many tennis games as he could, playing at the public courts in Pacific Palisades. He refused to join any "exclusive" clubs, tennis or otherwise.

Despite all the literary and cinematic opportunities coming his way in the mid-1960s, there was one movie offer from Paramount that he thoroughly relished. He jumped at the opportunity, for it was the first filming of a John le Carré work, *The Spy Who Came In From the Cold*, probably the most honest spy film ever made.

The Cold War itself is the villain of the movie.[57] Communist spies and Western spies are shown to be much more alike than different. There are no "good guys" and "bad guys" in international espionage; there are scheming, framing, betrayals, and murder. In *Spy* it is not the Communists who set up Alec Leamas (Richard Burton); it is the British. Alec speaks to a character in the movie, but he could just as well have been addressing his cinema audiences: "What do you think spies are? Moral philosophers? They are seedy, squalid bastards who let the moronic masses sleep soundly in their beds."

At the end of the movie Nan (Claire Bloom) tries to escape from East Berlin, and is shot to death. Though he has not developed any close relationship with Nan, Alec goes back to retrieve her fallen body. It is almost as though he knows what will happen to him. He is tired of the hateful acts of both sides in the Cold War. He, too, is shot by the East German volpos, and thus becomes "the spy who came in from the cold." His act is the "ultimate defection."[58] Dilys Powell, writing for *The Sunday Times* in London, said that "Martin Ritt could become known as the film producer who built the Berlin Wall."[59]

Filming of *Spy* went on through several months of 1965 and, all things considered, the period was one of the most miserable times of Ritt's life. For one thing, he had become quite overweight just as the filming had started. He went on a crash diet that kept him hungry—and crabby—most of the time. For another, it was finding the right location to create the ambience for *Spy*. Some of his associates pressured him to to do the interiors in Hollywood, but he refused. If his performers walked into a dark, dismal set out of a bright, sunshiny California day, he felt there was no way he could get atmosphere.[60] "I wanted a gray picture. None of the values in the story were black and white. I wanted rain or grayness in every scene—no sunlight." The movie was shot mostly in Ireland (around the area of Wicklow) because its weather was most like that depicted in the movie.[61] Other shootings occurred at London's Trafalger Square, Ardmore Studios, and in the German city of Garmisch.

Another matter that made Ritt's life uncomfortable while shooting *Spy* was that the studio wanted a happy ending. Ritt knew that a happy ending would ruin the entire mood of the movie. In addition, some studio people (and later, reviewers) faulted the movie for having too much dialogue (there were 32 speaking parts) and not enough plot. To all these points of view Ritt answered that he built the theme incrementally; one scene owed its entire existence to the scene that had just been performed. If he deviated from this procedure, again, he felt the movie would be ruined. He finally had his way in the matter; the movie's ending was definitely not happy.[62]

Worries about events back home in California kept Ritt in a tense condition. Patricia Neal, his Oscar-winning actress in *Hud*, and her family moved into the Ritt household during his absence. While living in his house she had an immense stroke that almost took her life. Ritt wrote a letter to Neal's husband, Daul, that contained the "best kind" of news: "No more rent!"[63] Later, when Neal was recovering, Dahl wrote to Ritt: "This place has been a real haven, a sort of tiny secluded paradise for Pat to recuperate in and no place could have been better."[64] It took real professionalism for Ritt to keep his mind on *Spy* when he was so concerned about his beloved friend.

Ritt told a reporter from *The New York Times* that "I had a miserable time making this picture in every imaginable way. The subdued understated quality of the picture, the small confining sets, the difficult characterizations—the whole thing was agonizing."[65]

And then there was Richard Burton. In the fall of 1964, when he signed Burton to play Leamas, everyone congratulated Ritt on his "good fortune." James Wong Howe, Ritt's principal photographer for *Hud* and *The Outrage*, wrote exuberantly to Ritt, "What a break for you to get Burton for *Spy*."[66] Such an arrangement, however, was to be Orson Welles and *The Long Hot Summer* all over again.

The kindest thing Ritt said about Burton during the ordeal was, "I'm used to working with both untalented bleeps and talented bleeps. Burton happens to be a talented bleep,"[67] but he definitely made no attempt to exploit Burton's glamorous and "sometimes infamous" reputation.[68]

On the contrary. First, Burton spoke his lines too loudly to suit Ritt. (It may be recalled that Anthony Quinn, in *The Black Orchid*, thought Ritt wanted him practically to whisper his lines.) Burton began to tell his associates that Ritt was "wearing him out" by insisting on "twenty-seven takes on every shot."[69] To this barb, Ritt replied: "I know what I want when I see it, and I haven't seen it yet, and he's getting $750,000. I don't say that's too much money, but I do say I'm entitled to a $750,000 effort."[70] (Ritt usually made $500,000 for each picture he directed.)

Though Burton annoyed him to no end, Ritt still admired Burton's artistry. "He's an immense personality," Ritt said of Burton, "and he's bright as a goddamn whip. He can charm you right out of your pants."[71] Difficulties off the stage included Burton's prodigious drinking, his chauffeur's son dying, and Elizabeth's father becoming ill.

In *Spy* there was a scene of a sleazy nightclub in Soho. In it, Burton was put to the floor, and his wrists and ankles were chained. He stayed in this position for a time, waiting for things to happen. An aide walked up to him and said, "Can I get you something, Sir?" Burton replied, "Get me Elizabeth." Right at that point the assistant director yelled "Quiet," and the director (Ritt) quietly and somewhat forlornly said "Action." Burton had the last word: "I'm going back to the mines."[72]

John le Carré was on the sets during much of the filming of his novel. He remembered that Burton became

Ritt's obsession and that their relationship caused the entire movie unit to become uptight. After one particularly stormy session, Ritt screamed at Burton, "I've got the last good lay in an aging whore."[73] Everyone thought Burton would explode at such a remark, but he said nothing, and actually cooperated for a time.

Ritt's relationship with le Carré was not all that pleasant, either. "Marty had a very triumphant and angry air about him," le Carré said.[74] Also le Carré recalled:

At first I think he was disposed to challenge me, I think on the grounds that I was English, and unfortunately I was wearing a black jacket and striped trousers on the first occasion when we met, since I had come straight from interpreting at a Foreign Office conference! . . . When Burton complained of the quality of his lines, Ritt summoned me from Vienna to rewrite them, but he warned me in advance that the production had no money for such contingencies, and I believed him. Our relationship was not made easier because he insisted on boasting about how little he had paid for the film rights in THE SPY[75] and it was further strained when I happened to read an interview he had given in which he made much of his acumen, and dismissed my next book as a failure. I don't think Marty meant any of this unkindly. I think he sometimes just talked from the hip. . . . My memory is of a kind-hearted man inside a pretty rough exterior.[76]

Ritt told a reporter in March 1965, during the shooting of *Spy*, that he was homesick for California. He missed the sauna at his home in Pacific Palisades, and he particularly yearned to see a baseball or football game. "I'm so American!" he exclaimed.[77] He may have become an internationally famous film director by 1965, but he was not beyond a few doses of self-pity.

All was not bleak for Martin Ritt while he shot *The Spy Who Came In From the Cold*, especially during the London sequences. A number of expatriates joined the movie's unit each Sunday morning at Hyde Park for hotly contested games of baseball, a fairly risky thing to do in a land committed to cricket. Ritt wore sneakers and his ever-present jumpsuit to these occasions, and he played a rather sloppy third base.[78] Playwright Neil Simon was in London at the time, and attended some of the ball games. He remembered

Ritt chasing a fly ball down the third-base line, and while trying to retrieve it, he ran headfirst into a big tree. The scene reminded Simon of a "Tom and Jerry" cartoon.[79] After the favorable reception of *Spy*, however, one of Ritt's friends wrote him from London: "Just saw *Spy*. Your two errors at third base are excused."[80] Another correspondent told Ritt that the baseball players left behind in London were thinking of building a monument at Hyde Park with "names inscribed of some of the great and colorful participants in the Sunday a.m. contest." The idea was scotched, however, he jokingly added, for fear that it would be an affront to the memorial to Prince Albert.[81]

When filming and cutting of *The Spy Who Came In From the Cold* was completed, Ritt knew he had a winner on his hands. Undoubtedly, it was this feeling that caused him to approach Paramount Studios about the publicity being planned for the movie. He wanted Paramount to advance him enough money to do his own publicity for *Spy*, a request the studio turned down. Instead, Paramount earmarked $25,000 for general publicity and $1,200 for magazine and newspaper advertising. These were sums, Ritt grumbled, that would hardly make a dent in getting the public interested in his movie.[82]

His friends and associates, however, surely did notice the movie. He received congratulatory telegrams from Claire and Rod Steiger and from David O. Selznick. A London correspondent found *Spy* "chilling, hard hitting, as well as sad, beautifully conceived, and directed,"[83] and a Pennsylvania friend called it a "masterful piece of work," where everything went together "with such unity."[84] Probably the letter he liked most was from a person he had only recently met. She wrote: "It is always an honor to meet a man whose movies *Hud* and *Spy* are a reflection of himself. Ballsy."[85] He was so buoyed up by these positive assertions that Ritt wrote to Oskar Werner (who played Fiedler in *Spy*) that the movie was on the way to doing "big business." Ritt felt that much of the positive image of the film was due to Werner's expert acting.[86]

With newspapers and magazines, *The Spy Who Came In From the Cold* was generally well received. The *Sunday Times* of London said *Spy* was a "deliberately low-key film" with no "flummery,"[87] while *The Boston Traveler* lauded it for combining all the qualities of "perfect entertainment," though it did "dull in its depiction of dullness."[88] Peter Bart, writing for *The New York Times*, noted that two of the Communist agents in *Spy* turned out to be less loathsome "than some of the Brits,"[89] while another journalist asserted that *Spy* "firmly established Martin Ritt in the vanguard of the better contemporary directors."[90] Respected film critic Stanley Kauffmann stated that "both the grubbiness and the norm have been trenchantly conveyed in Martin Ritt's good film of the book,"[91] and the *Washington Post* said that *Spy* was "realism in the contemporary field for the first time."[92]

The Christian Science Monitor argued that Ritt's characterizations in *Spy* matched the bleak backgrounds and "supported his cheerless anecdotes."[93] *The Guardian* believed that Ritt's film did not do "too badly" with atmosphere, but it fell "completely with the characters."[94] And the *Houston Chronicle* believed that Ritt's faithfulness to the book was one of the problems with the movie, because the "tone of despair" spiraled down to a "bottom of apathy."[95]

Again, Ritt's work went largely unheralded by those people in Hollywood who give out the prizes. A friend in London wrote soon after the 1966 Academy Award ceremonies that "we all took a pretty dim view of the Oscar nominations. The whole thing is a disgrace."[96] The picture was, however, voted one of the best ten of 1965 by the National Critics of Radio and Television Commentators. It also won magazine awards from *Photoplay* and *Film Daily*. But the best director award that so many of his colleagues felt he deserved continued to elude him.

Ritt's interest in and treatment of le Carré's novel could very well have been founded in the blacklisting period of the 1950s. Since he and many of his friends were its victims, he tended to attribute less than noble aims and purposes to governmental officials. Also, as he stated rather often, many readers and viewers thought of spy stories as involving only James Bond, a character he simply could not believe.[97] There were no clever gimmicks in real spying, he felt, and the "hero" did not always earn the company of beautiful women, as happened so often in the Bond movies made from Ian Fleming's books. They may been been entertaining, but they were not as factual and realistic as le Carré's work.

Martin Ritt returned to the United States toward the end of 1965, pleased with his efforts with *Spy*, but extremely proud to be home again. He was now more than ever in demand from studios and would-be film scripters, actors, and directors. He received hundreds of letters and dozens of manuscripts each month. He and Adele went through as many of them as they possibly could, and, of course, turned down most of them. He had to add extra secretaries to his staff to take care of all the incoming mail and to see that most of it was answered.

After resting for a time—mostly in his sauna and at the racetrack—Ritt and his friend Paul Newman came up with another idea for a western. It was ultimately to be labeled a "western day dream," a movie that started out as a "western" and ended up a Shakespearian tragedy. When it was released to the public, its title was *Hombre*, and it was the last movie Newman was to make for Martin Ritt.

Chapter 5

◆ ◆ ◆

Heroes and Villains:
From *Hombre* to the *Mollies*

Martin Ritt's settings may have varied between foreign and domestic, but his themes within those locales generally remained constant. Certainly this was true of *Hombre*, a 1967 Twentieth Century Fox release. Paul Newman, who played John Russell in the movie, said that *Hombre* had a theme "very dear to Marty's heart, and that is that competent people always pick up the tab for the incompetent."[1] Themes of universal corruption, determinism, and betrayal caused various critics to compare *Hombre* with classics like *Stagecoach* and *Shane*. Then, too, there was the familiar loner, the individualist, whom Ritt admired so much.

The movie is set in Arizona (though some of it was shot in Colorado). John Russell is a white man captured by Apaches as a baby. Then, a few years later, a Mr. Russell takes him away from the Apaches, only to have John run back to them. As the movie opens, a messenger tells John to leave his high-mountain retreat, where he rounds up and breaks wild horses, and come to see a freighter, Henry Mendez (Martin Balsam), who informs Russell that his father has died and that Russell has inherited from him a watch and a big boarding house.

The housekeeper, Jessie (Diane Cilento) tries to go into business with Russell. He refuses, because he has found a buyer for the house. Then Jessie proposes marriage to the sheriff, Frank Braden (Cameron Mitchell) who has been sleeping with her for the past year. "Not a chance," the sheriff replies. "I'm doing you a favor," he argues, because he has no financial means to support a wife and family.

As Jessie walks away from the sheriff's office, the camera fades into Dr. Alex Favor, Indian Agent (Frederic

March), and his wife (Barbara Rush) walking into the stage office. They want very badly, desperately even, to travel to Bisbee. Mendez tells them that the freight company no longer exists, that it has been run out of business by newly developing railroads. The Favors offer to take on other passengers (John Russell, Jessie, a young soldier, a young married couple, and a young boy), and to buy the wagon and horses if Mendez will put on a special run to Bisbee, an offer he can hardly refuse.

Just before departure, outlaw Grimes (Richard Boone) terrorizes the soldier into giving up his ticket, so Boone can have his seat. On the way to Bisbee the stage is confronted by outlaws, with Grimes revealing himself as their boss. One of the outlaws, incredibly enough, is Sheriff Frank Braden, who looks straight at Jessie, and says "I'm turning bad." Here is a betrayal that makes Jessie realize that Frank has indeed done her a favor by refusing her marriage overtures.

When Grimes and his men leave with some of the money Favor had stolen from the Indians, and the water, they take Favor's wife with them. A Mexican bandit comes back to the stranded passengers, and says that if they do not get the rest of the money and water, they will shoot Favor's wife. Russell replies, "Go ahead and shoot her. She's nothing to me." Russell has the reputation of despising white people for their depredations of the Indians. Finally, the outlaw gang catches up with Russell's group at an abandoned mining cabin. Favor's wife is brought halfway up the slope leading to the cabin, and tied to the railroad track. She will be untied only when Russell gives them the money; otherwise, she will die in the sun. Throughout the day and night, Favor's wife calls pitifully for him to rescue her. He will not. Finally, Russell goes to her assistance. He unties her, and then shoots Grimes and the Mexican bandit. They kill Russell in a hail of bullets. As the movie closes, a real-life photograph is shown on the screen, with the intimation that it is actually John Russell.

John Russell, "Hombre," gives the ultimate sacrifice to save a person he detested. (Favor's wife had forced him out of the stagecoach onto the top with the driver because he had lived with Indians.) He puts aside his own biases and concludes that "suffering is suffering, no matter the person, no matter the cause." It is this thought that propels him toward the wife's rescue.

Hombre, like *The Outrage*, is not a "Western" in the strictest sense of the word. It displays themes that could fit into any kind of setting, urban or rural, foreign or domestic, specific or universal. The sheriff and the Indian Agent personify betrayal and religious hypocrisy. The Mexican bandit symbolizes determinism; he exemplifies the idea that no matter what we do, we are going to die at the appointed time; Jessie is also a determinist, obviously believing that forces beyond her control are the guiding factors of her life.

The brilliant color photography of James Wong Howe propels the movie's themes. (Howe, as a young man, had done the camera work for many of the films made from the western works of novelist Zane Grey.) In one night scene on the Arizona desert, the wind is blowing to such an extent that it sounds very much like an ocean surf. Also, the camera pans the sand dunes in the distant background, making them appear to be waves breaking onto the shoreline. Years before, Zane Grey had made many analogies between the desert and the sea. They are alike, he said, in appearance and sound, and emotional feelings they evoke. One wonders if cameraman Howe remembered Grey in some of the scenes he shot for *Hombre*.[2]

In some ways, Ritt worked under duress with *Hombre*, for he was threatened with a suit from Twentieth Century Fox. He had contracted earlier for additional films with Fox, after *Hemingway's Adventures of a Young Man*, but had not delivered them; and besides he had gone over to Paramount with Salem Productions. "All film companies file charges almost promiscuously," said one authority, "since a lawsuit is a potent bargaining tool in any subsequent negotiations."[3] Ritt agreed to do *Hombre* for $250,000 if Fox would drop the lawsuit. Daryl Zanuck, head of Fox at the time, said "if we drop the suit, he only gets one fifty." After some "friendly negotiations," Zanuck was "agreeable" to $200,000[4] for Ritt's salary.

Certainly not helping matters while shooting *Hombre* was Ritt's continuing weight problem. He had been on a crash diet while filming *The Spy Who Came In From the Cold*, and now he decided that he would have to go to a professional weight-loss institute—a "fat-farm" as he called it—to get his body in trim. "The people who run the fat-farm," he said, "don't like me calling it the fat-farm. But I think it's a great name. Besides, for what they charge me [he did not publicly say] I can call it what I like."[5] One paper, in fact, had spoken of his "billowy figure."[6] He spent, he said, an entire week on 600 calories a day, and only lost a "lousy" five pounds. His blood pressure was normal after the week, but he still weighed—at five feet, ten inches—210 pounds.[7] Though his food for the period was low in calories, he believed it was high in cholesterol. "I could end up one of the thinnest corpses in town," he said.[8] "I don't smoke [though he did, while in production, smoke numerous small cigars] or drink," Ritt wistfully told a reporter, "but I do eat."[9]

Other difficulties in filming *Hombre* developed from illnesses of the performers. Newman was ill for six days, and Diane Cilento was off for five days.[10] Rains and heavy winds caused other delays in the filming. Also, Ritt and his crew had to be very careful to obey Arizona and Colorado animal laws. The Society for the Prevention of Cruelty to Animals had a representative on the scene, who insisted (although he did not have to, for Ritt was always careful to observe animal laws) that the scene that called for a falling horse be done with a trained animal who would fall into a soft bed. Early requirements for the movie called for a dead horse, and one that reared. Both of these representations were to be done by trained animals.[11]

An additional, possible, difficulty for *Hombre*, was the name of its main character, John Russell. The actor who played the leading role in the television series, *The Lawman*, was named John Russell. Also, the dean of the School of Astronomy at the University of Southern California was John Russell. The name, however, was deemed to be so widespread that little or no confusion would occur. Anyway, John Russell was said to have been a character based on a real person, from the novel by Elmore Leonard.[12]

Just before *Hombre* went into production, Ritt received a surprising but pleasant letter from his old Elon classmate and fellow football player, Walter Latham (who went on to become the principal of Bethel High School in North Carolina), whom he fondly called "Firpo." Latham had seen Ritt's name as director on numerous screen credits, so he decided to write to him. The result was that Ritt invited

Latham and his daughter to the sets of *Hombre*.[13] Latham observed the Arizona shootings of the movie, and kept a diary of the events. Of movies, he wrote, "it's rugged, dirty work. Each scene requires many tedious hours of work and sweat in the hot, dusty outdoors."[14] Ritt, said Latham, was a "perfectionist," who left "nothing to chance."[15] He wrote into his diary "Things I Have Noted": Cameron Mitchell (who played Frank Braden in *Hombre*) "believes in the strength of his beliefs. He is Amish and likes to be called 'Buck.'" Ritt, said Latham, "still appears to like me." He discussed and debated with Ritt on questions of "discrimination, religion, sentimentality, politics, and types of government." Latham ended his *Hombre* remembrances by saying: "The actors move around more off set than on. Lines are short, and repeated several times in rehearsal scenes. Sometimes the dialogue is read by a script girl to players just before a scene."[16]

Another small difficulty that arose with *Hombre* was how to distribute it. The studio wanted to release it on a multiple basis, including drive-ins and conventional cinemas. Seymour Poe of Fox Public Relations, said "We're all in this business for money and money is our motivation."[17] Irving Ravetch, who co-wrote the script with his wife, Harriet Frank, Jr., and co-produced the movie with Ritt, objected to a multiple release. He told Poe, "Audiences must be given time to be led. *Hombre* does not have the kind of total and immediate impact which will make it acceptable overnight to a mass audience. It's not that kind of film. For a western, the picture is slow and quiet. It has a purity of style. Its talk is literate and intelligent. It is not related entirely to action, but to an examination of mature people and their behavior."[18] Perhaps inadvertently, Ravetch summed up the problem of Ritt's films with the great moviegoing public in the United States. *Hombre* was not "slam bang," and it was not "bust for hell."[19] Again, it required people to think; and pensive necessity was not generally a part of the moviegoers' paraphernalia. Therefore, though one of *Hombre*'s stars, Diane Cilento (who earned $500 a week for her services as Jessie), was selected by *Cinema* Magazine as the best actress of 1967 for *Hombre*, the movie earned no other prizes.

Letters came in rather quickly about *Hombre*. Sydney Field wrote to compliment Ritt on his use of silence, not only in *Hombre*, but in numerous other films as well. "I think you're the only film maker in this whole country who thoroughly understands . . . the value of silence in film, allowing it to enrich the texture and mood. [Silence] has another dimension which is almost totally lacking from the American film today."[20] Another friend wrote that it was too bad Ritt was not a European and was not named Ingmar Rittburg, or something; otherwise, he would be hailed in the reviews.[21] Henry Rogers said, "I believe when the Martin Ritt cinema accomplishments are listed sometime way off in the dim future, I am sure *Hombre* will be at the top of the list."[22] Richard Guttman believed *Hombre* was "truly an extraordinary film," told with "tremendous conviction and honesty."[23] Stanley Meyer believed that *Hombre* "will rank with *Shane* and *High Noon* as the new champion classic western."[24] And Julio Mario Ronco wrote a simple fan letter about *Hombre* from far-off Argentina and told Ritt that he was the "most efficient and outstanding film director nowadays."[25]

Reviews of *Hombre* were either good or noncommittal. The *New Statesman* said that "*Hombre* resurrects memories of *Hud* and *Stagecoach*."[26] Bosley Crowther mentioned that in *Hombre*, "socially and morally disparate people" were thrown together. He said, "Take a large portion of *Stagecoach*, a small chunk of *The Treasure of Sierra Madre*, a dash of *Broken for Flavor*, and you have *Hombre*."[27] *Hombre*, Martin Ritt told the Los Angeles *Times* "is only nominally a western."[28] He didn't pretend to make another *Hud*, he said.[29]

Despite Ritt's insistence that he was not an auteur director, there were still films made in the mid- to late 1960s with the Martin Ritt imprint upon them. If a film had themes of loners, individualism, betrayal, and corruption, it could very well have been made by Martin Ritt. He remained, however, in his own mind, and in the mind of film critics, a generalist; someone who went from one subject to another in making films. His themes, however, stayed fairly constant.

Nowhere were his themes better expressed than in his next movie, based on the Italian mafia, entitled *The Brotherhood*, from a script developed by Lewis John Carlino. It was just like Ritt to make a "philosophical" movie about the Mafia at about the time *The Godfather* was coming into view for American cinema audiences. After all, he had made *The Spy Who Came In From the Cold* in the face of James Bond. Dramatically, perhaps, *The Godfather* and the Bond movies took the day; philosophically, and in portraying spies and the mafia truly, they did not even compare with *Spy* and *The Brotherhood*.

The Brotherhood is about dirty, squalid crime, but more importantly, about manipulations and fratricide. Frank Ginetta (Kirk Douglas) has many quarrels with his younger brother Vince Ginetta (Alex Cord) over whether Vince should join the group. Different objectives between the group and Frank propel the movie, and Frank finally ends up killing his own brother-in-law, Dominic Bartolo (Luther Adler). But then, in the long run, Vince Ginetta kills Frank, presumably for the good of the family. Frank is "old-fashioned," wanting to do things *his* way, rather than operating along the lines of the majority of the family interest. Frank has gone to Sicily, and when Vince arrives after some time, Frank knows exactly why he has come.

Kirk Douglas produced *The Brotherhood*, and apparently he first intended to shoot it with Warner Brothers. Even while the project was called "The Hoods," Warner threatened a suit against Douglas. The studio had, it said, spent $109,785 for the script and its casting, and Douglas "refused and failed" to render his services called for in the Warner contract.[30] The law firm of Mitchell, Silberberg, and Knupp, representing Warner, demanded an "immediate payment" of $109,785, with interest at 6 percent from 23 September 1966. "We will go to court otherwise."[31] Either the suit was dropped or Douglas paid the amount demanded, for the dispute did not go to court.[32]

Some of the movie was shot in Sicily, and the production crews did their best to keep a low profile—though this was next to impossible. One of Ritt's correspondents told him that "we are dealing, let us face it, with a mafia subject even though the framework of the script is within a very mystic and special atmosphere."[33] There were people on the island whose way of living and code of honor were—it could easily be maintained—being scrutinized by an American film company. In addition to extra sensitivity to local interests, Ritt's crew also had trouble getting all the materials they needed to shoot the movie. Endless negotiations went on between Ritt's business office and car rental companies, with Alitalia about flying in certain equipment and with officials about getting a "clapper" boy who was fluent in English.

Most of the filming was not done in Sicily at all, but on a stage in New York, and this situation ultimately bothered producer Douglas. He wanted to go on location in New York City instead of playing so many scenes in sets. He expressed his thoughts to Ritt, but rather tenderly, definitely not wanting to intrude upon Ritt's territory as director. "Before you start using all those four letter words and begin to attack me," Douglas wrote to Ritt, "please remember that I love you, that I am Jewish and that I am 1,000 miles away from you. When next we meet, I shall be so much less the producer and so much more the actor that it may frighten you. . . ."[34]

Upon completing the movie—which took 44 days and a half million dollars—Douglas and Ritt had to send it to the Motion Picture Association, headed by Jack Valenti. This rating agency suggested that some of the nudity in *The Brotherhood* be eliminated and that the blood spattering scene after the goat slaughter be toned down somewhat.[35] Likewise, a few swear words were excised from the movie. Douglas became quite angry when Valenti, without Douglas's knowledge or permission, sent a copy of *The Brotherhood* to President Lyndon B. Johnson, even before the movie opened to the general public.[36]

Ritt's and Douglas's friends were, of course, highly complimentary of *The Brotherhood*. One person claimed that his admiration for Ritt shot up "265 percent" because of *The Brotherhood*.[37] The film impressed one studio executive who earlier had expressed reservations. "I am the first to say I was wrong," the executive wrote. "I think you are going to have a big picture here. The performances are marvelous. Kirk is the best I have ever seen him, and I think Paramount is in for a big surprise."[38]

Martin Ritt made a great effort, said the *Times-Herald* in Dallas, to create a crime movie that was more than one-dimensional, "succeeding for the most part." The movie was an interesting study of the mood and character of the mafia.[39] The next day, Dallas's other paper, *Morning News*, called the camera work in *The Brotherhood* "imaginative," with the colors creating "a feeling of foreboding."[40] The

Oregonian in Portland, while believing the movie should have been made in black and white for dramatic effect, said that Ritt "played it straight" in directing *The Brotherhood,* but still got "powerful results."[41]

The *Cincinnati Enquirer* lauded *The Brotherhood* because it was "dramatically supercharged." Its narration never gets to a point of "sterile documentation;" nor does it "slide off" to "bombastic moralizing." The movie, the paper asserted, presents a "head-on collision of elderly feudal leaders and modern syndicate leaders."[42] Boston's *Record-American* spoke of Ritt's "sensitive direction" of *The Brotherhood,* stating that he had achieved "the flavor and color of Sicilian life. . . ."[43]

Vincent Canby, whom Ritt accused of being too partial to "auteurist" directors, said that Ritt "clearly opts for the old in movies of vivid incident," and that Ritt treated *The Brotherhood* with "dear solemnity."[44] The other tough reviewer of Ritt's films in New York was Pauline Kael of the *The New Yorker.* For her, *The Brotherhood* did not work dramatically. She thought the object of the movie could have been irony; to cause the viewer to feel perhaps a sense of pity for the passing of the old mob when compared to the increased brutality and machinations of the new. Ritt's direction, she believed, was commonplace and cloddish. "Not only does Ritt lack the style for irony but he keeps Frank in loving close-up so much that we seem to take up residence in the crater of Kirk Douglas's chin."[45]

Pauline Kael may have disliked *The Brotherhood* for aesthetic reasons, but the Americans of Italian Descent (AID) were furious, because they believed it was rife with ethnic stereotypes. The movie was a "disgraceful spectacle" that "denigrates, slurs, defames and stigmatizes 22 million Americans of Italian descent."[46] Douglas and Ritt wanted only to enhance their sensationalist Hollywood reputations, said the AID, but they would not succeed because *The Brotherhood* came at the expense "of the dignity and characters of millions of loyal, decent, honest hardworking American Italians."[47] In fact, AID fumed, "the entire motion picture is an insult to all decent Americans of whatever origin."[48]

Ritt was used to drawing fire with his movies, especially from critics, but this was the first time he had been attacked by an ethnic group. His opinion remained firm that *The Brotherhood* truly depicted a change in character and philosophy from one mafia generation to another. He denied efforts of stereotyping Italians, as he was fond of their literature and their music. The mafia, like gangsterism in America, was just one element of a society which did not at all reflect that society as a whole. Later, Ritt had this same problem when he started to make films about blacks. He ran the gamut of charges of racism, ignorance of black manners and ways, and exploitation of the black situation in the civil rights climate of the time.

Soon after *The Brotherhood* was shot (it took over a year from the time production started until it was finally showing in the cinemas across the country) Ritt took a sentimental journey back to the South, to Elon College, where so many years before he had played football for "The Fighting Christians." The honorary degree of Doctor of Fine Arts was conferred on Ritt by Elon President J.E. Danieley. He was reunited with "Firpo" (Walter Latham) and many of his other classmates of the 1930s.

Even though Dr. Ritt tried to get some rest after *The Brotherhood*, he was still bombarded with literally dozens of proposals. For one, Godfrey Smith, editor of the London *Sunday Times* sent four of his paperback novels to Ritt. "They are intended as a gift," the crafty Smith noted, "but obviously if you do see any film possibilities in them, I shall be delighted."[49] Almost as a postscript, Smith added that "similar sets of the novels are being sent out to a small selection of the best producers and directors in the United States and Britain."[50] Ritt found none of the Smith novels to be his "cup of tea."

Ray Bradbury's *Something Wicked This Way Comes* was offered to Ritt as was Larry McMurtry's *The Last Picture Show.* His old friend Arthur Miller sent him his play, *The Price.* Ritt wrote to Miller: "As I thought it through I felt that this play more than any of your others would simply look like a photographed evening in the theatre."[51] He also received and considered Leland Cooley's *Condition Pink*, Marian Winters's *All Is Bright*, Elmore Leonard's *Valdez Is Coming*, Goldie Kasnov's *Sea Wall*, Mitchell Brower's *The Mandarins*, Alan Abel's *The Great American Hoax*, Peter Matthiessen's *Fair Angelica*, Henry Weinstein's *Witness to a*

Killing, and Fletcher Knebel's *Vanished*, plus numerous others.

He even considered doing a movie about the Vatican because he wanted to delineate the total merging of church and state. Ritt was a dais guest at the Motion Picture Production Union's salute to Mayor John V. Lindsay for his efforts in bringing film productions to New York City. And, he agreed to attend a film symposium at Ohio University in early 1969 as long as he did not have to make a speech. He presided at several question-and-answer sessions, in which he told students that although it was tough to break into the movies, "real talent will always find an outlet." As recompense for his Ohio appearance, he only wanted his expenses to be paid and the $500 fee offered him to be given to a scholarship fund. Ritt had indeed come a long way from the days of blacklist inactivity to a schedule that had him busy every waking moment. He complained from time to time about the pressure, but all indications were that he loved it. He liked to be in charge of things, and one indication was that although he had a folding chair that had "Director Ritt" written on it, he rarely used it. In directing movies, Ritt was more apt to walk right along with the performers and the photographic technicians than sit in his director's chair.[52] He was, after all, an "actor's director," and he would rather work inches from them than feet, or worse yet, yards.

Some Hollywood directors, like some authors, will not take on another assignment until their current one is finished. Ritt was not one of them. Even in late 1966 negotiations were taking place on a movie that would become, at least in Pauline Kael's opinion, an "impressive failure." That movie was *The Molly Maguires*. Through the years, it probably remained Ritt's personal favorite, and he simply could not understand why it failed at the box office.

The movie is set in the 1870s in the anthracite coal regions of Pennsylvania. A group known as the Molly Maguires blows up mines and injures and sometimes kills mine supervisory personnel. Their leader is Jack Kehoe (Sean Connery). A newcomer, McKenna (Richard Harris) is at first distrusted, but later admitted into the Ancient Order of Hibernia. Only Kehoe's wife continues to have a "feeling" about McKenna. (In reference to stars for *The Molly*

Maguires, Ritt would not even consider anyone who was not born in the British Isles.)[53]

As it turned out, McKenna is an informer for the railroad police, known in the movie by the Irish slang term, "Peelers"; obviously, however, a reference to the Pinkerton Detective Agency, which sent hundreds of men into the Pennsylvania coal fields in the 1870s to subdue workers and discourage them from demanding higher wages and better working conditions from the owners. While Kehoe is in jail awaiting execution, McKenna—McParlan is his real name—comes to see him in his cell. Kehoe accuses him of coming for absolution; he wants some kind of punishment to set him free. Kehoe says, "Maybe it's my Christian heart, but I cannot stand the sight of a man bearing a cross." With that, he starts strangling McKenna and would have killed him if the guards had not beaten him off. Kehoe tells McKenna that he has no punishment this side of hell, to which McKenna replies, "See you in hell."

Who were, in fact, the Molly Maguires? One version had it that they were an Irish secret society first organized in 1843 to terrorize and murder rent collectors sent over to Ireland by wealthy English landlords. The "Mollies" were stout, active young men who blackened their faces and dressed in women's clothes. In Ireland their victims were frequently thrown down bog holes, or severely beaten. Apparently many such young men immigrated to the United States in the 1840s and 1850s, and perpetuated their organization. Its vendetta character against the English was quickly transferred to coal operators in the United States.

The coal mining industry became viable in the United States in the 1840s, and by the mid-1870s Pennsylvania was significant for its anthracite fields. Troubles flared often between the owners and the workers, and in 1875 there occurred the "Long Strike," accompanied by much violence. After the strike ended, explosions, beatings, and murders of mine officers and superintendents continued apace.

One version of the "Mollies," however, was that they were the imaginary creations of the coal operators themselves. It was only after the Pinkertons arrived on the scene that the "crime wave" appeared; and in actuality, it was not only the supervisory personnel who were victimized but ordinary miners and union leaders as well.[54] In reality, also,

James McParlan's testimony at the trial of the terrorists was "tortuous and contradictory";[55] nevertheless, 24 people were convicted, and ten were executed.[56]

Martin Ritt's movie *The Molly Maguires* was his most historically based work to that point in his career. His old friend Walter Bernstein wrote the script—for $15,000—and he said the material for it became "increasingly fictional."[57] Wayne G. Broehl, a professor of history at Dartmouth University, had published a book on the Molly Maguires for Harvard University Press,[58] but the book closest to *The Molly Maguires* script was Arthur Lewis's *Lament for the Molly Maguires*. Ritt's researchers found enough similarities between Lewis's book and Bernstein's script to recommend that Paramount offer Lewis $15,000 for use of his material, or at least give him screen credit. The studio did neither, however, its researchers finally arguing that it was best to eliminate any resemblances between Lewis and the script. Some examples of similarities included Mary Kerrigan (Samantha Eggar) in the movie being based on real-life Mary Higgins. John (Jack) Kehoe actually existed (though in actuality he became a saloon keeper after leaving the mines) and certainly McKenna (McParlan) existed; in fact, he went on to Denver after the events described in *The Molly Maguires* and was assassinated, presumably by an outraged unionist. There were enough composites, however, that Bernstein and Ritt were encouraged to use material in the public domain to film the movie without having to acquire any rights.

Bernstein had at first taken his idea and script for the movie to MGM, only to have it turned down because of fears of legal complications. Also, Paramount, the studio that ultimately made *The Molly Maguires* was approached by five different sources; it had declined the offers for various reasons, legal matters among them. Immediately, the question arose of whether Bernstein, who had now written a script on the subject acceptable to Paramount, had ever seen any of the previous proposals. He had not, he said, so there should be no difficulty from those quarters. (Some material for the movie came from the Smithsonian Institution, which refused to allow its name to be listed in the screen credits— perhaps because of a fear of legal implications.)[59] When Broehl wrote his book on the "Mollies," he had encountered some difficulties with the Pinkerton Detective Agency. There were strict usage regulations on Pinkerton materials in the Library of Congress.[60] Among other things, the author had to promise the agency that he would make no effort to film his book, or in any way try to get movie studios interested in it.[61]

The Molly Maguires was exactly the kind of movie Martin Ritt relished making. It was about a downtrodden group of Irish coal miners, who were, in the 1870s in the United States generally referred to as "white niggers." They lived on subsistence wages and worked in dreadfully unsafe conditions.[62] Their employers came from the wealthy, privileged classes in America, and in dealing with coal miners, they were uncompromisingly "capitalistic"; any semblance of unionism instantly earned their wrath. From the 1930s on, Ritt had been socially conscious, favoring the underdog, and those people who, generally, could not fight back. If and when they did retaliate, could their violence sometimes be justified because they had been brutalized by unfair systems in the first place? *The Molly Maguires* also has the strong theme of betrayal, another dramatic path Ritt liked to follow since the blacklisting days of the early 1950s: both he and Walter Bernstein had been blacklisted.

The Molly Maguires was filmed around the Hazelton, Pennsylvania, area—an event that certainly did excite the local population and press. *The Scranton Sunday Times*, *Sunday Eagle* from Reading, *Philadelphia Bulletin* and *Inquirer*, *Wilkes Barre Record*, Allentown *Morning Call*, and the *Pottsville Republican* had constantly on the scene reporters who described the crowds that gathered, and wrote feature stories on the performers.

Some of the shooting (again, James Wong Howe was the principal cinematographer) was done in Jim Thorpe, Pennsylvania; most of it, however, occurred in the small mining village of Eckley. It had been originally an Irish community on the lands of the Coxe Collieries, but now (1968) it was occupied by people mostly of eastern European background. The present owner was George Huss who lived in Ringtown, near Shenandoah, Pennsylvania, and ran strip-mining operations just at Eckley's limit. The little village had a population of between 150 and 200. There were some forty old red company houses stretched for half a mile along a road through Eckley, each renting for $8.00 a month. To get village cooperation, Paramount officials spoke with each head of household in Eckley and promised them, or their children, some part in the movie; not a difficult task.

The movie crew had to remove all the telephone and telegraph wires and put in underground cables. They built an entire store which would be burned down for the movie, and they renovated the old Eckley Sports club into a "saloon." All the roads had to be covered completely with dirt, turning them into vintage 1875. Ironically, there was a labor dispute during the filming. Ritt brought in specially trained Hollywood painters to render some highly visual creative effects, an action that bothered New York Local 892 of the United Scenic Artists, who thought they should be given the job. Ritt and Paramount ultimately convinced them that specialists were essential for the work they wanted done.

Ritt's headquarters while making *The Molly Maguires* was at the Gus Ginetti Motor Lodge in Hazelton. He probably came to regret that he did not accept Netti Postupack's suggestion that Paramount set up an Information Desk "to answer the questions of the thousands of visitors, many who drove hundreds of miles to come" to the movie site.[63] As it was, he was constantly barraged with letters, memos, and suggestions.

One person sent in an unpublished manuscript, "Ms. Gwilym of the Pen, or the Molly Maguires," which studio officials returned unread, while a film student from Chicago forwarded a book that dealt with creative uses of film in education. One mother was angered that her son's music designed for *The Molly Maguires* had been neglected. "The music hasn't been returned and that's the least you could do. No organization or man is that busy that they can't find some time to answer a bona fide first class letter."[64] Ritt agreed: he sent back the music with a note of apology. Ritt actually had never paid very much attention to the music in his movies. "I am very wary of music," he said, "and I never use it underneath a scene."[65] Ritt turned to noted musician and composer Henry Mancini for the music to *The Molly Maguires*. A movie must not start with music in mind, Mancini argued, especially with Ritt movies, which always subordinated music to the story line. Ritt never tried to tell a composer *how* to score his movies, but he did often insist on a time line.[66] Even so, Mancini gave a "big score" to *The Molly Maguires* as he filled it with American and Irish folk songs and rhythms. In fact, the music of *The Molly Maguires* was one of its most noteworthy features.

Bobbi Ann Warren, Miss Pennsylvania of 1967, was one of the extras, but she had a problem getting from her Edwardsville home to the shooting sites. "I do not drive," she explained, and felt it unfair to be given only a moment's notice about when her services were needed.[67] Ritt and his entire crew were "subpoenaed" to appear before the "Kangaroo" court of the Wyoming Valley West High School's Senior dinner dance.[68] He respectfully declined. Kathleen Reimold invited Ritt to be her guest at the Lakewood Musical Theatre.[69] Again, Ritt declined. Richard Tomasko would "give his right arm" just to view the shooting of *The Molly Maguires*.[70] Ritt invited him to the sets. Anthony Reznak, Jr., however, wanted to make still photographs of the filming; Ritt refused.[71] Clem McGinley asked if Ritt needed any whistlers for his film; Ritt did not.[72] Fred Henry wanted to know if Ritt would sponsor his bowling team; he would not.[73]

On and on these letters, suggestions, and proposals came. One correspondent proposed that at the end of each day's shooting, Ritt have all the principal performers in *The Molly Maguires* take walks along the edge of the location, so all the visiting fans could see them.[74] Ritt refused. Another writer complained of being pushed off the lot by a policeman.[75] Ritt replied by apologizing and inviting the lady to the sets. "The rudeness was uncalled for," he told her, "and we apologize." He told another woman that her son could observe the filming "if he wants to come and take care of himself which ever way he can." But then, he added, "even the go-fers are unionized and the unions are impossibly reactionary."[76]

Senator Joseph F. Clark of Pennsylvania put remarks about *The Molly Maguires* into the *Congressional Record*. "From this tragedy of the Molly Maguires, grew the seeds of rightful protest and from it and similar incidents labor unions were finally organized in this country. I salute producer-director Martin Ritt and his stars as they begin to film this important and meaningful segment of America's past."[77] Numerous citizens wrote to Ritt with the idea of turning Eckley into a coal museum after the filming was completed. David Golding assured Ritt that there was an ample supply of miners' cap lamps, picks, lunch and water pails, and boring tools to make the effort worthwhile. A small museum did begin to operate after the movie's completion. Otherwise, Ritt and Paramount would have had to restore Eckley in accordance with the agreement they made with Huss for use of the land.

The managing editor for the Foreign Press Association, Joe F. Sloan, got into a snit because Ritt did not answer one of his letters soon enough. He wanted to visit Eckley "to do a feature story for our newspapers but we haven't even received the common courtesy of an answer. If that's how Paramount wants it, okay by us."[78] Ritt replied apologetically. The lack of newspapers at the shooting locations certainly was no problem for Ritt and his crew; on the contrary, the fact that there were about a dozen papers permanently on the scene may have been instrumental in bringing on one of the crises while the film was being shot. Every time a reporter wrote a story about *The Molly Maguires* he invariably referred to the historical Pinkertons. (In the movie, it may be recalled, the police are called "Peelers," a common name for them in England and Ireland—after the Home Secretary of the 1830s and Prime Minister in the 1850s—Sir Robert Peel.) These newspaper references caused the contemporary Pinkertons to conclude that the movie itself was using the actual name of Pinkerton. Therefore, the Pinkertons began to demand that they be allowed to read the script to make sure their agency was in no way slandered. The request outraged Ritt, and he flatly refused. He did not know, however, how persistent the Pinkertons could be.

The problem started in January 1968, when the Pinkertons requested script approval. Ritt's attitude was "I really do not see how Pinkerton has any rights in this so long as we do not use their name."[79] Paramount lawyer Bradford Petersen tried to mollify the Pinkertons by telling them that Ritt "for reasons which would appear obvious wished to keep the story confidential."[80] Lawyer Petersen had, he said, read the script and could assure that there was no identification of the Pinkertons in the movie. "Accordingly, it would appear that there would be no point in having the lawyer from Pinkerton read the script."[81]

By April the 1968 Pinkerton's request had turned into a virtual demand. The agency feared that the picture might infringe upon its rights of privacy.[82] "All of the efforts of the movie makers [Martin Ritt, Walter Bernstein, et al.] might well be jeopardized," Pinkerton lawyers arrogantly claimed, "should our client be required at a later time to take appropriate legal steps to protect its rights."[83] Unfortunately, from Ritt's standpoint, the Paramount lawyers came around to an agreement. In August 1968, Ralph Kamon of Paramount strongly urged that "we permit the Pinkertons to read the script now,"[84] to avoid any "future unpleasantness in this matter."[85]

Ritt "held his nose" and turned over the script to the Pinkertons. In September Pinkerton lawyer Herbert C. Earnshaw wrote to Paramount that "We are pleased that the screenplay did not contain any material which would be objectionable to our client. The opportunity to read the screenplay has certainly allayed the fears it had."[86]

Martin Ritt and his associates thought that now the Pinkerton matter had been settled, and they went about filming their movie. They apparently overlooked one of Earnshaw's closing sentences in his letter to Paramount: "While we assume that the photography follows the screenplay in all respects, we would, however, appreciate the opportunity to see the picture at the earliest date when it may be screened in New York."[87] This was almost too much for Ritt. He fumed and raged and used up his repertory of four-letter words (which was immense) and then settled down and agreed to a Pinkerton private screening; otherwise, the whole movie would be threatened. The Pinkertons, in late December 1968, saw *The Molly Maguires* and gave their blessings: the picture could be released to the public. Such a release ultimately disappointed and baffled Ritt, because neither reviewers nor the public took to it in the way he would have preferred.

James Wong Howe's "use of space" in *The Molly Maguires*, gave the movie "an imposing solidity," said Pauline Kael, always a tough reviewer of Martin Ritt films. The movie carried a rather "dubious story," she said, "but it feels like a reminder of a bitter, tragic past, and when you come away, you know you've seen something."[88] Another reviewer said that the theme of *The Molly Maguires* should be "how honest, helpless, hard working and cheated miners were framed by the company which deliberately perpetrated dynamiting and arson themselves."[89] The Boston *Herald-Traveler* said that "Director Ritt gives the sounds and sights of the living conditions in the fields and of the violence which sought to change them."[90] Thomas Blakley of the *Pittsburgh Press* wrote that Ritt was known for his attention to "little details." He was not a "slave to brutality," presenting things honestly and simply, in an "unhurried manner."[91]

Perhaps it was the "unhurried manner" of *The Molly Maguires* that in part caused the movie not to catch on with the moviegoing public, though it did win a Bell Ringer Award from *Scholastic* magazine.[92] To capture the young audiences of the day, the action would have to be speeded up considerably, because as Ritt himself stated, the movies in the early 1970s were into car chases and, more importantly, were just ushering in the famous "tits and asses"[93] period of American cinematography. His movies offered neither of these diversions. Ritt mentioned to a friend that his movies portrayed "unfashionable truths"[94] to cinema audiences and he was aware that as a result he was not as popular as some of Hollywood's other "more auteur," directors.

To the older, more conservative movie audiences of the early 1970s, *The Molly Maguires* reminded them of some rather unpleasant recent occurrences. A United Mine Worker official, Joseph Yablonski, and his wife, had been murdered a few weeks before the release of *The Molly Maguires*. The movie thus focused attention on the coal mining industry,[95] and reminded citizens of the brutal strife that existed within labor unions of that day, and of the horrible relations between labor and management. Also, it was widely believed that *The Molly Maguires* tried to capitalize on some of the racial strife in the United States in the late 1960s and early 1970s. Was there not too perfect a parallel between the Molly Maguires of 1870 and the Black Panthers (whose members liked the film very much) of 1970? If you tell the truth about 1870, are you not also telling the truth about 1970?[96] Ritt, calling such accusations "bull," said that he postponed work on *The Molly Maguires* in 1965, because "Watts blew up"[97] The Panthers were not even on the scene in 1965; thus, it was clear, said Ritt, that *The Molly Maguires* was thought about long before the Panthers (or the Weathermen) appeared. If it seemed that there was a connection between the Molly Maguires of a hundred years before, and present-day radical groups, the similarity was, as they say in the movies, purely coincidental.

Another problem with *The Molly Maguires* was that it was difficult for audiences to figure out who was the hero. Was it Kehoe, who, with his organization, the Molly Maguires, was responsible for mayhem, injury, and murder in the Pennsylvania anthracite coal fields? Or was the hero McKenna, the informer? Definitely, in Ritt's mind, the hero was Kehoe. "I became myself in that picture," he told an interviewer.[98] "They [the audiences] should have understood that Kehoe, who was a murderer, was really the hero of that film, but they didn't." The villain was McKenna (or McParlan in real life), who wormed his way into the graces of his fellow workers, and then turned them in to the authorities. Ritt's disdain for informers was well attested; it was no accident that he directed this film—which cost $11 million—and that Walter Bernstein wrote the script for it. They had both suffered in the past because of the activities of "inside" informers.[99]

Still another factor that played against *The Molly Maguires* was the way films were distributed in the United States. It opened in February 1970, to "cool reviews,"[100] and then was essentially buried by Paramount. Late in 1970, *The Molly Maguires* turned up in several neighborhood cinemas throughout the country as a secondary feature to the main attraction. In Chicago, it was shown as a "second feature" to *Watermelon Man*. Noted movie reviewer Roger Ebert said this fate of *The Molly Maguires* was due to "our cruelly arbitrary film distribution system."[101] Ebert's cohort, Gene Siskel, also saw *The Molly Maguires* in late 1970. His view was that it was "so much better than the visual sewage which has floated into town . . . one is tempted to call it a masterpiece."[102] Siskel said that *The Molly Maguires* was not a "youth film." Rather, it was a traditional melodrama "which resembled many gangster films."[103]

Martin Ritt believed that *The Molly Maguires* was his most "American" film to date. After he had finished with the Communists, he told friends that he wanted to direct only "American" films. This genre of "American" films certainly did get him into the motif of the underdog and the minority.

Wherever there were needs for redresses of grievances, Ritt wanted to portray them on the screen. Throughout much of United States history, labor unions have unfairly been seen as a threat to property; in fact, the modified capitalistic society of the United States has practically sanctified private property. Anything that threatened that property—either in fantasy or reality—has been seen as a threat.

Martin Ritt came to the point in his movie career where clusters of movies created at least somewhat unifying themes. Individualism, independence, informing, betrayal, relative degrees of "morality,"—all were common to *Hombre*, *The Brotherhood*, and *The Molly Maguires*. In his next "cluster," Ritt went back to the American South, a part of the country he both loved and hated. In the early 1970s he began to film movies about the South with an emphasis on blacks (his earlier southern films, *The Long Hot Summer* and *The Sound and the Fury* were about white class conflicts in the South rather than racial strife).

Ritt's three racial films in the early 1970s were *The Great White Hope*, *Sounder*, and *Conrack*. In more ways than one, they are the films by which Martin Ritt is remembered.

Chapter 6

◆ ◆ ◆

Martin Ritt and the Black Experience:
The Great White Hope, Sounder, and *Conrack*

Martin Ritt's social consciousness was undoubtedly formulated by his youthful experiences in New York of witnessing Depression-era injustices. It was almost certainly solidified, however, by his stay in the South in 1932 and 1933. In the South, not only were there the economic down-and-outers whom he had seen in his home city; there were also blacks who had to bear the extra burden of racism. Even while at Elon College in North Carolina, Ritt noted the sometimes servile manner of blacks toward whites, and perhaps subconsciously determined someday to delineate their struggle toward equality.

His first great opportunity was in 1969-70, when he became involved with a New York play by Howard Sackler called *The Great White Hope.* By now Ritt was a highly respected director—much sought after by the studios—despite some of his spectacular "failures," such as *The Molly Maguires.* He went to see the play, "The Great White Hope," and, at first, was not interested in putting it on film. Several friends asked him about it, but he always said no, he wasn't interested. But then, Lawrence Turman, an important producer, telephoned and, with lures of salary and artistic satisfaction, changed Ritt's mind about the matter. Besides, Ritt had always loved boxing; he thought highly of its rhythmic, even poetic, movements.

The pull of the story for Ritt at this time was history. He had just finished his most "historical" movie yet, *The Molly Maguires*, and so it was a small transition to another historical subject. *The Great White Hope* deals with Jack Johnson, the world's first heavyweight black boxing champion. In 1908, Jack Johnson defeated Tommy Burns of Australia to gain the title. A black becoming champion deeply bothers the white-dominated world of professional boxing. "Prior to Johnson's time, fight promoters would not match black and white heavyweights in a title bout."[1] After Johnson's win in Australia, the "cry went up in America: 'Somebody has got to beat that big nigger.'"[2] Each boxer chosen by the white promoters to defeat Johnson comes to be known as "The Great White Hope." Frank Brady (Jim Jeffries in real life, who comes out of retirement in 1910 to face Johnson) fights the champ (who, in the movie, is named Jack Jefferson, played by James Earl Jones—to whom Ritt referred as "some kind of actor!") in Reno, and loses. The boxing officials will have to continue looking for a "great white hope."

As though "intrusion" into the white world of boxing is not enough to get him into trouble, Jefferson also comports with white women. In fact, on the boat back from Australia, he meets and falls in love with Eleanor Backman (Jane Alexander). Local law officials in Chicago determine to get Jefferson on whatever charges they can; they finally trip him by a questionable reading of the Mann Act, which prohibits taking a woman across state lines for purposes of prostitution. That Ellie is not a prostitute, and goes willingly with Jack Jefferson from Illinois to Wisconsin, makes no difference to the bigoted law officials.

Jefferson is given a sentence for violating the Mann Act, but he jumps bail. For the next several years he and Ellie wander throughout such European capitals as London, Paris, and Berlin. U.S. law officials, however, send word to him that if he will return to America, and throw whatever championship fight comes his way, he will receive a reduced sentence on his conviction, and for jumping bail. Many blacks are coming up to the North from out of the South, the lawmen tell Jefferson, and they must have someone other than himself to look to as a hero. Jefferson refuses, he and Ellie finally showing up in Mexico. The two quarrel and Ellie commits suicide. In despair, Jefferson agrees to a fight. He almost backs out of his agreement in the fight, coming close to defeating his opponent. He finally does, however, take a ten count, and tells all the reporters that he was beaten fairly and squarely—which is probably the truth.

The Great White Hope, Ritt's fourteenth movie, was in line with thematic developments he had fostered for the past several years. Jack Jefferson was a loner, and in being so, became a hero. He "step'n-fetched" his way around white people, and then either knocked them out in the ring or made fools of them. (In 1910, at the weigh-in before the fight, Brady weighs 204 pounds and Jefferson, 191. Jefferson quips to Brady: "They says I'se lighter than you.") He was the very kind of person Ritt liked and admired. Ritt said of the movie, "I liked it because it was juicy and full of beans and full of life and full of appetite and full of America. It's a very American film which appealed to me no end."[3] It dealt with the black-white problem, which was a "very American dilemma."[4] He even compared it to *The Diary of Ann Frank* in that it brought down to the "nitty-gritty" the abject condition of one man (Johnson) to all of his fellow human beings.

The film begins with a half screen in which the Australian fight is depicted showing just the legs of the boxers. The viewer knows that Jefferson wins when the white legs go to the canvas. Then, for the fight in Reno in 1910, Jefferson's victory is not specifically shown, simply montages of the bout; and again the viewer knows who is the victor. This viewer "knowledge by insinuation" was now a widely used practice of Martin Ritt. He believed that he did not have to "hit the viewer over the head" for him to understand the action. Ritt had never been one for much music in his films, and there was even less of it in *The Great White Hope* than in some of his other productions, due, perhaps, to the movie's being an adaptation of a stage play. Though the play, he said, was "filmic," he became less enamored than before of play material. "I am much more interested," he told a correspondent, "in an original screen-play or a novel that can be made into a film."[5] The film ends the way it starts; with half screens showing the "defeated" champ being led to his room while the proponents of the "great white hope" cheer their victory.

The film had a few problems with the censors. A black friend in the movie tells Jack that he is "itching for the white man's piece of poontang" with all his cavorting with white women. When Ellie faces the Chicago district attorney and finally realizes that he is trying to trick her into claiming that Jack Jefferson had committed some crime, she calls him a "no dick mother grabber." These expressions, plus several "hells," "by-gods," and "goddamns," caused some of those involved with the film to want to eliminate them. They won only in the sense that they kept the word "fucking" out of the movie: 1970 was still relatively early in cinema history to use such "risque" language. Ritt and his associates did use a technique becoming increasingly popular in the 1970s: they took their movie on a "test run" to an audience to try and learn in advance of general distribution how it would be received. Eighty-four percent of the audiences rated *The Great White Hope* as "excellent," 16 percent as "good," and two percent as "fair."[6] Even with this prognostication, the movie did not fare well at the box office.

The Great White Hope was filmed in Big Bear, California, and Barcelona, Spain, and it cost about $10 million.[7] The most expensive part of the movie was the fight scene purported to having taken place in Havana, where Jack Jefferson ultimately loses to the "white hope." Ritt always liked to film on location; justifying Barcelona, he said that audiences are sophisticated, and unless they get the genuine ambience of a scene, a movie is likely to be considered false.

Beyond matters of cost, the most significant questions about the movie dealt with the white-black issue. Was this movie a forum for supporting mixed marriages in America? Some people might believe such a theory, said Ritt, "but that's not going to bother me one way or another. . . . I've always said what I felt and let the chips fall where they may."[8] Did this film make a statement? Yes, it did, Ritt said; as did, indeed, all of his other films. If his films could not make a statement, then why do them? If the film worked emotionally (which it did for Ritt) then it would be only prejudiced audiences who would object to it and, as Ritt rhetorically asked, "What the hell do I care about them anyway?"[9] Did *The Great White Hope* have anything to say about the contemporary situation (1970) in the United States? Indeed it did, said Ritt: "I accept Jack's courage and his will and his fight for his identity."[10] Both Jack and Ellie fought for their rights as human beings, certainly a leading theme of the late sixties and early seventies.

Press reports about *The Great White Hope* were generally favorable. It was a "period piece,"[11] said one reporter, "but it is still about today." Ritt showed "consummate artistry,"[12] which bordered on being a "black passion play." For Judy Stone of the *San Francisco Chronicle* the film's message was "baby don't mess with me,"[13] while *Time*'s Stefan Kanfer thought it was staged purposely to be "razzed at a panther rally."[14] As with *The Molly Maguires*, Ritt had touched a painfully contemporary note by once again causing reviewers and audiences alike to surmise that he had black revolutionary groups in mind when he made his movies. It is nevertheless true that numerous black groups very much liked *The Great White Hope*. The NAACP, for example, awarded Ritt its annual Image Award for his directorial efforts.

The *Boston Herald Traveler* liked *The Great White Hope* because Ritt stripped it of the extraneous matter emanating from the Broadway play, and gave only the grueling basics of black reality in early twentieth-century America.[15] On the other hand, the *Philadelphia Inquirer* thought the movie suffered from being too *faithful* to the play.[16] The "stagy" quality of many of the movie's episodes kept it from being "a completely successful film."[17]

To the surprise of no one, Pauline Kael of *The New Yorker* did not like *The Great White Hope*. The movie "clunked along like a disjointed play,"[18] she said. "It's all so stagy that when Ritt splurges and shows us thousands of people at the final match, counting time with the referee, we are moved not by any meaning in the shot but its pathetic exhibitionism."[19] The writer for the *Examiner* in San Francisco agreed with Kael: "The film strains to be entertaining. . . . The incredible treatment with the whites played like villains and the blacks like saccharined saints destroys our faith in the script and causes us to wonder what really happened to Jack Johnson."[20]

Ritt's past southern films (*The Long Hot Summer* and *The Sound and the Fury*) did not have the plight of blacks as their major thrust. Blacks were, of course, in these films, but their roles were subordinate to white class struggles. *The Great White Hope* was Ritt's first film where he came directly to grips with biases and prejudices against the American black. The settings for the movie were not in the South, definitely an indication that by Ritt's time racism was not simply a sectional problem but one that had become horrendously national. One criticism of the movie that bothered Ritt somewhat was the charge that, as a white director, he could not really capture the nuances of the black experience. He answered such statements by saying that it was the "worst kind of racism";[21] if one believed such "logic," one would "also have to say that a black director can't direct white actors, and I don't believe that."[22] One newspaper, the *Press-Scimitar* of Memphis, came to Ritt's defense: "Martin Ritt was making movies about black people before it became either a popular or profitable thing to do."[23] Someone asked Ritt if he intended to film a black *Exorcist*. His response to such queries was: "I wouldn't make a *white Exorcist!*"[24] "In fact," it was pointed out, "Martin Ritt doesn't make black pictures or white pictures, much less demon pictures or devil pictures. Martin Ritt films human drama."[25]

Directly after *The Great White Hope* Ritt made *Pete 'n Tillie*, a tragi-comedy full of human drama, starring Carol Burnett and Walter Matthau (see chapter 7 for a full discussion of this movie). He was still, however, in a mood for black movies, and by good fortune came across a Newbery Prize-winning novel by William H. Armstrong that he very much wanted to film. In many ways, this movie became his signature film. It was *Sounder*.

Ritt received a letter one day from his friend Robert Radnitz, a former English professor at the University of Virginia, who had come out to Hollywood to be a producer. Radnitz had read Armstrong's novel, *Sounder*, and thought Ritt could be its director. The former professor had contacted the Mattel Toy Company and had received about a million dollars to pursue the movie. Radnitz told Ritt, "I can't pay you anything."[26] Ritt took an 80 percent cut in his salary to do *Sounder*. Since at this time he usually made about $250,000 for each of his pictures, this meant that he personally earned some $50,000 for *Sounder*. The entire movie cost about $900,000.

At first, the *Sounder* crew intended to film their movie in the Macon, Georgia, area. They encountered so much racial hostility, however, that it became increasingly difficult to get on with their work. Finally, Ritt had enough of it, and so he moved the entire cast and crew to the piny woods area of East Feliciana and St. Helen's parishes, near Clinton, Louisiana. The temperature there never "dropped below 95" each day. Ritt started out each day's shooting with an ice pack in his cap.[27] (The move caused Governor Jimmy Carter to ask Ritt what went wrong. In no uncertain terms Ritt told him. Carter asked Ritt to keep Georgia in mind for his next film. Ritt did so; his film after *Sounder* was *Conrack*.)

The place in Louisiana was the same general area where Ritt had made *The Long Hot Summer* so many years before. One of the big differences, he noted, was that in 1958 local catering companies would not furnish food unless separate black and white chow lines were formed; in 1972, there was no problem. In fact, the only real difficulty the movie people faced in Louisiana was being confronted by an outraged deacon of a local black church who thought Ritt's cameras were "instruments of the devil." It was reported that the good deacon actually held star Paul Winfield at bay for a while with a shotgun.[28]

Sounder, scripted from Armstrong's novel by Lonnie Elder, III, first and foremost, is a story about family love in the face of adversity. Nathan Morgan (Paul Winfield) and his son, David Lee (Kevin Hooks), hunt each night in the summer of 1933, hoping to put "sweet meat" on the table. At their cabin after an unsuccessful hunt, the mother Rebecca (Cicely Tyson) complains that David Lee has eaten some of the walnuts she has been picking for sale in the nearby town. "The boy's hungry," Nathan tells her.

Later that night Nathan disappears. The next morning David Lee and his brother and sister awaken to the smell of ham and sausages cooking on their wood-burning stove. When Rebecca looks at Nathan reproachfully, he says, "I did what I had to do, Rebecca." Of course he has stolen the meat, and of course the law comes after him. As the sheriff (James Best) carries Nathan off, the dog Sounder chases after them. A deputy sheriff, simply out of wickedness, shoots Sounder, who runs off into the woods and stays several weeks recuperating from his wounds.

Rebecca confronts the sheriff, but he will not let her see Nathan, who when tried, is given one year at hard labor for stealing the meat. He is spirited off to a labor camp, the name and location of which the sheriff will not divulge to Rebecca and her family. A kindly white woman, Mrs. Boatwright, finds that Nathan has been sent to the Wishbone Labor Camp. David Lee sets off by foot to find him. Ritt follows David Lee through a series of shots that dissolve into one another to express the journey; such technique, however, promoted "a kind of decorative and oddly inexpressive picture-making."[29]

At the labor camp, he cannot locate Nathan; and, in fact, a guard cruelly hits his hand with a billy stick. David Lee comes upon a school where Camille Johnson (Janet Mac-Laughlin) teaches a class of black students. She takes him in, doctors his hand, lets him attend classes, and introduces him to books about Harriet Tubman and Crispus Attucks, and quotes to him from the works of W.E.B. Du Bois. Finally he goes home, but it is clear that he wants to return to Miss Johnson's school.

Nathan finally returns, crippled by a dynamite blast. He comes to support David Lee's hope to go back to Miss Johnson's school. "School is good for you," he tells David, "like good air." He tells his son to "beat the life they [the white people] got all laid out for you in this place." As David heads out for Miss Johnson's school, he exclaims, "I'm gonna miss this old raggedy place but I sure ain't gonna worry about it!"

One of the first instances in making the movie where Ritt used his experience to good advantage was in coaxing Cicely Tyson through the scene with the sheriff. When he will not let Rebecca see Nathan, Cicely becomes increasingly angry and militant toward him. Ritt called her aside and told her that she is depicting a scene that belongs to 1933 in a manner that befits 1971. Blacks in Depression-era Louisiana were subservient to whites, and she had to "bite her tongue" and act accordingly.[30] Ritt always liked for scenes to be played quietly, even softly; certainly Anthony Quinn knew this from his experiences with *The Black Orchid*. The scene between Rebecca and the sheriff turned out to be one of the strongest in the movie, although she does tell him, "You got a low-life job, sheriff."

Music for *Sounder*, composed and performed by Taj Mahal (who plays "Ike" in the movie), is more abundantly used than in Ritt's previous films. Perhaps this increased amount was necessary to delineate family love, nobility of woman, and oppression of blacks by dominant whites. "Jesus, Won't You Come By Here?" is the theme song, sung in various forms throughout the movie. Again, though Ritt often derided it, he comes back to theology to help get his points across in a movie.

Ritt's old friend cinematographer James Wong Howe had died, and so Ritt turned to John A. Alonzo to shoot his movies. Never using more than two cameras, and most of those hand-held, Alonzo caught the stark beauty of the Louisiana countryside, as he depicted moss-laden trees, sugar cane fields, cow pastures, fetid swamps, and rolling streams. There were, however, "no brilliant cuts or breathtaking camera angles."[31] The cameras were not intended to make a comment: they were used to support the story line rather than the story line supporting the cameras.[32] Within this milieu was the sharecropper black man who struggled to provide for his little family in a rickety cabin, even if he had to steal to do it. Easily the most dramatic scene in the movie is when Nathan returns. Sounder sees him first and runs to him. Rebecca and the children tearfully follow, and all five embrace in a touching scene. In fact, Cicely Tyson put "such a storm of emotions" into her run that cameraman Alonzo was himself overcome. His eyes were "so clouded by tears" that he could not vouch for the quality of what he had shot. Thus, another shot was done, the one that was seen in the finished film.[33]

Ironically, Ritt had problems with dogs. He said he did not like them (although he owned one in his Pacific Palisades home). "The damn dog that played the part," he said, "couldn't even run."[34] The dog's big scene—where he was shot by the deputy sheriff—took 36 days until Ritt was satisfied with it. When Nathan returns from his imprisonment, Sounder runs to him, jumps up on him, and licks his face. The only way Ritt and his crew could get the dog to lick Nathan's face was to put syrup on his face. Even then, the scene had to be shot from a distance rather than close up.[35] "I suppose I sound like a bad guy talking this way. The poor dog died two weeks after we finished the film."[36]

While the filming of *Sounder* was in progress, Ritt and Radnitz gave a ride to one of the observers. As they drove along, Ritt asked the man what he thought so far of the movie. Though he said he liked it, Ritt detected a negative tone in his voice, and pressed him for a response. Finally, the man mentioned a kissing scene between Rebecca and Nathan. What's wrong with it, Ritt wanted to know. The man answered that "those people don't kiss like that." By "those people," he of course meant blacks. This stereotyped response infuriated Ritt. He had the car stopped immediately and evicted the hapless northerner right there on the street.[37] Normally regarded as gruff and short of patience (as the northerner, with good reason, came to believe), Ritt said of *Sounder,* "I thought I knew where we were going with it." When all the shooting was finished, however, and he and the film's editor got a first look at *Sounder,* he rather incredulously asked, "Guess who cried?"[38]

Sounder was an immediate artistic and commercial success. The praise that came in for it from Ritt's friends and acquaintances could in some instances be likened to poetry. It seemed the whole country fell in love with *Sounder,* a development that convinced Ritt that one can go further in this world by preaching love than by expounding hate.

Why the praise? Besides exemplifying family love to such an extent, *Sounder* was true to the black (and to some extent, the white) sharecropping experience in the south. Sharecroppers on the whole were "family-oriented, hardworking, and intent on providing a better education for the next generation."[39] It was this care and love between Nathan and Rebecca and then between the parents and the children that made *Sounder* reach such classic proportions.

One correspondent said, "I'll remember the images of *Sounder* 'til the day I go. . . . My God, Marty, it's a remarkable work of art. I felt I'd lived the experience."[40] Delbert Mann reported that "I never go to see films twice and I never cry twice at a film. I did both things at *Sounder.* Damn, it's a good picture!"[41] Another admirer told Ritt that he didn't make a picture but "painted a masterpiece." Susan Hamner attested that at the end of *Sounder* she left knowing "that for at least one evening I'd been involved in an artistic and honest appeal to human understanding."[42] Julian Lewis exclaimed about *Sounder,* "Marty, you're all heart and ten feet tall. Not bad for an agnostic."[43] The distinguished actor Ossie Davis wrote that *Sounder* was a "poetic tribute to endurance and strength."[44] *Sounder* portrayed the plight of minorities in the United States so well that some people wrote to him, asking for movies about other ethnic minorities. Raymond Schiff's letter was typical: "I am sure that with your understanding of minority groups, you would make an ideal director for a film dealing with the American Indians."[45] Ritt was interested, but he felt that with *Hombre,* he had already done what Mr. Schiff suggested.

Ritt was always proudest of receiving letters from common, ordinary theatergoers in reference to his movies. Nevertheless, he relished also hearing from his peers. The internationally acclaimed actor David Niven wrote to Ritt that "you have always been at the top of the class, but now you get the prize."[46] Niven saw *Sounder* in New York. The theater was packed, he said, at 3:00 p.m., and he was most intrigued by the audience. "The audience included many enchanting black children, one of whom sitting next to me, held my hand . . . and he jabbed loudly when it looked as though Sounder was lost. Periodically, the little fellow called out for him and nearly broke my arm when the dog finally did come back."[47]

Another prominent actor, Jack Lemmon, wrote enthusiastically to Ritt about his experiences of seeing *Sounder*. "I was totally and completely absorbed in every single frame and I honestly cannot remember when I have felt such empathy for the characters up there on the screen."[48] Lemmon reported that "when that son of a bitch [the deputy sheriff] shot the dog I jumped out of my seat and screamed at him. This scared the shit out of the lady sitting behind me and she promptly screamed and all hell broke loose for the next thirty seconds."[49]

The most touching tribute from an established actor, however, came from Joel Fluellen (who played "Tick" in *The Great White Hope*). *Sounder*, he said, caused him to react to his childhood experiences, as he grew up in the vicinity of Monroe, Louisiana. "I openly and loudly cursed when Sounder was shot. I cried in remembrance of the old church hymns ["Old Time Religion," for example] which were a part of my childhood. I marveled at the beauty and depth of your understanding of black people in that particular era which even now exists. Every one of your characters was real. . . . Each time I try to speak to someone about the beauty and depth of *Sounder*, the emotional impact overwhelms me. I cry like hell. You, Marty, are a great director, a marvelous human being, with a tremendous amount of understanding of people."[50] Ritt responded to Fluellen's letter: "Dear Joel; your letter made me a bit teary."[51]

Not all correspondents, however, were complimentary. A Mobile, Alabama, writer was "sorry" that Martin Ritt had "such a biased and slanted view of the South," as in *Sounder*.

In Ritt's line of work, she said, he had seen only "one side" of the South (obviously forgetting or being unaware of Ritt's tenure at Elon College). If Ritt ever found himself in or near Mobile (which he did, just a few years later, with his movie *Backroads*), he might change his mind about the racial question.[52] Characteristically, Ritt answered the lady's letter by telling her that he thought she and her husband were "fine people." However, "the record of your section of country on the black question is inhumane and indecent. . . ."[53] Ritt had not minced words since the 1930s, and here, 40 years later, he certainly was not inclined to change the practice.

Even some members of Congress got in on the praise of *Sounder*. Charles C. Diggs, Jr., member of the House from Michigan, exclaimed, "I believe 'Sounder' marks a turning point in the art of the motion picture. This is a black film to take pride in."[54] The congressman quoted several tributes to *Sounder* made by various personalities of the day, including Mrs. Martin Luther King, Jesse Jackson, Wilson Pickett, Roy Innis, and Lofton Mitchell. He urged his colleagues and "all those across the country who are interested in quality entertainment" to see *Sounder*. "And I congratulate Robert Radnitz, Martin Ritt, 20th Century-Fox, and all those connected with the film, for creating a film Blacks—and everyone—can be proud of."[55] Later, Diggs sponsored a luncheon in Washington, D.C. for Tyson, Winfield, Radnitz, and Ritt. On this occasion, he said that *Sounder* "will endure as a classic work of art and a classic look at the humanity in each of us."[56]

Senator Claiborne Pell of Rhode Island joined in the praise: "It is all too seldom that the entertainment industry . . . succeeds in reaching beyond commercialism . . . to produce a work of art."[57] *Sounder*, the senator exclaimed, was a black film, "but it transcends easily and gracefully the barriers of race and appeals to all of us as human beings."[58] Pell closed his remarks by asserting that *Sounder* "has set a standard of excellence toward which I hope the motion picture industry will strive."[59]

Predictably, *Sounder* was compared with numerous other recently produced black films. The difference, however, between *Sounder* and these black films was that the latter demonstrated blacks' anger and the former depicted their love. Ritt vigorously denied that he was getting into "blaxploitation" films like *Blackula, Shaft, Cool Breeze, Nigger Charley*, and *Superspade*. He did not particularly denigrate these films; on the contrary, he noted that *Shaft* director Gordon Parks, who was black, had an "enormous talent," who would, given the opportunity, make serious black films.[60] However, if *Shaft* and similar productions represented films exclusive to black audiences, then "the future of films about blacks is in jeopardy."[61]

Some blacks objected to Ritt about *Sounder* that they did not want to know about their mothers doing laundry; they simply wanted to win the civil rights revolution and they wanted to win now, without looking back at the past.[62] Ritt finally quit responding to such criticisms because they were essentially unanswerable. And then there was the old canard that blacks and whites could not work together creatively on any matter that dealt with race. Even the process by which *Sounder* came to the screen belied this notion. William Armstrong, who wrote the novel, was white, while Lonnie Elder, III, who penned the screenplay, was black. Both Armstrong and Elder were pleased with each others' efforts. Armstrong told Radnitz: "[*Sounder*] is so graciously and beautifully done, the end results reflect such sincerity, complementing what I was aiming for in my book, that my feeling is one of unqualified praise and thanks."[63] For his part, Elder stated that "in terms of what Marty Ritt accomplished [in *Sounder*], the results confirm that maybe nobody else could have directed it better."[64]

The most significant thing about the "blaxploitation" films, according to Ritt, was that black cinemagoers were able to see blacks on screen not only as heroes and heroines, but also as villains. The blacks in these films ran the entire gamut of experience of real-life blacks. These movies, he said, gave vent to some of the "accumulated and very understandable anger that has been stored up all these years."[65]

He was, however, adamantly opposed to a proposal which recently had come from the Congress of Racial Equality. CORE wanted to create a review board to approve or disapprove proposed scripts about blacks. Even after shooting of such films had been completed, CORE wanted to edit them before they reached the nation's cinemas.[66] Of course, in Ritt's view, this was censorship, and "I am and always have been opposed to censorship in any form, shape, or color."[67]

(Actually this was not the first time blacks had suggested a "review board" to deal with black roles in movies. As far back as the 1940s, Walter White of the NAACP, had wanted to create the "Hollywood Bureau" for just such a purpose.)[68] At about the same time as the CORE resolution, a "Coalition Against Blaxploitation" was formed in Hollywood. The coalition charged that the film industry denied the black artist the right to work at his craft "with a sense of dignity." Also, the mind of the entire nation had been "warped" by movies that glorified "the absolute worst image of the black community."[69] Neither the CORE resolution nor the coalition received much attention.

Ritt began to distance himself from criticisms of *Sounder* by asserting that the movie was neither a black nor a white film. "I believe it is a human film. The family could have been white, but in this story they are black."[70] (Ironically, Ritt bought the cabin where the black family lived from a white sharecropper in the area, who in real life was just about as bad off as the black family depicted in the movie. He paid the white $1,000 for the cabin.) He was heartened, too, by the profuse praise of *Sounder* that came from the black leadership. Letters and testimonies from Ossie Davis, Roy Innis, Jesse Jackson, and Mrs. King cheered him immensely. He was greatly pleased, too, when the National Council of Negro Women praised *Sounder*, joined by such black journals as *Ebony*, *Soul Magazine* and *Black Education*. Ritt and his movie drew praise also from the southern California branch of the American Civil Liberties Union: "This sensitivity we saw will remain with all who were privileged to view it."[71]

Not even Ritt was prepared for the deluge of reviews that came from the country's press on *Sounder*. Perhaps the most astounding turn of events was that even Pauline Kael of *The New Yorker* liked it! She was so entranced by *Sounder* that she actually telephoned Ritt at his home to offer her congratulations. "Who would have believed," she asked, that "an inspirational movie about black strength and pride . . . could . . . become the first movie about black experiences in America which can stir people of all colors?"[72] Ritt, she claimed, endowed his performers "with the dignity that accuses us when we look at photographs [of the Depression South] by Walker Evans or Dorothea Lange."[73]

Ritt had made *Sounder*, said one reviewer, "without reverting to the saccharine contrivances of another boy and his dog."[74] There was nothing maudlin about the story, yet it contained a wide spectrum of emotional power, which never seemed forced. The drama rose "spontaneously from the depths of character and situation,"[75] and audiences felt the "texture and the pace of the land and the people directly and immediately."[76] The political and economic slavery of the Depression was "recaptured with a fidelity and a sensitivity which is both heartbreaking and heartwarming."[77] *The Christian Science Monitor* saluted Ritt for his "sure, realistic, and tender" directing of *Sounder*.[78] This movie, the *Monitor* believed, "may just be the first classic film about a black family."[79] The *Philadelphia Inquirer* gave an opinion that *Sounder* "is the kind of movie the civil rights organizations have been hoping Hollywood would make,"[80] while its sister paper, *The Philadelphia Daily News*, called the film "decent and noble," and "the first movie in a long time which doesn't exploit blacks."[81]

Only Vincent Canby in the *New York Times* could not see the value of *Sounder*. It was, to him, a film of "well ordered tepidity." He added sarcastically, "after all *Sounder* has been endorsed by everybody with the exception of God, but God doesn't have an outlet. *Sounder* is so sweet and inoffensive that I don't want to kick it. . . . [However], *Sounder* patronizes the 'littleness' of its characters."[82] (Canby's remarks about God brought a quick retort from script writer Elder. He was pleased to note Mr. Canby's "unexpected humility.)"[83]

Another reviewer for *The New York Times* was not quite as callous as Canby. Roger Greenspun said that even the plot in *Sounder* "has the feel of historical demonstration."[84] While Ritt was an earnest and conscientious director, the reviewer said, "he seems to strive for classical plainness, but to succeed only in being ordinary."[85] Ellen Holly, also of the *Times*, argued that "in terms of film technique, *Sounder* offers nothing new."[86] She did, however, advise her readers to see the film.

The pedantry of *New York Times* reviewers notwithstanding, there were some New Yorkers, besides Pauline Kael, who appreciated *Sounder*. *Time,* noting Ritt's "erratic talent" with some of his previous movies, asserted that he "has never seemed surer of himself or in greater control than in *Sounder*, which he invests with simple beauty and insight."[87] *Newsweek* spoke of Ritt's "delicate hand," and great sensitivity in directing *Sounder*.[88] Other reviews of *Sounder* emphasized Ritt's compassion for the downtrodden,[89] and his theme of universality: "*Sounder* is not just true of the bottoms of Louisiana; you can find it around the corner in Minnesota."[90] From England *The National Observer* said that *Sounder* was "Martin Ritt's best ever,"[91] while the staid *Guardian* grumbled that if the movie had been made 25 years before, "it would have been a significant break-through film."[92] Though the makers of *Sounder* "can quote from Du Bois, they haven't advanced beyond Booker T. Washington's solutions."[93] Patrick Gibbs of the *Daily Telegraph*, however, said that Ritt had "always seemed likely, since he first came into the cinema, to do something masterly, and now he does so with *Sounder*."[94] London's *Evening Standard* echoed Gibbs: "Martin Ritt's unobtrusive direction [of *Sounder*] is a minor victory for race relations,"[95] while the *Daily Mirror* believed *Sounder* "is going to be a landmark in film history."[96]

With all these reviews, mostly in the rave category, one would have thought that *Sounder* would walk away with the Academy Awards for 1972. It was, in fact, nominated for four awards: best actress, actor, screenplay, and picture. It won none of them. Incredibly enough, Ritt was not nominated for anything. The entire membership of the Academy of Motion Picture Arts and Sciences votes for actor, actress, and best picture nominations for the Oscar. Only the Directors Guild votes for best director. And, one could say, there is probably more room for politics in the Directors Guild than in the Academy as a whole. Bob Fosse won as best director in 1972 for *Cabaret*. (The best actress award went to Liza Minelli for *Cabaret*, the best actor award went to Marlon Brando for *The Godfather*, which was declared to be the best film of 1972.)

Definitely, Ritt was not the first director ever to have such a fate. Ralph Nelson's movie, *Lilies of the Field* had been nominated for several awards, none of which included best director. Nelson wrote to Ritt: "Ten years ago you were kind enough to call me when 'Lilies of the Field' received five academy award nominations, but I was not nominated as best director. I certainly didn't expect that the same fate would befall you."[97] Richard Morris sent a telegram: "*Sounder* is a great directorial achievement. I feel blindness of Academy a sad reflection on their credibility."[98] Another correspondent told Ritt, "Please be assured that all your friends, members of the industry, critics, and TV commentators felt that you should have been nominated and beyond doubt won the Oscar for the best director of the year. The Academy failed this year, not you."[99] Despite this "unforgivable injustice," brought on by "lethargy and prejudicial influences," everyone knew Ritt would "continue to contribute to the industry with increasing merits."[100] A telegram from fellow director Carl Foreman told Ritt: "How ridiculous and stupid you were not personally Oscar nominated. It's insane."[101] Thanking Foreman, Ritt quipped "I think I'm too old to expect justice."[102]

Even if the Directors Guild could not see its way clear to award Ritt an Oscar for best director, several other groups and associations in the United States and elsewhere did. He was, for example, proclaimed as the best director of the year, for *Sounder*, at the International Film Festival in Belgrade, Yugoslavia, while Cicely Tyson won the best actress award for the Stratford Film Festival in Canada.[103] *Sounder* also won a Bell Ringer Award from *Scholastic* magazine, and the Christophers, a New York based religious organization, gave its award for 1972 to Ritt and *Sounder*. This was the first of three movies (*Conrack* and *Norma Rae* were the other two) for which Ritt won a Christopher Award.

The loners and individualists whom Ritt had amassed in so many of his previous movies are missing from *Sounder*. Family love is the overwhelming force in this movie. In the face of ignorant, prejudiced whites this black family grows increasingly close. Nathan Morgan's "crime" of "stealing" food for his hungry family is an action that decent men all over the world would take under the same circumstances. Thus, *Sounder* is *authentic*, made up of situations that are all too painfully real.

Definitely, the theme of the underdog is in this movie. The sheriff (James Best) and his insensitive deputies always refer to black males, no matter their age, as "boy." Even the kindly Mrs. Boatwright regards David Lee in more a maternalistic manner than as a fellow human being. The Morgan family work the sugar cane fields while Nathan is incarcerated; they succeed against all odds, a condition that most whites do not expect. That success and the love of the Morgan family are the two things that caught black and white attention for *Sounder* in 1972. Ritt was now established as never before as a sensitive filmmaker of social sentiments. Moreover, to many blacks, Ritt had become their hero; one of the few white men of the time who could hold that distinction.[104]

As might be expected, a multitude of suggestions came to Ritt for his next movie. Some of his admirers wanted him to make a documentary of the civil rights movement. Others urged him to film the life of Harriet Tubman, the "Moses of her people," who had led literally hundreds of slaves to their freedom during the first part of the nineteenth century. He was interested in these proposals, he said, he and Adele trying conscientiously to read all of them. The proposal that caught his attention, however, was the winsome story of a young white schoolteacher in South Carolina who taught at an all-black school. Adapted from one of Pat Conroy's early novels, *The Water is Wide*, Ritt filmed it under the title character's name, *Conrack*.

Conrack concerns a young, white, idealistic substitute schoolteacher who teaches 21 black children for almost a year on an island just off the coast of South Carolina. He finds them unsophisticated at the beginning; they cannot pronounce the word "Conroy;" it comes out either as "Patroy" or "Conrack." They do not know what country they live in, they cannot do arithmetic or recite the alphabet. Their principal, Mrs. Scott (Madge Sinclair), has lost any idealism she might once have had in teaching. Blacks need the whip, she told Conrack, because they are going out in the world to please The Man. "That's a bunch of shit," Conrack replies.

At the end of the year there is a certain sophistication about the children; they have become much more aware of the world than previously. He uses a teaching technique that was employed in *Sounder*. He deliberately gives false information to the children ("The first president of the United States was Conrack"), so they will take delight in correcting him. In fact, it is Conrack's taking them to Beaufort for Halloween celebrations that first brings them into contact with the larger communities, as most of them have never left their island.

The film was shot in Georgia: on St. Simon's Island, just off the coast of New Brunswick. Ritt had remembered the unsavory, racist "greetings" when he had tried to film *Sounder* in Georgia. Governor Jimmy Carter asked him to think about Georgia for his next film. Ritt contacted the governor, who went out of his way to welcome Ritt and his associates to Georgia. According to one report, Carter even had jet planes at a nearby airport diverted one day, so Ritt and his crew could get on with the shooting.[105] He contacted the Reverend E.C. Tillman of the Shiloh Baptist Church who talked with a local schoolmaster to get the children. Ritt cast them on an "educated guess," which turned out all right. To get them to play their roles, Ritt "teased them, bullied them, flattered them . . . and did just about everything short of getting physical with them." Mr. Carter "met personally" with Ritt, "made sure that all state agencies cooperated on *Conrack* and attended the premiere along with all the black children who took part in the film."[106]

John Alonzo, Ritt's principal photographer with *Conrack*, shot a lot of back light, and used sepia tones, "with the full knowledge that if we didn't like it, we could go back to normal color at any time."[107] This procedure, however, bothered the studio people in Hollywood, who kept giving Alonzo a "lot of static." Ritt got on the telephone and "screamed" at them and the harassment stopped. He quipped that he had screamed at studio executives in some of his earlier pictures "and almost got fired."[108] That he could do so now with impunity, he said, was perhaps a mark of how far he had come in moviemaking circles.

One question that gave everyone pause was the matter of once again shooting—or trying to shoot—a movie in Georgia. Racism had run them out with *Sounder*, and many wondered now whether it was worth the time and effort to try Georgia once more. As it turned out, the relations between the blacks in the film crew and the local white citizenry became something to celebrate.

In addition to Governor Carter's help with state agencies, there was also Ernie Phillips, a black man in charge of painting and decorating the sets. (Ritt's son, Mike, also worked as a carpenter on the sets of *Conrack*.) At the beginning, the local white craftsmen were somewhat stand-offish in taking orders from a black supervisor. As time passed, however, it became apparent to them that Phillips was a superior craftsman, and they began to enjoy and appreciate his knowledge and workmanship. After a time, some of the white carpenters invited Ernie to their homes for dinner, a development that caused Ritt to pronounce in some understatement, "I feel that was something significant."[109]

At another time, Ritt tried to engage the services of a local boatman to transport the film crew, including all the children to and from St. Simon's Island to New Brunswick. He refused, telling Ritt that when the movie ended everyone connected with it would go back to Hollywood, but he would have to continue living in Georgia with his neighbors who, he believed, would not look kindly upon his mixing with blacks. Ritt told him that, while he disagreed with the philosophy behind this reasoning, it was still understandable.

A few days later, however, John Alonzo and his wife wanted to go to New Brunswick where the fishing fleet was being blessed at the start of a new season. As they left Taylor's fishing camp on St. Simon's Island, they noted Ernie Phillips standing on the pier, wearing overalls. The boatman waved to him, steered his boat to the dock and invited him to get in the boat. He did so in the full view of the local white community. Ernie and the boatman shook hands and were laughing and conversing with each other as the boat headed for New Brunswick. It turned out that Ernie Phillips and the white boatman were both 32nd-degree Masons. It was Masonry that made the initial cut through the racial barrier, and it was the two men finding that they had more in common with each other than differences that overcame it.[110]

Conrack initiated an extensive dialogue among film critics and scholars. Was Conrack (played by Jon Voight) simply trying to imbue his young, black students with Anglo-Saxon ideas and values? The idea was absurd, Ritt said, too absurd even to answer, but it was possible that some bigoted viewers might come to such a conclusion. Film scholar Ted Lange believed that *Conrack* was a "white exploitation" film. Whites could see it and "feel very good about a white man who goes into the South to educate some black kids out of the kindness of his heart."[111] Then, after he gets fired, the movie plays a bit of Beethoven and never really explores the black experience in America.[112] Ritt said that this description of *Conrack* really was "another picture" and encouraged the critic to make it.

Was there any interrelationship between the white teacher and the black children? Was it only the black children who learned anything? Did the white teacher learn something? Was he in any way changed by his experience of teaching in a black school? (His name was changed, from Conroy to Conrack.) Yes, replied Ritt. Conrack comes head-on with the authoritarian bureaucracy that runs the South Carolina school system. Superintendent Skeffington (Hume Cronyn) fires Conrack for bringing the children to Beaufort against orders. Conrack's feelings about the wrongness of segregation and his philosophy that it is talent rather than color of skin that should be the determining factor in a person's life are cemented as they never have been before. He also meets an ancient midwife who tells him some truths about life, both black and white. So, yes, Conrack is changed and does learn a great deal by the experience.

Should Conrack have been turned into a black teacher for the purpose of teaching black children? No, replied Ritt, because the movie is based on the truth, "and I'm too old to be bullied."[113] Moreover, the question had the same vintage as the one about whether white directors could successfully direct black performers. *Conrack*, he felt, could just as easily have been about a black teacher going into white Appalachia, to get the same points across: it was a love story between a teacher and his pupils.[114]

Ritt argued that his experiences in the South in the 1930s and then his early movies dealing with southern white-class structures made him as knowledgeable, or more so, about the South as most southerners, black and white, themselves. ("I have lived my professional life in the South," he told one reporter.)[115] He could not understand the criticisms that he should depict blacks only as contemporary and well educated. Blacks, like whites, ran the entire spectrum of human experience. There were a few heroes in both races, a few criminals, and a whole lot of common, ordinary people. There was no point in deliberately filming either the best or the worst, for that *would* put a tincture of class and propaganda to his work that he wanted to avoid. The South was full of ferment and conflict, and it was out of these two conditions that drama was created. Thus, his personal knowledge of the South and his sense of the dramatic enabled him to make successful southern films.

Friends, colleagues, and fans wrote numerous letters to Ritt to express their appreciation for *Conrack*. Jet Fore wrote that 1974 just had to be Ritt's year. First, he became a "brand new poppa" (one of his race horses had foaled), followed by his third film hit in a row (*Sounder, Pete 'n Tillie* and *Conrack*). "Now if the baby will just win the Kentucky Derby we'll have it made."[116] David Hartman told Ritt that *Conrack* "was one of the best produced, written, and directed movies" he had ever seen.[117] In his reply, Ritt said *Conrack* was a movie he "loved making."[118]

Another correspondent thought Ritt's directing of the black children was done "especially well."[119] Their playing of Beethoven's Fifth at the end of the movie was a "wonderful directorial idea and very moving."[120] He "thanked God that Ritt was not afraid of true emotions and because of that you never allow sentimentality to creep in."[121] Fellow Elon alumnus Thomas Bass told Ritt in reference to directing the children, "How you managed to evoke the responses and yet maintain such control, I'll never know."[122] Actor Hume Cronyn told Ritt that when he watched *Conrack* there was a "marvelous dead quiet" at the end of the movie, followed by a "great burst of applause."[123] Gordon Stulberg took a poll among the viewers of *Conrack*. There was a significant degree of difference between those who knew it was a true story and those who did not. Those who—at the beginning of the movie—knew it was true were "more emotionally aroused and broken up" than the others. In fact, those who found out that it was true only after they had seen the movie "somehow felt cheated."[124] Other letter writers suggested that study guides be prepared for use in classrooms, that school teachers should be required to see the movie (a thought quickly rejected by Ritt), and that other "Conracks" be found throughout the country and duly honored.

The letters Ritt treasured the most, however, came from the black students who played in *Conrack*. He and they became very fond of each other and just leaving at the close of shooting was difficult. "The kids were cool 'til the last moment," Ritt reported, "and then they broke down."[125] Many wanted Ritt to take them to Hollywood with him, but he told them that performing in *Conrack* was just one experience of their lives and—unconvincingly—that there would be others that would probably be "even better."[126]

Ronnie Harris "enjoyed seeing" *Conrack* and remembering the filming. "The way you directed us to act—you must be one of the best producers in the world. I think so anyway."[127] Madge Sinclair was in a "state of shock" when she saw *Conrack*.[128] Rebecca Cobb told Ritt not to work too hard "because we won't want anything to happen now to Old Martin, will we?" She and all of the children missed Ritt very much, and would always remember him as "Old Uncle Martin" and would think of themselves as "your babies."[129] Ritt wrote back to Rebecca that "I'll remember all you children for the rest of my life."[130]

To Kathy Turner everything seemed as a dream. "It doesn't seem real any more. I wonder, was it really true?"[131] In her prayers she prayed for Ritt and his family, and "I hope you do me the same."[132] She would always "love and remember you," for the experience of *Conrack*, and then she wanted to know about Ritt's weight. "Have you gained that weight back?" she asked him. "I bet you are as big as a cow," she told him. She had decided to go into acting; Ritt told her to "educate yourself as much as possible" to prepare for a life on stage and in film.[133] This was, in fact, his stock answer to just about everybody who asked him about an acting career. Though Martin Ritt had many honors to come his way throughout his life, among his most cherished memories were the children of St. Simon's Island who acted in *Conrack*.

Press and journal reviews of *Conrack* ranged from good to rave. Pauline Kael said it was a story about an "unrepressed man fighting a slowly dying system of repression."[134] Russell Light of *Iconoclast* complimented Ritt for continuing to make socially conscious films at a time when most other directors would not because such films would not make enough money for them.[135] A.H. Weiler, in *The New York Times*, called *Conrack* the "son" of *Sounder*,[136] while his colleague Eugenia Collier said that *Conrack* was a "serious attempt to deal with a human situation."[137] The movie, she believed, was more about the young white liberal than the black children.[138] Integration efforts had just been started throughout the Southeast at the period represented by the movie, and white revelations about blacks at that time were probably more startling than black knowledge of whites.

The only real flap that occurred in the press about *Conrack* was when the review board in Memphis, Tennessee, gave it an "R" (audience restricted to those 18 and above except when accompanied by a parent or guardian) rating for reasons known only to itself; presumably because it contained a few "goddamns" "asses" "hells," "shits," and "bitches." The action infuriated Edwin Howard, amusements editor for the Memphis *Press-Scimitar*. He suggested that Ritt and Twentieth Century sue the board. "If you should decide to institute legal action against the board," Howard told Ritt, "I am confident you would win on this film, and I can promise you full support by me and my paper."[139]

Ritt declined. The Board of Review, in his opinion, had "acted childishly," but if he became involved in legal actions, he would find himself "making no films and just suing for the rest of my life."[140] His best course of action, he believed, was to render his "attacks against that kind of mentality through the films I make."[141] He dropped the matter then and there and never came back to it.

Definitely the most emotional aspect of *Conrack* dealt with an unfortunate interview Pat Conroy gave to Jim Stingley of the *Los Angeles Times*. It came at the end of a difficult and tiring promotional tour Conroy made on behalf of the movie, and so perhaps he was vulnerable to the manipulations of an overzealous newspaper man. What else would cause him to agree that *Conrack* was a "syrupy, fact-lacking affair that thrills pie-in-the-sky liberals with its fairy-tale fight against bigotry?"[142] He had taken the job on Yamacraw Island teaching black children, he said, not because of any idealism—ending segregation or otherwise—but to escape conscription in the Vietnam War. "There was this here war going on," Stingley quoted him as saying, "and I was feeling a draft."[143]

In reference to his "babies" on Yamacraw Island, "I can't get fired up about teaching a 12-year-old kid how to count to five. . . . And when they started to read, it was a total miracle. Because there wasn't one damned thing I'd done to make it happen."[144] Why then, if he felt this way about the matter, did he write his novel *The Water Is Wide* about his experiences with the black children? "I was mad and unemployed. When they fired me for fighting their system, for trying to improve the deplorable situation just a little bit for those children, I looked for other jobs."[145] He could not get any more teaching positions, for, apparently, his reputation as a "flaming rebel" had spread on into Georgia, and superintendents of education would have nothing to do with him.

Finally, about his tour, Conroy showed little but disdain. Though he traveled first class, stayed in the "finest" hotel suites, and was "fawned over" and applauded, he still yearned for Dixie. "I ain't never lived like this in my whole life," he told avidly waiting reporter Stingley. "And I'll tell ya . . . if I don't get back to Southern soil pretty soon, I just don't know what's gonna happen."[146]

Very soon after the Stingley interview, Conroy apparently realized that playing country bumpkin to a big city reporter was not exactly the thing he should have done. The day after Stingley's article appeared, Conroy fired off a telegram to Martin Ritt: "I am sorry from my heart. Suggest new title for movie, 'Conjerk,' or "Conmouth.' Forgive me. I bleed."[147] Shortly after the telegram, Conroy wrote to Ritt that the worst thing about the interview was that it hurt Ritt's, Irving Ravetch's, and Harriet Frank, Jr.'s feelings. (The latter two had written the script for *Conrack* and had invited Conroy to be present on the sets during much of the shooting. Conroy, they said, liked the movie, until someone "got to him" and "changed his opinion.")[148] The second worst thing about the interview, Conroy said, was that it was so "pompous and self serving."[149] He claimed to be somewhat quoted out of context. With some of his previous interviews, he said, he had greeted reporters with the statement, "The movie's a piece of shit, isn't it?" The reporters would protest and Conroy would then tell them that "the book's worse."[150] He explained to Ritt, "Now if one of them [the reporters] had reported that first line cold, without any other description of the conversation, we have an example of how one can be stung with a simple, unfinished recitation of a quote."[151]

Then Conroy became a bit defensive. He wrote testily to Ritt, Ravetch, and Frank that "if Hollywood friendships can be broken up on the basis of newspaper articles, then you folks are much more entrenched in the silliness of that town [Hollywood] than I thought you were." He hoped that this "unfortunate incident" would not mark the end of their friendship, but if it did, "then it was the shallowest, briefest, and most gristleless friendship I have ever made."[152] He had, in effect, he said, been "new journalized," and he hoped the affected parties would understand.

In addition to the telegram and the letters, Conroy also wrote a disclaimer to the *Los Angeles Times*. He had hurt Ritt and the Ravetches, he said, very much, and he wanted publicly to apologize. When "little Southern boys," he wrote, get movies made about them, they "often grow heads the size of watermelons."[153] It was true also, he said, that when "little Southern boys" get their "first taste of fame," they tend to forget to be grateful." They also talk too much and try to impress reporters with how "magnificently cynical and unaffected they are."[154] He closed his letter by saying, "I love the movie *Conrack*. I love the people who made it. I served them reprehensively."[155]

Apparently Ravetch and Frank did not write back to Conroy, but Ritt did. The article was a shock, he told Conroy. He felt from the beginning that Stingley's intent was to "assassinate" the picture, and Conroy had been had.[156] In no way, however, did "being had" exonerate Conroy for his foolish behavior. Ritt had been betrayed in the past, he told the author of *Conrack*, and each time it happened it was a "bitter pill." The wounds from the article, Ritt maintained, had not totally healed, but he was prepared "to meet you again as a friend."[157] Apparently the two never met again.

From racial prejudice against black athletes in *The Great White Hope* to the triumph of family love against all odds in *Sounder* to the uplifting of the human spirit in *Conrack*, Martin Ritt depicted and explained the black experience in America. His black-oriented movies corresponded with much of the later civil rights revolution in the late sixties and early seventies. Though the subject matter of *The Great White Hope* and *Sounder* was from different time periods (1910-14 and 1933), the theme was still pertinent to the last half of the twentieth century.

Ritt was probably a more logical person to present the black experience than any other director in Hollywood. Many northerners who have never visited the South automatically condemn it for its racism and seemingly slow social ways. Many southerners who have never visited the North automatically condemn it for its arrogance and "better than thou" attitudes. It takes a person familiar with both great sections to understand that one must condemn what is wrong, but at the same time be able to see redeeming factors. Martin Ritt was such a person, and that is what made him so successful in filming the South. He *knew* the South; there was nothing artificial about his southern movies, in dialect, characterization, or setting. Within the scope of their own subject matter and the way that subject matter was treated, Martin Ritt's southern films were genuine depictions of life and conflict.

After *Conrack* Ritt did not make any more films specifically about the black experience in America. He did, however, continue to film various aspects of the South, based, as were some of his earlier movies, on white class struggles rather than purely black-white issues. Among these were some of Ritt's most remembered films, like *Norma Rae*, *Back Roads*, and *Cross Creek*. After *Conrack* Ritt became even more eclectic than before, filming whatever interested him personally, continuing totally to reject the auteur theory, so much regarded by many of his Hollywood colleagues.

Sally Field, Martin Ritt, Beau Bridges, at the Cannes Festival, 1976. Photo by Y. Coatsaliou. Courtesy of Adele Ritt.

Martin Ritt, with various players from *Sounder*. Courtesy of Robert Radnitz.

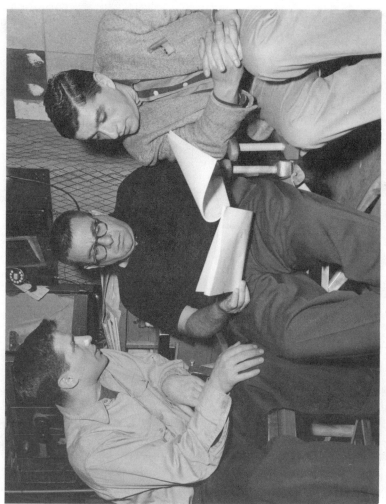

Edge of the City. John Cassavetes, Martin Ritt, Robert Alan Aurthur (author). Courtesy of Adele Ritt.

The Long Hot Summer. Martin Ritt, Lee Remick, Tony Franciosa, Jerry Wald, at the Cannes Film Festival, 1958. Courtesy of Adele Ritt.

The End of the Game. Martin Ritt, Jacqueline Bisset, Friedrich Durrenmatt, Maximilian Schell, and Jon Voight. Courtesy of Adele Ritt.

Adele and Martin Ritt. Photo by Ron Phillips. Courtesy of Adele Ritt.

This photo is believed by some of his friends to be the last one ever taken of Martin Ritt. Others in the photo are Terry Nelson, Robert Radnitz, and Joe Sargent. Courtesy of Robert Radnitz.

Cross Creek. Mary Steenburgen, Martin Ritt, and Robert Radnitz. Photo by Ron Phillips. Courtesy of Robert Radnitz.

Martin Ritt wearing a new jumpsuit, a birthday present from his friend Robert Radnitz. The inscription on the photo reads: "So you've made me a fashion plate. Love, Marty." Courtesy of Robert Radnitz.

Pfc. Martin Ritt, U.S. Army Air Corps; ca. 1944.

Martin Ritt at his Bar Mitzvah, 6 March 1927. Courtesy of Adele Ritt.

A young Martin Ritt, with his father, Morris. Courtesy of Adele Ritt.

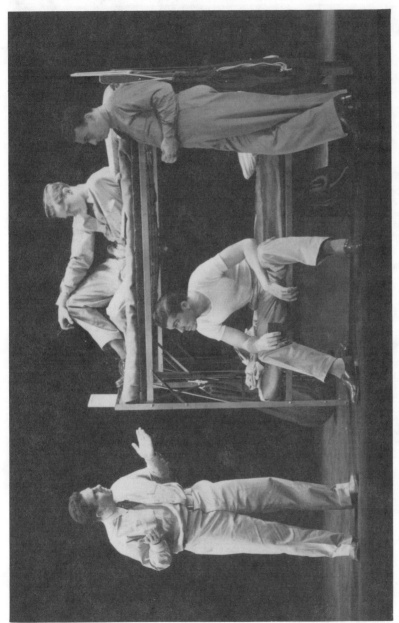

Martin Ritt (left) in Maxwell Anderson's *The Eve of St. Mark*, which opened in New York just before Ritt was inducted into the military. Courtesy of Adele Ritt.

Sophomore Martin Ritt, all dressed up to play football for the "Fighting Christians" at Elon College, 1933. Courtesy of Adele Ritt.

Chapter 7

◆ ◆ ◆

Full Circle on the Black List?

It was a tribute to Martin Ritt's remarkable versatility that he could make such disparate movies as *Sounder* and *Pete 'n Tillie* at roughly the same time. *Sounder* deals with a poor black tenant-farming family in the Depression South; *Pete 'n Tillie* is a treatment of two contemporary wisecracking urbanites who suffer personal tragedy. Never had he shown his eclectic qualities better than in 1972 when he worked on both these movies. He could move from one mood to another, and from one set of performers and personalities to another with equanimity.

Pete 'n Tillie is an adaptation of Peter De Vries's novelette, *Witch's Milk*, about the loss of a dear child through leukemia. Set in San Francisco, it stars Walter Matthau as Pete Seltzer and Carol Burnett as Tillie Lane. After a while of seeing each other on the social scene, Pete asks Tillie if she wants to come up to his apartment for a spell of heavy breathing. Once there, the two automatically begin to unclothe. Tillie remarks, "I have a feeling I'm being stripped for surgery." Afterwards, Pete proclaims the "operation" a success.

After some time, Pete tells Tillie that "the honeymoon's over; it's time to get married." Their marriage soon produces a son, Robbie. Pete and Robbie are inseparable. Even as an infant, Robbie loves to listen to Spike Jones, and as he grows, Pete teaches him to recite "Who's on First?" because it ranks right up there with the Song of Solomon, the sonnets of Shakespeare, "and the speeches of Spiro Agnew." The two go fishing; Robbie catches one and begs Pete to let it go. They play pranks on their next door neighbor by secretly pouring gasoline into his automobile, making him think he is getting better mileage than he actually is.

Then it turns out that Robbie is fatally ill. Pete denies reality by stepping up his wisecracking and by playing "Piano Roll Blues" on his apartment piano, wearing only a straw hat. Tillie, on the other hand, curses God for bringing this affliction to her and her family. "Bastard!" she screams out at God. "Suffer whose little children? Mary, where are you now? I spit on you, Mother of Mercy!"

Even in acting, Carol Burnett could not easily commit blasphemy. Ritt "struck" on the first night of shooting this scene (that is, he quit). On the second night, things were not too much better. At 3:30 a.m. Ritt was able to get the performance from Burnett that he wanted. Just as Ritt had had to induce Cicely Tyson through the scene with the sheriff in *Sounder*, so he had to persuade Carol Burnett in *Pete 'n Tillie*—through continual rehearsals and reassurances—to play her part. The scene in question turned out to be the most powerful and dramatic one in the entire movie.

Pete and Tillie's subsequent relations are rocky, to say the least. Pete keeps watching football games on TV, "hoping for injuries," while Tillie again becomes interested in religion. When she tells Pete that she is thinking about becoming a Catholic, he asks her why. "Because I need something," she replies. Tillie wants to know if she and Pete are being punished for something. Pete incredulously replies, by whom and for what? Tillie tells Pete that most of his true feelings are hidden behind his jokes. Pete responds by saying that most of his true feelings deserve to be hidden. And, finally, Tillie asks Pete, "How did we stay married eleven years?"

Tillie goes into a rest home to pull herself together. Pete moves from their old apartment into a new one. Pete visits her one day and, as usual, is wisecracking. Then in the midst of their conversation Pete begins to cry, and Tillie knows he is weeping for Robbie. "We'll be all right," she comforts him. They are still separated when the movie ends, but the strong implication is that they will get back together.

Ritt explained to a reporter that he was drawn to Julius Epstein's script of De Vries's novel because he wanted to do something "less heavy" than his previous movies.[1] Though the movie was poignant and tragic, it was also, he felt, an "affirmative picture about a middle class marriage."[2] He had not worked with middle class subjects to this extent since *No Down Payment* of many years before. John Alonzo was again his principal photographer—shooting the film in crisp Panavision-Technicolor—with John Williams writing the musical score.

When *Pete 'n Tillie* was in the planning stages, actress Lee Grant wrote to Ritt wanting the role of Tillie. Ritt's preference for the part was Joanne Woodward, who had played in so many of his previous movies. She wrote to him, saying, "I didn't feel right for the script. I think I just want to stop playing parts that start out 'she sits crying in her bathrobe.'"[3] Ritt replied that he had thought the part of Tillie was "extraordinary" and "very funny" as "evidenced that I took Carol Burnett when you were unavailable."[4]

Perhaps it was the effusive outpouring of love and praise for *Sounder* that caused *Pete 'n Tillie* to suffer by contrast, though it did receive its share of plaudits. One reviewer believed *Pete 'n Tillie* was the movie that *Love Story* tried to be, but wasn't.[5] Robby's death and the events leading to it could have been maudlin, but Ritt absorbed "the painful fact of a young boy's death . . . by simply immersing it in fun."[6] Ritt's direction, said one critic, used comedy "not only to counterpoint tragedy but also to accentuate it,"[7] while another maintained that Ritt's direction was as much for warmth and simplicity as for style."[8]

The *Financial Times* of London proclaimed that with *Pete 'n Tillie,* Ritt had revealed a "hitherto unsuspected ability with sentimental comedy,"[9] supported by the view of the *Sunday Express* that Ritt's "taut direction" produced scenes of "marvelous slapstick."[10] The *Daily Telegram* echoed its Fleet Street brethren by saying that although Ritt had never before directed comedy, "he makes up the deficiency very agreeably with Pete 'n Tillie,"[11] and the *Daily Express* asserted that films the quality of *Pete 'n Tillie* "are few and far between."[12] And the *Sunday Telegraph*, noting that comedy's not usually being Ritt's line of work was probably the reason why *Pete 'n Tillie* was outside the usual "domestic comedy rut."[13]

One reporter noted that Ritt's direction of *Pete 'n Tillie* was a reaffirmation that "sensitivity and gentleness" are more valuable than flamboyant tricks and spite."[14] This philosophy was augmented by Jane Fonda, who acted several years later in Ritt's last movie, *Stanley & Iris*. She said that Ritt's directing always reminded her of her father's acting: "You could not see the wheels turning, but you always knew they were there."[15] Ritt went for the basics, she said, the human interest, and the movies that were "non-stylist."[16] Such descriptions perhaps explain why Ritt never received an Oscar for best directing, but at the same time they delineate why he was such an extraordinary figure in the history of Hollywood filmmaking. *Sounder* and *Pete 'n Tillie* fit very well into the mode of which Fonda spoke.

Negative responses to *Pete 'n Tillie* were equal to the positive ones. Charles Champlin of the *Los Angeles Times* complained because the "'n," was "homespun" and trivializing. Even Ma and Pa Kettle, he maintained, rated an "and."[17] Walter Matthau, he said, had played characters like Pete many times, but Carol Burnett, who was made to look drab as Tillie, was underplayed.[18] George McKinnon of the *Boston Globe* exclaimed that it "doesn't seem possible that director Martin Ritt could have crammed any more contemporary cinema cliches into 100 minutes of playing time"[19] than he did with *Pete 'n Tillie*. With *Pete 'n Tillie*, Ritt had grafted two "rather incompatible" stories into "disagreeable Siamese twins," grumbled a newspaper reporter.[20] One critic spoke of Ritt's "ghastly direction"[21] while another suggested that Ritt's work with this movie showed that in his life he had reached a "period of amiable dotage."[22]

In a way *Pete 'n Tillie* is a masterpiece, and it is underrated compared to Ritt's other works.[23] For one thing, it balances good times with bad, laughter with tears, and social life with loneliness. These are attributes of life itself; thus, the movie becomes almost a metaphor for life. Also there is still this coming back to theology by self-acknowledged agnostic Martin Ritt. Time and again he tells newspaper reporters that he has no use for religion. Time and again he uses religion either as a point of reference in his movies or as a means of unity. If he did not believe in religion, why did he use it so much in his movies? Certainly he believed in his movies, as he said repeatedly to hundreds of critics and reporters. Perhaps it was a case of taking a social institution that, whether one believed in it or not, nevertheless had a huge impact on the society that he wanted to describe in his films. There was a time when he even wanted to make an "incisive, pragmatic" picture about the Vatican, to see what it was like in "that kind of isolation," a situation in which church and state are totally merged.[24] Whatever the reasons, Martin Ritt came back more to religion in his films than to any other social institution of his day.

After *Pete 'n Tillie*, as we have seen, Ritt directed *Conrack*, and then thought about going on to other projects. One such was *First Blood*, about the war in Vietnam. It was to be a "harsh story" about a Vietnam veteran going on a killing spree.[25] Though it would be a "terribly violent film," he said, "I think it can be of philosophical importance."[26] When negotiations began on *First Blood*, he thought of Kentucky as a filming site. This elicited a letter from Edward Spivia of Georgia, saying that North Georgia had "truly beautiful mountains" with a variety of elevations, lush with vegetation and scenery. He was certain Georgia could duplicate or improve anything Kentucky had to offer.[27] Perhaps with the positive experience of Georgia and *Conrack* behind him, Ritt would have chosen Georgia to shoot the picture. Unfortunately, the writers' strike of 1973 was instrumental in halting immediate plans for the picture. A year or so later, Ritt expressed an interest in renewing the matter, but other things seemed always to intervene. He never did film *First Blood*. Another movie he thought for a time about making, but one that never materialized, was *Old Mani and the Boy*, to have been set in India.

Throughout much of 1974 Ritt was involved with things other than movies. For example, he had always been an avid horse-racing fan, never losing his affinity for the sport, from the days when he made much of his living betting on the races during the blacklist period. He spent the entire summer at La Jolla, close to the racetrack, "since that is my major degeneracy."[28] He also played a great deal of tennis at La Jolla beach and at the local tennis club. As noted earlier, he would not join any "exclusive" clubs.

Ritt was a great handicapper of horses, regarded far and wide as the standard by which everyone else bet on horses. He would go to the tracks for two or three weeks at a time and take notes before he got into any serious betting. (If the odds were no better than, say, six to five on the horse he felt was the best, he would not bet. "It's against my religion to bet at that price," he always explained.)[29] When he did bet, it was because he had studied the horses and their jockies. He was not particularly fun to be with at the races; for him, the whole matter was serious business.

He and Walter Matthau went to the races often, and Matthau frequently brought along his young son, William, "as any good father would do."[30] Ritt would not tell William which horse to bet on until fifteen seconds before the race started, and in more cases than not, he won.[31] Did Ritt have any further influence on Matthau's son, William? "Yes, I suppose so," said Matthau. "He's now a director."[32]

In addition to betting, Ritt also got into race-horse ownership. In 1974 he bought three Argentine race horses, Frisante, Persuavio, and Carape. (He already owned a horse named Tina's Cat.) He raced Frisante, which did "pretty well," though he offered no specifics. He intended to use Persuavio as a breeding horse.[33] (Later on in the decade, he owned Martin Ritt Stables, housing $150,000 worth of weanlings, yearlings, and brood mares.)[34] Roald Dahl reminded Ritt that he had said many times in the past that he would like to film a movie about horses. Dahl suggested that Ritt purchase the books of Dick Francis.[35] Ritt replied that he had thought about the matter, but unfortunately, all of Francis's books had been optioned.[36] Ultimately, Ritt did make a horse movie. Starring Walter Matthau, its title was *Casey's Shadow*.

By the mid-seventies Ritt was well off and comfortable. He had made about twenty movies by now, and his fees ranged anywhere from $200,000 to $500,000 for each of them. He had invested wisely, and now owned several horses and participated in horse partnerships. In addition, he owned numerous paintings and other objects of art, cars, and apartments in Venice, San Remo, and La Jolla. He definitely did not flaunt his status, as so many other Hollywood directors did, although he did once tell a reporter that "I make more in a single year than my father made in his lifetime."[37] His house in Pacific Palisades, though roomy and comfortable, was said to be "modest" by the usual Hollywood standards. His life was consumed by movies, horse racing, tennis, sports, and his family. He continued to wear jumpsuits, many of which came down only to his ankles; in fact, he became a familiar sight as he walked along the streets and lanes of Pacific Palisades. (He was so addicted to jumpsuits that he and a friend planned to go out for dinner in one of New York's finest restaurants. When Ritt showed up in a jumpsuit, his friend told him, "Marty, you can't go to a New York restaurant at night in a jumpsuit!" Ritt replied, "Hell, then, let's go to a delicatessen." They did.[38])

His status did not keep him from being summoned to jury duty. He received his "greetings" in late August 1974, to serve on a Beverly Hills jury. He wrote to the court that the nature of the motion picture business required much travel for long periods of time, and that, as of 1 October, he was leaving the country to do a film in Switzerland.[39] Even when he returned, he said, he would be at home for only two months; he was going to New York to make another picture. The court excused him from jury service. The movie in Switzerland to which he alluded was *The End of the Game* and the movie in New York was to be *The Front*. In the first one, Ritt was the lead actor and in the second, the director.

The End of the Game is based on Friedrich Durrenmatt's psychological thriller, *Der Richter und Sein Henker* (*The Judge and his Hangman*). Maximilian Schell directed the movie, and he thought his old friend Ritt would be a perfect Inspector Hans Baerlach. Ritt told Schell that he had not acted for twenty years, and then asked who else was in the picture. "Robert Shaw," replied Schell, "and Jacqueline Bisset." Ritt interrupted him, "Say no more. I'll be on the next plane."[40]

Ritt played a large "cigar-ingesting" detective "whose stomach is so rebellious he gurgles as he walks."[41] Later, when he saw himself on the screen, he exclaimed "I couldn't believe I was really that fat and that old."[42] Ritt did not bother to acquire an accent for the movie, speaking for the most part as though he were a "cop from New York," but still playing a convincing role for his audiences.[43]

The movie starts out at Mahmud Bridge in Istanbul in 1945 when Gastmann (Robert Shaw) bets Baerlach that he can kill a young girl drifter and no one will ever be able to prove it on him. After the girl is shoved into the Bosporus, the movie comes forward 30 years, to 1975, in Switzerland. Gastmann is now a master criminal and manipulator of government officials. Baerlach has become a policeman, working his way up to become commissioner. By now, he is ill with an ulcerated stomach, and is constantly told by his physician that with an operation, he might have one more year to live. Baerlach always answers such advice with an excoriation against "fat-ass scholars." Though he tries to watch his eating habits, he does smoke cigars soaked in cognac.

If Gastmann cannot be proven guilty of a crime he *did* commit, then perhaps he can be found guilty for a crime he *did not* commit. How this feat is accomplished and by whom make up one of the more thrilling aspects of the movie. As the film ends, Baerlach visits an inn he has frequented in the past before becoming ill, and in his joy that the case has been solved, orders a huge meal of soup and sauerkraut and wieners. Is Baerlach's literally eating himself to death the "end of the game," or is it finally disposing of the evil Gastmann?

Jon Voight, as Walter Tschanz, and Jacqueline Bisset as Anna Crawley, play major roles in this movie. Pinchas Zukerman, however, plays a part that lasts only 30 seconds—a figure in a fog—but Donald Sutherland plays the briefest part, that of a corpse. The movie is in part allegorical, full of fog with figures moving back and forth in it; mysterious, haunting music; surprise turns in the plot—so much so that one reporter referred to Ritt as an "untidy version" of Porfiry in *Crime and Punishment*.[44]

For his part, Ritt loved participating in the movie. "It felt good to sit three months in Vienna [where the movie was shot, although the setting was Berne, Switzerland], having nothing to do but perform."[45] He spent his days on the set and then had "leisurely" dinners and got eight hours of sleep every day. "It was luxurious not being in control."[46]

The End of the Game did not receive much press attention in the United States. What there was of it, was usually favorable. "There is an outrageous vitality to it that gives it a bumpy appeal," said one critic.[47] "What a glorious return to the screen" Ritt made as Commissioner Hans Baerlach, proclaimed another.[48] The *Globe & Mail* in Toronto, however, disliked the cinematic effort. Only Ritt's part, it said, contained the breath of life, "and we are grateful that Ritt radiated a bit of warmth in this otherwise cold, bleak film."[49]

Though *The End of the Game* was a success, certainly by artistic, if not box-office, standards, it would be ten years before Ritt again played a role in a motion picture. (That was *The Slugger's Wife,* in 1985.) As soon as he returned to the United States he began planning for the movie he told friends he "was meant" to make. It was the most auto-biographical movie he ever made, dealing with a particularly painful period in his life. It was *The Front.*

Throughout his career, Ritt had spoken freely to reporters, friends, and acquaintances about the blacklist of the 1950s. He had lost his own job in those days, and for six years he and Adele had to struggle to make a living. He always believed it was ironic at best and despicable at worst that people could be fired from their jobs and then persecuted in a country that boasted First Amendment rights of free speech, and Fifth Amendment rights of due process. He was not maudlin or sentimental, or even particularly bitter, about the matter—just angry. Even so, he usually spoke passionately about HUAC and the McCarthy hearings. In fact, as one of his admirers attested, he loved talking about the blacklist, because he was intractably opposed to injustice.[50] Harriet Conrad, who played in *The Front* "clearly recalled" Ritt talking about the blacklisting and gaining such empathy "that tears welled up in my eyes."[51] Once, in Connecticut, Ritt was at a friend's house for dinner when, just before the meal was to begin, another guest arrived. Ritt took one look at him, ran upstairs, and would not come down during the entire evening. Finally the host got him to say what was the matter. The guest, Ritt stated, had turned in his own wife to HUAC several years before. Ritt absolutely refused to have anything to do with him.[52]

The Front dealt exclusively with television productions, and its origins dated back to the time when Ritt and Bernstein worked on *The Molly Maguires.* He and Ritt talked for "countless late-night hours" about a movie dealing with the blacklist. They did not want to be preachy, so hit upon the idea to make it, to some extent, a comedy.[53] They spoke often about trying to get Robert Redford or Dustin Hoffman for the part, and then in a moment of inspiration, Ritt asked Bernstein, "What about that kid?"[54] "That kid" turned out to be Woody Allen, whose role helped Bernstein and Ritt to approach the movie "ass-backward," and make a success of it.[55]

The movie opens with a background of Frank Sinatra singing "Young at Heart," with a collage of McCarthy's wedding, bomb shelters, MacArthur's parade, new cars, the Korean war, Ike and Adlai, Joe DiMaggio, and the Rosenbergs. Allen plays Howard Prince, a down-and-out coffee-shop employee who is contacted by blacklisted writers to take what they had written and present it under his own by-line to the producers of the various television networks. At the beginning Howard stands in for three writers for ten percent of each of their earnings on the scripts they give him. As the movie progresses, complications arise as he takes on additional writers. For example, how will the taxes on all these earnings be paid, and then Howard—who has been reading Eugene O'Neill—begins to advise the writers about how to write their scripts, creating some friction. He befriends Hecky Brown (Zero Mostel, who in real life had been blacklisted). Brown, however, becomes so despondent over the blacklist that he commits suicide.

Finally, Howard himself—through being such a famous "author"—comes to the attention of HUAC. At first he refuses to appear before the committee, and when he finally relents he refuses to give them any straight answers. He finally jumps to his feet and tells the members of HUAC to "go fuck yourselves," a statement that might have accounted for the film's ultimately being more popular in Europe than in America. As the movie ends, Howard is led away in handcuffs, again to the music of Frank Sinatra.

Almost everyone connected with *The Front* had been blacklisted in the 1950s. Martin Ritt, the director; Zero Mostel and Herschel Bernardi, the actors; and Walter Bernstein, the scriptwriter, had suffered at the hands of HUAC. Of course, there were—and still are—rumors that a blacklist never even existed; that it was merely coincidental that all those people fired from their jobs had real or supposed affiliations with the Communist Party. In fact, Ronald Reagan denied that there was a blacklist; and it was further reported that while Reagan was president of the Screen Actors Guild, he may have been an informant for HUAC.[56]

Since *The Front* dealt with television, one big question was whether or not the networks would screen it. Yes, said CBS (where Ritt had been working when he was blacklisted), because "it deals with a subject that is now comfortably historical."[57] Such statements, said Ritt, pointed out the essential hypocrisy of the entire HUAC-McCarthy period. First, the studios during the blacklist period knew they were getting material from fronts, and they relished it. Second, just exactly how many Communists did McCarthy expose? None. And almost certainly there were many of them around. Yet, many of the best creative people "had their voices stilled, and it was a terrible, terrible time."[58] Though the networks looked forward to seeing the movie, NBC was not cooperative while the movie was being shot. The network refused to allow some of the shots to be made on its eighth floor headquarters in New York. Ritt was "too sophisticated" not to know why. "They are not dissimilar," he wrote indignantly, "to the unspecified reasons that the networks gave for submitting to McCarthyism and allowing the blacklist to flourish."[59] He believed that at least NBC had not learned anything from its previous mistakes.

Ritt always told his friends that in no way was *The Front* a "typical" Zero Mostel–Woody Allen comedy.[60] "Instead, what the audience will get is a film filled with a bitterness and irony that reflect the ludicrousness of the time of the blacklist."[61] In a way *The Front* was a morality play, and, of course, it induced questions about whether or not a period of McCarthyism could ever occur again. Ritt always liked to shock the people who asked him this question by saying that the young people of the 1970s would, quite frankly, tell McCarthy, as Howard Prince told the HUAC, to "go fuck yourself."[62] Ritt always saw a connection between HUAC-McCarthyism and Richard Nixon's election to the presidency in 1968, and the creation of a political system that allowed such things as Watergate. (This same thesis was outlined in Lillian Hellman's *Scoundrel Time*.) The political constituency in 1975 was, he believed, smarter than the one in the late forties and early fifties. It would be up on its "hind legs" in a hurry if another McCarthy came along.[63] Woody Allen was less sanguine than Ritt on the matter of a reoccurrence of McCarthyism. It can definitely happen again, he said. "I feel we're just six inches away. I have no trust in government. I was cynical even before Watergate. I always get a queasy feeling about guys in blue suits."[64] However, he felt that the government had "disgraced itself" so consistently in the recent past that perhaps the general public would not let McCarthyism occur again. "If it does happen again," Allen said, it will be in some "new and more sophisticated manner."[65]

Ritt claimed that he would have made *The Front* for nothing—and he did make it for $250,000, half his normal fees. It was a "terribly political film," he told a friend, one that he had been wanting to make for the past twenty years.[66] Some of Ritt's associates told him that *The Front* would have been more pertinent in 1953. He responded to such suggestions that it would not have been acceptable in that year, and "as a matter of fact, I have doubts whether it's welcome even today [1975]."[67] It was shot entirely in New York, causing some city officials to claim that the movie implied that New York had been the blacklisting center of the country. Ritt quickly dispelled such notions. Also, he had criticized some officials for not responding to his needs for settings, such as courtrooms, as quickly as he thought they should have. He later believed his criticism had been unfair to those officials, because the city was in a "genuine state of crisis at the time"[68] and it had more important things to consider than the making of a movie." (New York in 1975 faced a major sanitation strike, the mass transit authority was almost bankrupt, and a federal grand jury returned a 44-count indictment against the chairman of the cultural affairs committee.)

One correspondent accused Ritt of conjuring up anti-Irish, anti-Catholic feelings with *The Front*. The major inquisitor was Irish, and seemed to be a "blurred image of the goyem world,"[69] some sixteenth- or seventeenth-century "Jesuit dressed in a business suit"—or if not a Jesuit, at least a racial stereotype of an Irish Catholic."[70] Ritt was up front with his answer: "I don't disagree with your feelings about the Irish Catholics."[71] (He had dealt at length with the Irish, it may be recalled, in *The Molly Maguires*.) His only defense was that *The Front* was a true story. Ritt, however, had made a film about the victims, not the inquisitors, and thus he believed he had no apologies to make to any religious or ethnic groups.

As might be expected, some of the most ardent supporters of *The Front* were the very people who had been blacklisted. "The screening room was filled with gray heads and sad eyes," reported one correspondent.[72] He was pleased that the few young people attending the movie "responded with a great deal of interest and lots of laughter."[73] (A few months later, however, Ritt was shocked to learn that many students at a famous university, Stanford, had not only not seen *The Front*, but had never even heard of Joseph McCarthy.)[74] Edward Eliscu said that "we who survived the blacklisting, the runarounds, and rebuffs, the backdoor fronts, and the tragedies," owed Ritt a debt of gratitude for bringing out *The Front*.[75] He was in tears, he said, as he left the cinema, and just writing the letter to Ritt caused a lump in his throat to well up again. "In short," he proclaimed, "we who are not about to die salute you."[76]

Shepard Traube "howled with laughter" at *The Front*; some of it ironic, "but we were able to go back to what was a traumatic time . . . and to know that most of us are still here to recall it."[77] Lee Steiner had participated in some of the hearings of the HUAC-McCarthy era, and he thanked Columbia Studios for making an "accurate and entertaining" statement about "this ugly area in American history."[78] Laura Bock wrote to say that the audience applauded each name on the credits who had been blacklisted.[79] Henry Hack was most impressed by the suicide scene in *The Front*. It could have been maudlin, he believed, but it was "clean and almost surgical."[80] (The movie does not show the suicide; only Mostel walking toward an open window, and then the curtain blowing in the wind.) Roger Woodis, saluting Ritt's courage for making *The Front*, nevertheless told him that "people fed on an endless diet of Clint Eastwood and monsters of various sizes are unlikely to be attracted to a movie that deals with a real disaster."[81] John P. McLaughlin believed it should be mandatory (again, as with *Conrack*, Ritt did not like the word mandatory) that young people see *The Front* to learn how "easily freedom can slip away when we allow irresponsible politicians to create that kind of hysteria."[82] Ritt's good friend Dino DeLaurentiis sent a congratulatory telegram for "a wonderful picture."[83]

Press reviews of *The Front* were mixed. Pauline Kael, not surprisingly, did not like it. She believed Ritt was paralyzed by the subject of blacklisting. For her the sequences did not flow; hence, the movie was sterile, unpopulated, and passionless.[84] It did have an appealing theme, however, one that decent people could not oppose; it was just the way the story was delivered that bothered her. Her review did not anger Ritt, for, with few exceptions (such as *Sounder* and *Conrack*), Kael had been one of his most persistent critics. It did trouble Ritt's friend Ted Allan. "This [Kael] is the lady who described *Last Tango in Paris* with . . . enthusiasm. It is clear that she is so self involved and so self oriented she didn't see the significance of this very significant movie."[85] A writer for the *New York Post* believed Ritt had handled a "touchy subject" with "intelligence, feeling, and humor;" however, the movie failed at several points due to "sloppy errors of direction, writing, and casting."[86]

Variety was not too enthusiastic, either. Neither director Ritt nor screenwriter Bernstein had made the McCarthy madness either "romantically credible" or "absurdly incredible."[87] Some reviews blamed pedestrian aspects of the movie on Woody Allen, intimating that he was out of his element in *The Front*. He "painfully" and "awkwardly," though "sincerely," tried to play a straight role,[88] and he did not succeed.

That Ritt had been a long-time critic of the auteur method of filmmaking, yet made *The Front* on a very personal level, was not overlooked by the press. *The Christian Science Monitor* believed that Ritt had been "legitimately attacked" in the past for his lack of "a personal filmmaking style,"[89] but perhaps *The Front* at least somewhat redeemed him. Whatever else could be said about the movie, it was nonetheless true that it was the first non-documentary feature "to deal directly and intelligently with McCarthyism."[90] Staying away from heavy-handed political polemics caused the filmmakers to opt for a format half comedy, half drama, and "satisfying as neither."[91] Vincent Canby in *The New York Times*, called *The Front* "incomplete" and "oversimplified." It did, however, "work on the conscience" and recreate "the awful noise of ignorance that can still be heard."[92]

The only nomination for an award *The Front* received was to Walter Bernstein, the scriptwriter. At a dinner in Hollywood, a friend told Bernstein that his nomination was as far as *The Front* "was going to go out here."[93] There was probably no way *The Front* could have won any awards in the United States in 1976. Though it dealt with television, and did not indict Hollywood, there was still enough of a difference of opinion on HUAC-McCarthyism among the acting community that films dealing with the blacklist were treated gingerly both by the Academy of Motion Picture Arts and Sciences and by the Directors Guild, perhaps showing once again that Hollywood is populated by some of the country's most dedicated conservatives.

The Front, however, did indeed receive an award—and perhaps its reception was the most ironic thing about the movie. It received the Golden Ibex Award at the Teheran, Iran, film festival. The award was presented to the makers of the film by none other than Farah Pahlavi, wife of the Shah of Iran. That a film about unfair blacklisting of a nation's most creative element should win an award in a country that was almost completely despotic just has to have been the strangest, if not the most bizarre, thing that ever happened to Martin Ritt's moviemaking career.

In a letter to David Golding, Ritt spoke about how some idealist intellectuals around the country were receiving The Front. "All the right wing liberals [he did not define what he meant], the Trotskyites, and all the disaffected left have jumped on the film."[94] For some reason, Ritt came to believe that two of his greatest detractors concerning The Front were historian Arthur Schlesinger, Jr., and columnist Hilton Kramer. Although Ritt had always considered himself to be a liberal—at least in rejecting establishment societal standards —he lashed out at Schlesinger and Kramer for being "venal liberals."

In Ritt's opinion, both Schlesinger and Kramer "behaved like McCarthyites" during the blacklist period,[95] and now, 1976, they did not want that era to be "dredged up and the truth to be aired."[96] He said that Kramer had charged The Front as a convenient revision of history,[97] and he bet his friend Nancy Green that she did not know "how many of your liberal, intellectual friends were potential McCarthyites."[98] The more he wrote on the subject, the angrier Ritt became: "At the end of one of Hilton Kramer's articles, he said if there had been no Communists there would have been no McCarthy." Ritt felt this sentiment was "just one step from saying that if there had been no Jews, there would have been no Hitler."[99]

For his part, Schlesinger was perplexed that Ritt "should have got so mad at me."[100] He had praised Hud and The

Molly Maguires when he was a film reviewer, and had "rather liked" *The Front.* "I do remember running into Zero Mostel on the street after it came out and having a genial conversation with him. He was not mad at me."[101]

At about the time *The Front* came out, Lillian Hellman's book *Scoundrel Time* (which stayed for many weeks on *The New York Times* bestseller list) was published.[102] Kramer, in his piece for *The New York Times*, argued that the real scoundrels in the literary and artistic community in the late forties were the Stalinists and their fellow travelers. Schlesinger thought Kramer's article "a useful corrective of leftwing cliches and so deposed in a brief letter to the *Times*," in which he said, "I wish Hilton Kramer's article could be made required reading for everyone born after 1940."[103] Professor Alfred Kazin also wrote to the *Times*, approving Kramer's article. (Kazin's review of Hellman's *Scoundrel Time*, was turned down by the *New Republic*.) The letters outraged Lillian Hellman, and she did not speak to Schlesinger for the next two years.[104]

Kramer's article mentioned *The Front* as an example of left-wing sentimentalization of the Stalinists, and of "revising history."[105] He felt that *The Front* was a vast over-simplification of "good guy" versus "bad guy," when, in fact, the witnesses before HUAC had been the Communists the committee claimed they were. Ritt must have joined Kramer's article with Schlesinger's and Kazin's letters, and concluded that they were McCarthyites in disguise.[106] Schlesinger was surprised "that as late as 1976 Martin Ritt would equate anti-Stalinism with McCarthyism. He should have known that anti-Stalinists of any persuasion were vigorously anti-McCarthy too. . . ."[107] He wondered if Ritt might have had "residual Stalinoid emotions."[108] The truth is probably as Schlesinger supposed: Ritt read Kramer's article which, among other things, faulted *The Front*, and then he read Schlesinger's praise of Kramer's letter—and this produced the flash point. He was probably more angry than ideologically motivated in his outburst against Kramer and Schlesinger.

It is obvious that the most sensitive subject to Martin Ritt over the years was the blacklist and, perhaps one might say, almost every movie he made had some theme or other from it. Social injustice (*Edge of the City*) and coercion

(*Sound and the Fury* and *Norma Rae*), individualism (*Hud*), betrayal (*Hombre* and *The Molly Maguires*), guilt by association (*The Front*), social reform (*Cross Creek* and *Stanley & Iris*), and supporting the underdog (*The Black Orchid, Sounder*, and *The Great White Hope*) were his chief interests. These and other themes emanated at least in part from Ritt's experience of being blacklisted.

Did *The Front* settle the score with Ritt's feelings about the blacklist? No, indeed not. He continued to make movies from themes that arose from the blacklist, and also to speak to both broadcast and print media about that era. Why? Was it a way to draw attention to his own career? Did he want reporters to view his blacklisting as the central focus of his moviemaking? To some extent, yes. More significantly, however, he sincerely supported the free movement of ideas and opinions that art must have if it is going to survive and succeed. No government at any level must dictate the theme or subject matter of artistic creation. Majority public opinion must not, either. The public has a right to reject an artist's and moviemaker's work, but not to set down beforehand the rules by which it is to be judged. Art brought into being to serve the particular purposes of interest groups or governmental agencies is probably not art at all; more likely, it is propaganda. Ritt was interested in art, not propaganda.

He had had numerous opportunities in the past to enunciate his philosophy of art. He had spoken, taught, and offered symposia on his work at such places as the University of Southern California, UCLA, the University of Kansas, and Brigham Young University. Also, he had participated in numerous film festivals in Canada, England, and other parts of the world. One of the most memorable gatherings he ever attended was in March 1977 at Eastern Illinois University, in Charleston.

An instructor at Eastern, Rebecca Smith Wild, happened to run across Ritt's name in a newspaper and wondered if he was the same person who had been her classmate at Elon. He was, indeed, and she immediately began plans for a Martin Ritt retrospective to be held at Eastern. She was not able to get funding for the event, the university administration was not very helpful, the entire affair had to be rescheduled during spring break, and then the weather turned bad.[109] Undaunted, Professor Wild forged ahead with her plans for the retrospective. Some 40 people attended, and by all accounts it was one of "the very best artistic programs ever presented at Eastern."[110]

Ritt was "informed, gracious, vital and energetic, witty—everything a one-man show required.[111] Even so, he bemused several people at a dinner party, using his fingers more than his fork, and being a "very audible eater."[112] He kept talking at the table about the "fuckability quotients" of actors and actresses in casting them for particular roles.[113] He used this phrase quite often; in fact, he used it in reference to Paul Newman. "Paul always had that cool sexuality, what I call a great fuckability quotient, which, let's face it, is part of what makes a star."[114] While such a phrase may have been common and ordinary to Martin Ritt, it certainly was not to his midwestern audience. He never even noticed the "hitch" that the phrase came close to causing in the retrospective.

After the retrospective, Wild wrote to Ritt apologizing for the small turnout. Ritt told her that quality made up for quantity. What mattered, he told her, "was that people of good will got together to examine their times and the work of one of their constituents."[115] He also told James Quivey, chairman of the English Department at EIU, that he found the retrospective "stimulating," and he believed that filmmakers should visit academia more often for meaningful give and take between directors and sophisticated viewers.[116] Ritt always treasured his visit to Charleston, and the small but perceptive audience at Eastern Illinois University. He worked best in question-answer series. He did not like to give lectures, either public or private. He relished, however, the one-to-one contact of discussion. EIU gave him that opportunity, and he was forever grateful.

Even while he was enjoying himself at Eastern Illinois University, and even before that, while *The Front* was being shot, things were happening unknown to Ritt that would have an important impact on his life and career. David Begelman, head of Columbia Studios, went on a check-writing spree, starting in 1975, that ultimately impacted a great many people, Ritt included. In fact, Ritt and Begelman had known each other for years, and for a time Begelman was Ritt's agent at MCA. As president of Columbia Studios, Begelman was one of few executives in Hollywood who gave

Ritt and Bernstein a serious hearing on the possibilities of filming *The Front*. He finally stuck out his neck, and approved the project.

Begelman was accused of embezzling $40,000 from Columbia Studios between January 1975 and May 1977. He allegedly forged actor Cliff Robertson's name on a $10,000 check, restaurateur Pierre Groleau's for $25,000, and Martin Ritt's for $5,000.[117] When the check to Ritt was written, *The Front* was in production, so it was natural for various payments to be made to Ritt by Columbia Studios during that period, "payments that could easily have helped camouflage a single forged check."[118] A young lawyer, Nancy Barton, found the check made to Ritt. On the back, there had been two endorsements. The first one was Martin Ritt; the second one was David Begelman.[119] David McClintick, in *Indecent Exposure*, explained:

The handwriting looked familiar. Nancy Barton had become the [investigative] team's expert on Begelman's handwriting. She knew his nuances. She knew that he wrote differently with a felt-tip pen than with a ball-point, and that his signature differed from other forms of his writing. The endorsements on the Martin Ritt check appeared to be in Begelman's handwriting. . . . Barton passed the check around the room. The studio's file on Martin Ritt was summoned and revealed that Ritt's handwriting was different from that on the check.[120]

Ritt was queried by Robert Elias of the Burbank police department about pressing charges against Begelman. Ritt had no intention of doing so. "The answer is no," he told the police official. "I am not interested."[121] Also, Mike Wallace of *Sixty Minutes* wanted to feature Ritt on the Begelman affair. Ritt turned him down, saying that the matter was of no importance "except as the aberration of a former agent."[122] Though *Sixty Minutes* was a "consistently excellent" show, he said, he really did not know all that much about the charges against David Begelman. He was not "in the business" of "heaping rumor upon fact."[123] Apparently, the personnel at *Sixty Minutes* kept telephoning Ritt, trying to get him to change his mind. As an alternative to Begelman, Ritt apparently suggested that Wallace do a segment on Judge Irving Kaufman, who had sentenced the Rosenbergs to death.[124] "Wallace, said Ritt, told me to 'get off his fucking back' and hung up."[125] Wallace vehemently denied that this ever happened: "This is pure bullshit!" he exclaimed. "Why would I hang up on Marty Ritt? He was a friend of mine; not close, close, but a friend."[126]

Ritt considered Begelman a friend going through some troublous times, and he was not about to kick someone when they were down. Begelman had "totally blocked" Ritt's check from his mind,[127] and Ritt accepted the explanation—and the apologies that followed. It was a piece of personal business, he felt, between David Begelman and Martin Ritt—and should be of no concern to police departments or television shows.

For Ritt, however, the situation turned ugly by the publication of an article in *New West* magazine, entitled "The Incredible Past of David Begelman." Its author, Jeanie Kasindorf, wondered why no one apparently wanted to prosecute Begelman. (Cliff Robertson ultimately did file charges.)[128] She quoted Ritt as saying that Begelman was his friend, "and until he does something that is destructive to me, I'll support him."[129] Everyone, it seemed, considered Begelman to be their friend, and they came to his support during his time of trouble. Or, at least, that was a general impression.

According to Kasindorf's article, however, there was another reason for lack of prosecution: fear. All the writers and directors, she said, "worked in a very small business, where it was easy to be up one day and down the next."[130] They may have had their own private opinions about the matter, but "they knew what their public opinions had to be."[131] What came next was, for Ritt, a point of no return. Kasindorf interviewed Sid Luft (whose wife, Judy Garland, was widely reported as having an affair with Begelman) for her article. Luft was reported as saying that he had tried unsuccessfully to get Ritt to talk with reporters about the Begelman affair. Luft "understood" why his old friend was so reticent: "Marty's a rich man today. He's a horse owner. He's scared. Here's a guy who's reinstated after the years of the McCarthy blacklist. You can understand how he doesn't want to get involved."[132]

Ritt waited a few days after reading Kasindorf's article, to "let his anger simmer down," before writing to the author. She had allowed a "very cheap shot" to be taken at him, Ritt said.[133] (She had asked Ritt for an interview about the Begelman affair, and he refused.) Even though Luft's statement had been put in quotes, Kasindorf, he thought, had handled Ritt's name in a "cavalier" fashion. "The least you could have done was to call me to check out what Sid Luft had said. The notion that I would kiss anybody's ass to keep working could not be supported in any way by my record."[134] She had allowed Luft to "philosophize" about Ritt's reactions to the Begelman affair, and that was journalism, "at best sloppy," at worst "vicious."[135]

If Ritt was angry at Kasindorf, he was absolutely outraged at Luft. In fact, he broke off their friendship over the matter. He did it precisely, almost surgically. "You characterized me as a long time friend. Your loose mouth estimate of my character makes it clear to me that you are anything but my friend. I would appreciate it if you would just forget that I exist from now on."[136] Apparently, the two never saw or spoke to each other again.

For anyone to have suggested that Ritt acted out of fear for his career simply showed that they did not understand either his personality or background. He was a person who had refused to cooperate with HUAC, who had broken his bonds with one of his best friends, Elia Kazan, over the matter of "friendly testimony," and had bucked much conservative Hollywood tradition from the first day he got into town. His was too independent a mind to have supported Begelman out of a fear of not being able to get work; if he had been willing to "pick up the tab" at an early point in his career when he had neither money nor influence, it would seem incredible that he would stop the practice at a point when he had all the money he would ever need, and was a person of international moviemaking influence. Definitely, people could disagree with him and still be his friend; they ran into danger only when they assumed too much. He was a "man apart," as John le Carré characterized him, "not because he's a power man or vain, but because in a painful and ambitious life he has learned that his own judgment is the only one he can trust."[137]

Ritt quickly moved on from one event in his life to another, without allowing himself to brood or sulk over matters. He cared about things, because he cared about people. But life, he reckoned, like his movies, was made up of small brush strokes that were meant ultimately to cover an entire canvas. Thus, he refused to dwell on any personal adversities, and to stay busy.

Staying busy was Ritt's forte. After such movies as *Sounder*, *Pete 'n Tillie*, and *The Front*, many directors would have been content to rest on their laurels. But not Martin Ritt. Many times, even before he had finished one movie, he was thinking about the next one. Such was the case with a subject about which he had always wanted to make a movie: the atomic bomb, the most surpassing example of power—and terror—in our time. He wanted to center such a film around the personal struggles of Robert Oppenheimer, Enrico Fermi, and Klaus Fuchs, as they worked on the bomb during World War II.[138]

As the news of Ritt's proposal to make a film about the atomic bomb became known, he learned that he was not the first movie person to think about such a project. Back in 1955, Dexter Masters had written a novel, *The Accident*, and none other than David O. Selznick had wanted to film it. Selznick International had fallen on hard times in the late fifties, and, hopefully, *The Accident* would have been his comeback film. Selznick hired Masters to write the screenplay; three months into it, Selznick telephoned Masters with the news that the "project was off."[139] "Why?" of course, was Masters's first question. "They won't give me an export license," the film producer explained.[140] Who were "they?"

Masters found out a while later. At an acting school in New York Masters heard a student refer to *The Accident* as a "banned novel."

"What do you mean?" Masters asked him. "Who banned it?"

"The State Department wouldn't give Selznick an export license. Everyone in Hollywood knew what that meant," he said. "The government banned it."[141] As a result, Selznick had dropped the project.

Now, some 22 years later Ritt and his friend at Columbia, Ray Stark, revived the matter. Masters wrote to Ritt, "I am curious to know why if you are interested in making a film on this subject you have not considered *The Accident*."[142] He mentioned the State Department's past hostility which had cut short Selznick's money-raising efforts on the matter. But to Ritt, Masters said, all of these past difficulties "would not affect you, of all people." He was certain the barrier that Selznick could not leap would by now be gone.[143] Ritt told Masters that he had not had any "real awareness" of *The Accident* when he started the atomic bomb project.[144] From Masters's first letter on, however, *The Accident* was at the forefront in the planning stages. Ritt and Stark still referred to their projected movie as "The Oppenheimer Project," but it was clear that it was going to be based on Masters's work.

Ritt thought of William Goldman as the scriptwriter for *The Accident*. He found, however, that Stark already had his own writers, and would have to wait until they presented him with a total first draft before either approving their work or moving on to some other writer.[145] A few weeks later, Ritt was having second thoughts about the entire Oppenheimer matter. Because of the nature of the project, it was "quite explosive" (whether he was punning here or reacting to some differences of opinion with Stark is simply not known), and "I'm not sure I will be able to make it, but I'll try."[146] He may have tried, but he did not make it. *The Accident*, plus another project of the time, *The Electric Horseman*—scripted by Walter Bernstein—did not materialize for Ritt. The latter was ultimately turned into a movie; the former, never.

Perhaps one reason why *The Accident* did not come to fruition for Ritt was that Stark wanted him to direct another picture—the one about horses that Ritt had always said he wanted to do. When it was made, it was called *Casey's Shadow*, with Walter Matthau as the star.

From *Pete 'n Tillie* to *The Accident*, with *End of the Game*, *The Front*, the EIU symposium, and the Begelman affair in between, Martin Ritt stayed busy, living life to the fullest. He was, in fact, in the prime of life during the mid-seventies. He had "arrived," but he refused to let his "arrival" satisfy him. He kept looking for what to him would be the "perfect" film. He almost found it in *Norma Rae* which, along with *Sounder*, became one of his two most famous and remembered movie efforts.

Chapter 8

◆ ◆ ◆

"Martin Ritt *Is* Norma Rae"

Martin Ritt was astute at both horse racing and poker playing; he could usually come out ahead in both enterprises. Though his movies always returned their costs (among his other accomplishments, he was also known as a director generally "on time" and "under budget"), he was not so expert in predicting how they would fare at the box office. He was well known for his artistic leanings and the themes he followed in his movies. Entertainment with substance was the quality that kept bringing movie producers back to Martin Ritt's direction. Such a producer was Ray Stark, who wanted his friend Martin Ritt to make a horse movie.

His love of horses and their feats on the track made it predictable that Ritt would one day do a racing movie. Starring Walter Matthau, his horse movie—made in 1977, and released in 1978—had working titles like *A Horse of a Different Color, Cajun Colt*, and *Coon-Ass Colt*. This last title was abandoned because of ethnic and racial considerations,[1] although Dr. John—Stark had wanted Waylon Jennings, Willie Nelson, or Kris Kristofferson—did sing a song with such a title in the movie. The movie's title derived from a young colt, born to a sickly mare, but sired by a prize-winning thoroughbred, who is the pride and joy of young Casey Bordelle.

Casey's father, Lloyd (Walter Matthau), has never seen a horse run as fast as Casey's Shadow. Unfortunately, his son, Casey, cannot resist the temptation to see *how* fast Shadow can go, well before the time he is physically fit to race. Casey almost "blew him out" in a run. He takes good care of the horse afterward, but then, a young female jockey bets him $5.00 on a race over rough ground. Fourteen-year-old Casey cannot resist, and the race results in a sprain in Shadow's leg.

Beer-guzzling Lloyd Bordelle, whose wife has left him, and whose old Chevy truck is difficult to start, dreams of winning a million dollars and going on a vacation to Tahiti, "where the women walk around without any tops on," stakes everything he has that Shadow will win the eighteenth running of the American International at Ruidoso Downs in New Mexico. "I know it's wrong," he explains to his sons and friends, "but it's my one chance to be somebody."

Shadow runs in the race at Ruidoso Downs, and wins. Afterwards, however, it is found that he has a three-way break in a shin bone. One of Lloyd's sons bitterly asks him, "Was it worth it, Dad?" The veterinarian recommends that Shadow be put down. Contritely, however, Lloyd talks him into operating, saying that he will keep the horse immobile long enough for its leg to mend. The operation is a success. The movie ends with Lloyd apologizing to his sons for the way he handled the matter, and taking Shadow home to Louisiana with the intent of making a stud horse out of him. This is another Martin Ritt "happy ending," said by some critics to be contrived.

Casey's Shadow may have its humorous moments, with Matthau's Cajun accent and mannerisms, the bars, and horse-racing jargon. The movie shows essentially, however, that Lloyd Bordelle let his principles slip away from him in his quest of big winnings. He had had opportunities to sell Shadow, but refused, holding out for the big race at Ruidoso Downs. Contrary to good horsemanship, he races a horse he knows has been injured and is likely to be injured again by continued competition. Apparently what gold can do to the prospector, a race card can do to a professional horse-man.

Ritt used two horses, one of which he bought from Burt Reynolds, to portray Casey's Shadow, and his movie about the horse cost approximately $3.5 million. Ritt was angered when a preview, or trailer, was released which had a "low level of technical excellence."[2] He was "pissed off" and amazed that someone would care so little about *Casey's Shadow* to let a "raggedy" piece of work go out to the public.[3] There were some test showings of the movie: only four percent rated *Casey's Shadow* as "poor," while the remaining 96 percent rated it "good" or "excellent."[4] These test ratings showed that Ritt was not adept at predicting how his movies would do with the general public. He wrote a friend a while after *Casey's Shadow* opened that it was an "outstanding critical success,"[5] but the "business" for it had been "very uneven."[6]

Apparently, Ray Stark was not the easiest person to work with. Perhaps it was Ritt's unhappiness with the trailer of *Casey's Shadow* that caused Stark to tell Ritt that some of the movie's scenes were "hokum"; this at the time the movie was just being publicly released. Though Stark and Ritt were the best of friends, Ritt could still be very blunt: "I believe I gave every scene in *Casey's Shadow* what I felt it deserved emotionally. If it is hokum, you know there are plenty of other directors you could go to in this town. What I have to sell is a much rarer commodity."[7] He did not, he hastened to add, write this letter in anger, but out of desire to make Stark understand what he did, and why, with *Casey's Shadow*. Anyone, including Sid Luft in the Begelman affair, who thought Ritt would cower toward his superiors and do their bidding because he did not want to lose his career, should have been disabused of that notion by Ritt's relationship with Ray Stark in the making of *Casey's Shadow*. Ritt had his own ideas of art and entertainment, especially art, and he would not allow himself to be intimidated or manipulated by anyone, be they friend or foe.

Although one person called *Casey's Shadow* the "*National Velvet* of the 1970's,"[8] the movie did not get wide press coverage. What there was of it, however, tended to be favorable. Ritt was cheered, for example, when he learned that prominent film critic Judith Crist selected *Casey's Shadow* to include in the Dallas eighth annual film festival.[9]

Because Ritt was a "lifelong horseplayer and racetrack habitue" he could bring knowledge and "affection" to *Casey's Shadow*.[10] The larger issue in *Casey's Shadow* deals with the relationships between the father and his sons. There is a balance of obedience and independence as the sons join Lloyd in the horse-racing business, but then show off their own specific lifestyles as the movie progresses. The reconciliation of these diverse threads makes up much of the movie's dramatic impact. Ritt tackled "familial emotions head-on, with unaffected squareness," that produced a memorable movie. It was "Americana" with a rural tinge.[11] The movie was "tough enough to cry for," said Rob Baker of *The Soho Weekly News*. There are deep feelings among the men in

Casey's Shadow, and how they express their emotions to one another is important, not just in terms of horse racing, but in terms of life itself.

Lloyd Bordelle's having dreams and ideals fit well into the motif of Martin Ritt's moviemaking. The "slow deterioration of [the character's] values"[12] in a racetrack atmosphere, and then his ultimate redemption in making things right between himself and his children probably caused audiences to have an empathy for him. *Playboy*, perhaps understandably, noted the lack of any sex and romance in *Casey's Shadow*.[13] How the contagious "feverish will to win"[14] stacked up against the human emotions of father and sons was, *Playboy* said, the chief impetus of the movie.

Vincent Canby, a long-time critic of Ritt's films, apologized in print for giving *Casey's Shadow* a somewhat negative review. It was such an "easygoing, understated" film, one that produced such "good feelings," that it would be almost rude to fault it.[15] There were, however, far too many horse-racing cliches, so many in fact, that the average viewer would be lost with the "inside" jargon. On the same day as Canby's review, the *Valley News* echoed him by complaining that *Casey's Shadow* "for the most part keeps us outside, looking in."[16] There was no explanation of what the terms meant, giving the movie a "stable ambience" that "stalled" as often as Lloyd Bordelle's old pickup truck.[17]

Even while depicting Lloyd Bordelle's idealistic goal of "becoming somebody," Ritt began to make plans to film the life of another person who came to have idealistic ambitions. He went to a nuclear-freeze rally one day, and there he made the acquaintance of a young actress named Sally Field. Martin Ritt took her under his tutelage, and made a major motion picture star of her. In turn, she made the film that many critics and viewers judged to be the one by which Ritt would be remembered. It was *Norma Rae*, for which Sally Field won the Oscar in 1979 as best actress; of course, Ritt won nothing.

Ritt complained several times throughout his career about the strict rules and regulations of such Hollywood unions as the Screen Actors Guild, and the Extras Guild. (He even advised his daughter, Tina, to bring suit against the Screen Directors Guild for its persistent refusal of her application for membership. He also told many people who aspired to any kind of movie work how tough the unions were; that, often, they would have to join a union before they could even observe a picture in progress.) Nevertheless, he liked the idea of trade unions. From the time he was a social activist in New York, he felt that trade unions came closer to representing the true needs and wants of the working person than any other organization. "I like working people," he often exclaimed to newspaper reporters.[18] Therefore, when he got an opportunity to film a story about trade unionism, he jumped at it.

Norma Rae was based on the real-life experiences of Crystal Lee Sutton, who had helped considerably to unionize the textile industry, particularly the J.P. Stevens Company, in Roanoke Rapids, North Carolina. (Ritt stayed away from the Stevens Company during the filming of *Norma Rae*. Just as he had not been able to mention the Pinkertons in *The Molly Maguires*, he could not mention J.P. Stevens in *Norma Rae*.) Ritt's interest in the matter was piqued when he read Henry P. Leifermann's article in *The New York Times* about the hardships union activists and organizers faced: hostility from the community, ostracism from their fellow workers, and physical threats to their persons. He could not believe, he said, that he was not reading a period piece instead of one that was contemporary; he had no idea that working conditions were really that bad in the textile industry in the supposedly enlightened period of the 1970s. He bought the film rights to Leifermann's book, *Crystal Lee, a Woman of Inheritance*, and set about trying to find a Hollywood studio that would make it.

When negotiations first started for the movie, most producers told Ritt they did not want to produce a "downer."[19] Alan Ladd, Jr., president of Twentieth Century Fox, echoed this sentiment about *Norma Rae*: it would be too depressing. What was depressing, though, Ritt wanted to know, about depicting a girl who turns into a woman, "who is as close to a complete woman of superior dimensions as any in film history?"[20] Ladd bought this argument and decided to produce the picture.

Largely because of the past favorable experience with *Conrack*, Ritt decided early on to shoot *Norma Rae* in Georgia. According to press reports, however, the state textile commission got wind that Ritt planned to visit some textile mills, with a view to selecting one of them as the chief set for his movie. Allegedly, the commission sent letters to every textile-mill owner in the state, advising that Ritt be barred from entering.[21] The Georgia situation caused Ritt to move to next-door Alabama, whose governor, George C. Wallace, was touting his state's desirability as a place to make movies, and also trying to live down his segregationist past. Even in "The Heart of Dixie," however, Ritt faced difficulties. Every mill owner Ritt approached turned him down. Apparently, Alabama's textile commission was as powerful as Georgia's. Ritt was getting somewhat discouraged, thinking he might have to move Norma Rae out of the South entirely, when he got a letter from two textile-mill owners. While they did not agree with the premise upon which Norma Rae was based, they nevertheless did not like to be "bossed around" by the textile commission. One owner backed out of the matter altogether, and the other said he would be killed by fellow owners if they ever found out he let his mill be used for such a movie. Ritt "upped the ante" for the use of the mill from $25,000 to $100,000, and the owner said he would have to "re-examine his scruples."[22] He and Ritt struck a deal. Though the scenes in Norma Rae depicted North Carolina, the entire movie was shot in Opelika, Alabama.

Even though Ritt tap-danced in the streets of Opelika and was jovial by day, he was restless by night. "A film is a living organ,"[23] he proclaimed. Sometimes he could not get to sleep at night for worrying about mistakes that might have been made in the previous day's filming. The next day he had to erase everything that went badly the day before, and start afresh. Moviemaking was a nerve-wracking business.[24]

Filming Norma Rae was such a big occasion that Governor Wallace himself came to town, and invited Ritt and his crew to lunch. At first Sally refused to dine with the Alabama governor because of his reputation as a die-hard segregationist. Ritt told her to quit being childish,[25] and so she changed her mind (the Ravetches, however, never did). Ritt explained to her that Wallace's days of power were over, and he was harmless.[26] They did dine with the governor, and had a "civil conversation."[27] Sally did not change her opinion of Wallace, but did conclude that he had been a pawn of his era.[28]

Wallace as well greatly enjoyed the encounters with Ritt, his stars, and crews. "I watched one of the scenes that was being recorded for the film, and Sally Field came in and kneeled down by my chair and had a picture made with me."[29] "[She] was a very beautiful young lady and was very gracious to me in allowing me to have her picture made with her."[30] Wallace's visit to the set of *Norma Rae* to some extent proved one of Martin Ritt's long-standing theses: it is possible for people to change for the better, to redeem themselves for past illogical behavior, and through the "civil conversation" that Ritt mentioned, people from diverse cultures and backgrounds can finally be made to see that there are more similarities between them than differences. Perhaps it is, as historian George Bancroft said so long ago, that the drift of history is upward.

Ritt and his film crew had to blow cotton dust into the mill to give it a realistic ambience.[31] During most of the scenes in the mill, Ritt could not even hear his actors and actresses speaking to each other above the deadening noise of the looms. Once, when a scene at the mill was "wrapped," Ritt pronounced it "perfect." "How do you know?" asked someone, "you couldn't even hear your performers." Ritt replied, "I never listen to actors."[32] He explained: "When I say I never listen to actors, what I mean is that since I've already worked very carefully on the script, I never *hear* what an actor says when he's playing a scene, he or she. I'm *watching* them."[33] He put actors in a situation, tried "to set them on the right road, and let them go."[34] The good ones would make it, he said, the bad ones would not. Sally Field definitely made it as Norma Rae. Ritt said that she came to her parts externally: "she's unafraid, she'll plunge in and just play the shit out of a scene."[35] Both Cicely Tyson and Sally Field were expert, he believed, at playing the "lumpen proletariat";[36] perhaps this was why *Sounder* and *Norma Rae* became his two most remembered films.

Norma Rae Webster comes from a family of mill workers. She is divorced, and supplements her wages by sleeping with prominent men around the community, most notably the police chief. (Sally Field's role here of a worldly, independent woman who guzzles beer when things bother her, and listens to country music straight from Nashville, is a far cry from her previous major film offering of *The Flying Nun*.) Early in the movie, Norma Rae becomes a "spotter," that is, a worker who reports to management if any of the other laborers are goofing off or not doing their job properly. Naturally, this position causes all of her friends to hate her. And then, her father (Pat Hingle), who has always had the usual southern abhorrence of labor unions, collapses and dies because of being worked too hard.

Norma Rae quits being a spotter and begins to support the ideas of Reuben (Ron Leibman), a union organizer. Reuben hands his notice of a union organization meeting to management, who is required by law to put it on the bulletin board. They put it up so high, however, that only "Wilt Chamberlain on stilts" could see it. The scenes where Reuben confronts management are shot laterally alongside the men, and then the camera "swings in front of them to dolly backward with the men advancing rapidly toward the camera."[37] Such camera technique allows audiences "to see Reuben through the workers' eyes."[38]

Norma Rae becomes increasingly union minded, working so much at organizing that she neglects her new husband, Sonny Webster (Beau Bridges), and her children. (In real life, "Norma Rae" was born Crystal Lee Pulley; then, by her first marriage, she became Crystal Lee Jordan; and finally, with her second marriage, Crystal Lee Sutton. She is 53 years old [1994], has six grandchildren, and lives in Burlington, North Carolina. Her husband works in the textile mills, and she still gives occasional lectures on behalf of labor unions.)[39] She even leaves her church when the pastor refuses to allow the building to be used for union meetings.

Of course, the company strikes back. It appeals to racial prejudice by telling the predominantly white working crew at the mill that if a union comes in, it will be run by blacks. Norma Rae is arrested inside the mill for disorderly conduct when she holds up a big sign in block letters on a piece of pasteboard that say "UNION" (an event that actually happened to Crystal Lee Sutton), and is carried off, screaming and kicking to the police station. Company agents put out propaganda that Norma Rae has made pornographic films with the local police chief.

And, of course, her relations with Reuben, the union organizer, are suspect as well. They are frequently together late at night, and sometimes take walks and rides with each other through the countryside. On such an outing, Reuben slips on a big pile of cow manure. As he sits on the ground trying to clean himself, Norma Rae laughs, and says, "It's only grass and water, Reuben." (As noted earlier, this was a line that came out of Ritt's own experiences in shooting *Hud.*)

On one of their walks, Norma Rae and Reuben even go swimming together, and still, their relationship remains platonic. Ritt said he could not allow Norma Rae and the organizer to have an affair; it would jeopardize the moral fiber of the film. Reuben had to go on from one town to another in his unionizing efforts, and if, as Ritt said, he "screwed every dame that he made connection with," the movie's theme would definitely be altered.[40]

The creek-swimming scene also brought a mild rebuke from a viewer in Arkansas. Reuben says, while swimming, that minnows are biting him. The Arkansan noted that southerners do not say "minn-ow"; they say either "minn-ah," or "minn-er," depending on one's "sense of gentility."[41] This scene, the viewer reported, "broke the sexual tension" that had been building between Reuben and Norma Rae. Another misconception of "southernisms" in the movie was the use of "Y'all." Southerners do not usually say "you all," as northerners would have it, and they do not say "y'all" (pronounced "yawl") in the singular, only in the plural. "Y'all" is used in *Norma Rae* in the singular, clearly an error. One of the millworkers uses the decidedly non-southern word, "fink";[42] Norma Rae speaks of buying something at the "five-and-dime" when the correct southern usage would have been "ten-cent store,"[43] and when Reuben asks, "How come everybody down here has three names?" he was perhaps depicting more the southwest than the historical Old South.[44]

As the movie approaches its climax, the situation is set for a vote by the employees of the textile mill as to whether or not to have a union. Dramatically, the votes are counted, and at the end, the union is approved, 425 to 373, among cheers and accolades for Norma Rae and Reuben. There is "instant jubilation as first the black workers, then the women," begin to chant "Yoon-yun, yoon-yun!"[45] As Reuben prepares to leave, the two express a hint of romantic feeling for each other. Reuben says to Norma Rae, "I think you like me." Norma Rae replies, simply, "I do." The movie ends to the sounds of Jennifer Warner singing "Bless the Child of the Working Man."

Ritt told reporters that *Norma Rae* was as much about women's liberation as it was the trade union movement. An extraordinarily large number of women worked in these mills throughout the South—most of them at subsistence wages. *Norma Rae* changed her life through the process of unionization. She learned that she and thousands of women like her need not be thrust into an industrial feudalistic society; that there was a way out, and with dignity. Norma Rae grows up because, among other things, she ultimately sees the great need for education, and the necessity to fight for what one believes in. All her life she has been conditioned to accept the mill owners' attributions of capitalism and the "American Way of Life" (which invariably means their own privileged way of life), and even her own parents acceded to these explanations.[46] The mill workers in the South were somewhat like coal miners: everybody wanted the product they made, but "polite" society did not want to mingle with them. They were the "trash" workers of the much vaunted American industrial system. Perhaps coming to the conclusion that there are no absolutes in this world is the most valuable lesson Norma Rae learns and, by extension, the thousands of female viewers of the movie come to the same conclusions. Martin Ritt had always been a maker of social films; never was he better at it than with *Norma Rae*.

As one might expect, the labor movement throughout the United States hailed *Norma Rae*. The Amalgamated Clothing and Textile Workers Union, wrote Ritt a letter of thanks,[47] as did the United Automobile Workers.[48] One of the effects of working in textile mills for protracted periods was the development of lung ailments (just as coal dust for miners helped to cause "black lung"). The Carolina Brown Lung Association congratulated Ritt for *Norma Rae*, and agreed with him that the movie should be viewed by all mill workers, especially those in the Roanoke Rapids region, where Crystal Lee Sutton had first been a union activist.[49] A union official in Michigan urged Ritt to make a movie about the fights that had occurred in trying to unionize the non-editorial aspects of newspapers around the country.[50] Ritt made no commitment, but he did write back that he was largely unaware of any historical labor struggles within the fourth estate.[51] From a Portland, Oregon, labor editor came word that *Norma Rae* had a "sticky wicket" during its first release because the theater chain showing it had had "less than cordial relations" with the County Labor Council.[52] William Maness, a Methodist preacher from Jacksonville, Florida, told Ritt about his and other ministers' work with migrant farm workers in the United States. At first, Ritt was intrigued with the idea of making a movie about their endeavors,[53] but a month later he had backtracked. He wanted to meet all the church people involved in trying to help the migrant workers as they scratched out an existence on the great farms of America,[54] but at the same time, returned all the material that Maness had sent to him. Professor Robert C. Allen from the Virginia Polytechnic Institute wanted Ritt to make a film about the Loray (Gastonia, North Carolina) textile-mill strike of 1929. Ritt declined, saying that in terms of working conditions and fair wages in the textile industry, 1929 and 1977 were one and the same. On and on these letters came, reflecting their widespread agreement with the philosophy behind *Norma Rae*, and wanting more of it.

Interestingly enough, the Screen Actors Guild co-sponsored a fund-raising event for Crystal Lee. Some 900 people came to the Berwin Entertainment Center in Hollywood for the occasion, at which a screening of *Norma Rae* was presented. During the festivities there was a telephoned bomb threat from a male caller; the entire building had to be evacuated. One wag was quoted as saying that former SAG president, Ronald Reagan, would "turn over in his grave" if he knew of the guild's "emerging identity as a 'working class' union."[55] The bomb threat was fake, but the reactions engendered by it were real.

Individuals not representing anyone but themselves also wrote dozens of letters to Ritt, extolling the virtues of *Norma Rae*. The inimitable Virginia Durr of Wetumpka, Alabama, wrote a letter that Ritt treasured for the rest of his life. She was glad there were no overt sex scenes in the movie, thus lifting *Norma Rae* several cuts above the "cold-bloodedness" of most contemporary films.[56] Current motion pictures, Mrs. Durr claimed, were like earthworms. They were so promiscuous that one earthworm would copulate with every other earthworm; even if you cut one in half, it would copulate with itself. "That's what movies today are like," she said. *Norma Rae*, she believed, was an "honest film" and so "hopeful and encouraging," showing indisputably that poor white southerners are *not* trash.[57]

Another Alabaman, Ralph Vickery, president of the University of Montevallo, was an invited guest when some of the scenes of *Norma Rae* were shot, and he hoped Ritt's stay in Alabama had been "pleasant and profitable."[58] If Ritt ever shot a "campus movie," Vickery said, he should consider the "red bricked streets, stately trees, and imposing old buildings" of the University of Montevallo.[59] Ritt had never heard of this university, but noted that "it does have a lovely, exotic sound."[60]

Fellow movie person John Randolph told Ritt that *Norma Rae* was "absolutely splendid," and it made him "glad and proud" to have come, like Ritt, from the Bronx. The only member of his family who might not like the movie was Randolph's wife, and that was because her brother was a vice president of a big cotton mill in Spartanburg, South Carolina.[61] Kirk Douglas thanked Ritt for making such a "wonderful movie."[62] His old friend Joel Fluellen sent Ritt a congratulatory telegram, saying *Norma Rae* was a superb winner. David Brown, of the Zanuck-Brown Company was "wiped out" by *Norma Rae*[63] and Alfons Sinneger of Zurich "learned something about life."[64] Ritt's friend Ted Z. Danielevsky saw *Norma Rae* with his daughter, Ann, in Provo, Utah. She said the movie made her know about unions; "they are about people who help one another."[65] Albert Maltz, one of the "Hollywood ten," however, believed Ritt had not adequately dramatized what a union could give to the mill workers. If a worker broke an earplug, and the company charged $10.00 for a replacement, or if, when the father complained of having beans for supper three nights in a row, the mother replied that "we can't afford meat," one would "be aware of something tangible" in the movie.[66] Ritt disagreed with this line of reasoning. If he had gone the way of Maltz's suggestions, *Norma Rae* would have become too "polemical" to reach the kind of audience Ritt wanted.[67] Regardless of these points about "tangibility," Maltz believed that few films had immediate impact on social problems; *Norma Rae* was one of them. He compared the movie to

Harriet Beecher Stowe's *Uncle Tom's Cabin*, and Upton Sinclair's *The Jungle*.[68] Heady stuff, this; particularly from a man Ritt admired as much as he did Albert Maltz.

Not all was pleasant for Martin Ritt in the aftermath of *Norma Rae*. Crystal Lee was upset with a number of ways the movie was developed. First, according to reports, she wanted the movie to be more documentary, with less of a dramatic plot. Then she wanted to change some of the scenes, and finally, she wanted, so it was reported, control of the script. (According to Crystal Lee, it was Eli Zivkovich, the union organizer who was the prototype for Reuben, who wanted control of the script. "He was the most intelligent person I've ever met."[69]) Ritt—though he said he understood why Crystal Lee would want the movie to be more documentary than it was—would not accede to any of these wishes and demands.[70] By the time the shooting of the movie ended, there were threats of lawsuits from Crystal Lee and her lawyers. Though Twentieth Century Fox had bought Crystal Lee's life story, according to reports, neither she nor Eli Zivkovich had received any money.[71] Crystal Lee was now divorced, out of a job, and blacklisted in every textile mill in the South. "Hell," she exclaimed, "they've [Ritt and Twentieth Century Fox] taken pages from my life and it's all gone down the drain."[72]

To be sure, Ritt struck back at these accusations. He was really "pissed off" at being accused of immorality by Crystal Lee and her lawyers.[73] The record was quite clear, he said, of how he had behaved all his life, and he had nothing for which to apologize. Sally Field excoriated Crystal Lee as well: "Crystal's going around saying 'Norma Rae' is her life story—even though it was based on the stories of five different women."[74] Pamela Woywad, who was Crystal's publicist for *Norma Rae*, stated that the idea of a composite was "not true."[75] Crystal Lee herself said it was "interesting that I make up five different people. I'd like to meet them."[76]

Sally felt it wrong for Crystal Lee to give the public impression that Ritt and Fox had exploited her, and that she had never been offered any money. In fact, Sally claimed, Crystal had been offered $50,000, but had been talked out of taking it by her attorneys.[77] Always a staunch defender of Martin Ritt, Field said it was a shame that Crystal Lee had not yet taken the time to thank Ritt for the movie; without it, she would never have received the public recognition that came to her because of *Norma Rae*.[78] Apparently, through the pro bono efforts of an entertainment lawyer, Robert Levine, Fox offered Crystal Lee an additional $25,000, "based on justice,"[79] beyond what it had paid to Leifermann for her biography, and the matter was dropped.[80] No suit was ever filed.[81] Crystal does not bear any grudges against Martin Ritt, remembering him as "real friendly," and "courteous."[82]

Reviews of *Norma Rae* were almost as enthusiastic and gratifying as they had been for *Sounder* several years before. The *Boston Globe* noted that Martin Ritt "fell in love with Norma Rae."[83] She had an indomitability, like a "bulldog that grabs hold of your cuff and won't let go."[84] She was, in short, Martin Ritt's kind of woman. *The Seattle Times* likened *Norma Rae* to *The Grapes of Wrath*[85] in its dramatic conflict and intensity. One Seattle audience thought, before it went in to see the movie, that it was about the Depression of the 1930s. About half still thought that way when the movie was over.

Norma Rae opened in New York on 2 March 1979, Ritt's 65th birthday. Archer Winsten of the *New York Post*, spoke of the movie's "perfection of detail." Ritt, he said, had never done "a better job."[86] *The New York Times* cadre of movie reviewers generally acquiesced in Winsten's opinion. Aljean Harmetz described *Norma Rae* as "abrasively concrete."[87] And Vincent Canby said that Sally Field rose above "senti-mental temptations"[88] in *Norma Rae*—the "plum role"[89] of her career—and performed as big "as the screen that presents it."[90]

"Unlike the wonderboys of the recent American cinema," *The Boston Herald American* announced, "veteran director Martin Ritt has a point of view, a set of beliefs that extend beyond his ego,"[91] and he exemplified these values with *Norma Rae*. The *Soho Weekly News* was pleased that Ritt "still has a way with actors," and can "limn an entertaining, one-sided parable as assuredly as the next Hollywood director."[92]

Again, as with *Sounder, Norma Rae*'s favorable press coverage caused people to speculate that *Norma Rae* would win several academy awards. By this time, Ritt was probably resigned to the fact that he would win nothing. He was happy when he learned that Sally Field had been nominated as the best actress, and thrilled when she won it. In Sally's acceptance speech for her Oscar, she let her audience know in no uncertain terms that she was quite displeased that Ritt had not even been nominated as best director. "He was very hurt," she said, "and I don't blame him. I feel terrible about it."[93]

"Martin Ritt *Is* Norma Rae," she indignantly reported. This remark angered some of the textile-mill workers, especially those in North Carolina, and upset Crystal Lee, who said she did not care "whether or not Sally mentioned my name, but she should have honored some of the workers."[94] Sally repeated her opinion that Martin Ritt took the risks with the movie and gave recognition to the trade-union movement in the textile industry; therefore, he was the "pioneer," the "Norma Rae" of the movie world. At least Sally got Ritt to do two things that no one else had accomplished: first, she got him to attend the Academy Awards, and then, most astonishingly, he wore a tuxedo, black tie and all. His friends teased him after the meeting, telling him that instead of jumpsuits, he was "born to wear a tux." Imperturbably, he brushed off such remarks.

He received many telegrams and letters, indignant that he had once again been overlooked for an Academy Award. Fellow director Carl Foreman sent a congratulatory telegram, telling Ritt "you have my Oscar."[95] Joel Fluellen's telegram blessed Sally "for her honesty," and pitied the Screen Directors Guild for its "blatant prejudice."[96] The Ravetches telegraphed Ritt that "we would rather be directed by Martin Ritt than anyone else in the world,"[97] while David Chasman wanted indignantly to have a word with the Directors Guild.[98] Kirk Douglas said, "I still don't know how you didn't get a nomination. You certainly deserve it."[99] Eric Roth's message, however, said it all: "Dear Marty. What do those pricks know? I still love you."[100]

Again, the question came up of why Martin Ritt could not win an Academy Award. The consensus seems to be that he was too independently minded. He was the "consummate proletarian."[101] He did not play the Hollywood game. He felt his job was to interpret a script that had been laid before him, or at least to remain rooted to its original idea and perhaps improvise upon it, but not to undo and re-create it, as so many auteurist directors did. By never getting an

Oscar, Ritt joined an "elite group," such as Charles Chaplin, Sidney Pollack, and Martin Scorcese, Sidney Lumet, and others who maintained a sense of cooperative movie making rather than always trying to put their own personal, egotist stamp upon a production.[102]

Did failing to receive an Oscar hurt Ritt? He told people it did not, that he was too old to be bothered by such things, but he was nevertheless grateful for Sally's defense.[103] He quickly became involved in another movie, *Back Roads*, again starring Sally Field, but it was apparent that he chafed at apparently being "blacklisted" by the Directors Guild. He became fairly testy, for example, with some of the people in charge of his horses. He had brought a filly, Twice Judged, over from Europe, and apparently wanted to race it at Del Mar right away. Barry Irwin urged him to let Twice Judged rest for a time, and win some races "next winter."[104] Barring this action, Irwin believed he could sell the filly for $100,000.[105] Ritt was "pissed off" at Irwin because he had not kept him as informed in the matter of Twice Judged as he had Ritt's racehorse-owning partner, Jeff Siegel.[106] Whatever happened with his horses, Ritt said, "I ought to be kept specifically informed about every element concerning my money."[107] Ritt had always been blunt with people, and at times quite temperamental. Asked if she had ever seen Ritt angry, Sally Field, responded "Puh-leeze!"[108] He certainly did keep up his general good humor, but by the end of 1980 it was apparent that he was growing tired and somewhat querulous.

The Directors Guild's not seeing fit to honor Ritt for *Norma Rae* was a distinctly different position from that of the United States Congress. On 11 June the movie was screened at the Dirksen Senate Office Building for members of both houses,[109] with good attendance. Some members of the National Committee for Justice at J.P. Stevens were present. *Norma Rae* had an important impact on them and the congressional members in attendance. Ritt and Sally attended in May 1979 the film festival in Cannes, and its participants chose Sally as actress of the year.[110] The National Board of Review (a group of "independent, public-spirited" individuals who maintained that the responsibility for good motion pictures came not just from the studios who made them but also from the public who watched them) awarded a David Wark Griffin prize to Sally Field as best actress, for *Norma Rae*.[111] The New York Film Critics Circle also honored Sally by citing her as the best actress of 1979.[112]

Ritt's alma mater, Elon College, saw fit to honor him, not just for *Norma Rae*, but for all his other filmmaking efforts as well. He had received an honorary doctorate from Elon years before, and now he was invited to return to receive a Distinguished Alumni Award. Apparently through the years, Ritt had made regular contributions to the "Fighting Christians," the football team at Elon, and had kept in touch with his old friend and teammate, Walter "Firpo" Latham, sending him congratulations when he was elected to Elon's Athletic Hall of Fame. Ritt had a wonderful time at Elon in the spring of 1980, relishing the award in ceremonies held at the Carlton Building, just a few doors away from his classrooms of the early 1930s. Governor James Hunt presented Ritt with a gift: a book on North Carolina history.[113] The governor did not quite let Ritt get away before asking him good-naturedly why he had never made any movies in North Carolina. Ritt's answer was never recorded.

Though, as he had said many times, he loved the region, Ritt exclaimed about 1980, "Will I ever get out of the South?" He asked this question more out of bemusement than despair. He continued to note a great irony of his life: he was a Jew from the largest urban area in the country, who appreciated and even loved the ways of the South. Just after *Norma Rae* was completed, CBS contacted Ritt for another movie—this one to be made for cinema and television. It was the first venture of the newly formed theatrical films division of CBS. It had gone into filmmaking because of what it considered the exorbitant prices of the studios when selling their productions to television networks.[114] Ritt immediately contracted Sally Field, in the belief that one success generally leads to another. By this time, Ritt was the "preeminent male in her life"[115] (after her breakup with Burt Reynolds). He was a father figure to her, a mentor, a teacher. She admired Ritt for what he had done with his talent—and hers—and how he had taken life, "the jolts, the good and the bad."[116] Ritt liked to tell reporters that Sally Field could play anything Bette Davis could. A working title for the movie was *Lovers*; when it was released to the public, it was called *Back Roads*.

Ritt had seen Tommy Lee Jones in *Coal Miner's Daughter*, and liked his style. He believed that Field and Jones might catch on with the American public, because they "sported" a "lot of chemistry."[117] Rather naively, he claimed that the pair might even be compared with Clark Gable and Carol Lombard. Again, John Alonzo shot the movie on location, (they had started out in Brownsville, Texas) in Mobile, Alabama—and Henry Mancini wrote what some reviewers called a rather "syrupy" score,[118] with Sue Raney singing "Ask Me No Questions and I'll Tell You No Lies." (Milton L. Brown wrote a song he hoped would be used in the movie. He called it "Back Roads," and it spoke about wild geese, full moons, freedom, and "knowing something deep inside." Perhaps its philosophical undertones turned the moviemakers away from it.) The movie was obviously shot with two audiences in mind. The version that went to the cinemas, and later transferred to video, was full of the word that automatically earns a movie an "R" rating. Definitely, it had to be "edited for television."

Shooting most of the movie in Mobile gave Ritt a few problems. He was usually early to bed, but much of *Back Roads* deals with Alabama hookers, which meant—at least in his opinion—staying up half the night shooting scenes. He grumbled about "jet lag" caused by heat and humidity and by such a disrupture of his schedule.[119] Ritt's production hairstylist, Terri Cannon, as a joke, donned a wig, makeup, and tacky clothes and passed as a hooker. Chief photographer Alonzo's wife, Jan, joined her in the charade. For a time, none of the film crew recognized them.[120] Several local socialites, mostly wives of the members of the Alabama Film Commission, were given parts as hookers. Some crew members were confused "as to who were real, passing, active, and/or retired."[121] After each day's shooting, Ritt sent the cuts to Los Angeles, to Sidney Levin, who viewed them closely and then talked to Ritt about them on the telephone. Their conversations dealt primarily with the content of the developing film, so that Ritt could change a scene here and there if need be.[122]

Any doubt that Sally had left her "Flying Nun" image behind is dispelled, in part with *Norma Rae*, but definitely with *Back Roads*. In Amy, she plays a prostitute, and Jones Elmore is a drifter. Whatever the theme of the story, it is definitely not that "opposites attract." They are both "losers," at least in the view of the outside world. (In fact, Ritt caught some flak from the "moralistic" community for making a movie about two such people. Ritt replied that he did not care much about their opinion, on *anything*.[123]) As the story develops, however, the two express wishes to change their lives. As Amy says, "When I was born, the Doctor didn't deliver a little girl whore." She wants to be a beautician. Also, she is the mother of a young boy, whom she gave up for adoption at his birth. She frequently goes by his school to stare at him, only to be chased away, with threat of police action, by the boy's adopted mother. The movie makes clear that Amy came to her position in life, not through wickedness, but through circumstance. Elmore is a washed-up boxer (not that he had ever been a good one), who, despite slugging policemen and rolling drunks, shows a tender, protective side in his developing relationship with Amy.

The movie begins with Amy plying her trade out of the A Lede Hotel in Mobile, and Elmore patronizing her. At the end of the sex act, Elmore tells her he cannot pay her the $20 she has demanded for her services. This revelation causes a hue and cry through the streets of Mobile. Amy is propositioned again, only this time by an undercover cop. Elmore knocks him out, and he and Amy are now on the run. Elmore apologizes to Amy for ruining all her business for a night. She says, "not really. Tonight's Monday. It's Monday Night Football." (Ritt was a regular viewer of *Monday Night Football* on ABC.) They get a ride with a man who talks incessantly about "law and order" while his daughter steals Amy's wallet from her purse. Without money, the two have to rely on "wit and grit" to get to California. In fact, getting to California becomes the propelling motive of the movie. At one point of despair, Elmore laments, "There probably ain't no California."

In a western town, Elmore gets a prize fight. Someone tips him that his opponent is always late coming into the ring after the bell. When the bell rings, Elmore runs across and lands a haymaker, winning $100—evidence to him that he is definitely not a loser. He loses the money, though, a while later when he returns to his and Amy's motel room, only to find that the local madam and her henchman are roughing up Amy. They knock out Elmore and take his money. After this incident, the two begin bumming rides from truckers going west. At the movie's end, they are out on the road hitchhiking, and it is clear by now that they love each other. "I still owe you twenty dollars," Elmore tells her. "That's all right," she replies. "I figure you're good for it." And they ride off into the proverbial sunset, another "uplifting" Martin Ritt ending.

There was a bit of a ruckus with officials at CBS as the shooting of the movie came to an end. Apparently, Ritt had not conferred with them as much as they wished. One of them indignantly told the movie's producer, Ronald Shedlo, that "The best movie making . . . is a collaborative effort and I'd like *Back Roads* to be just that."[124] (This statement must have surprised Ritt, for he had always thought of himself as a collaborator on his movies.) Donald March of CBS liked the movie, but still felt "emotionally shortchanged" by Amy's and Elmore's relationship. "In other words, we want more."[125] Only a director with Ritt's experience and clout could have his way so completely with the producers of a film.

For example, consider the following exchanges:

MARCH: Is there any way to bring Sally in earlier?
RITT: No.
MARCH: Can Tommy's "hitting on" Sally not be so abrupt?
RITT: No.
MARCH: Could we hold a bit longer on Sally after she saw her son?
RITT: I don't like it.
MARCH: Can we perhaps tone down Sally in the back of the truck?
RITT: No.
MARCH: Can we see David Keith picking Sally and Tommy up?
RITT: No.
MARCH: During the pinball scenes, where is Sally?
RITT: She's right there.
MARCH: Could we extend the mud scene?
RITT: I don't like it.
MARCH: In the bus station, Tommy's line about needing money is not audible enough.
RITT: It's o.k.[126]

Martin Ritt was used to having his way with "sassy producers," even in a "tough comedy" that cost $7 million to make. (*Norma Rae* cost $4.5 million.)[127] "I'm willing to listen to management's woes," he said sheepishly, "but not at the expense of my own scar tissue."[128]

A few of his friends and acquaintances wrote to him about *Back Roads*, but certainly not to the extent as about *Norma Rae*. Ritt had always told Allan Burns that he wasn't a comedy director. "Well," Burns exclaimed, "you'll never convince me of that. The comic moments in that picture are to be treasured."[129]

Vincent Canby of *The New York Times* said *Back Roads* was a "sentimental canonization of two waifs" who would have trouble surviving in heaven, much less the real world.[130] The movie was appealing to Canby, always a tough reviewer, as "gutsy and very funny."[131] Canby's colleague at the *Times*, Elin Evans, could feel Ritt's affection for working-class women in *Back Roads*—"whether they work all day in a textile mill or all night on the honkytonk side of Mobile."[132]

The atmosphere of *Back Roads* was actually more important to reviewers than plot. "Down-home backdrops of bars and brothels and seedy bus stations"[133] captivated audiences. Ritt adopted a "relaxed attitude" toward the plot[134] and came up with a movie that was "respectable, if not outright entertaining."[135] Does one loser crave the company of another loser of the opposite sex? No, said the *Washington Post*; more likely, they will despise each other and "lust after those who are out of their reach."[136] *Back Roads*, the latest "Marty movie," was based, the paper said, on such an illusion.[137] Thus, it was the skilled acting, the atmosphere, the brilliant directing of Martin Ritt and the photography of John Alonzo—not the plot, created by Gary Devore—that made the movie so appealing. Archer Winsten, of the New York *Post*, said that Ritt had pulled out all the stops on "the low-life circuit."[138] He believed the movie had more of Hollywood's atmosphere than "genuine hangouts for working whores."[139] Turning the South into a "regional time warp," Ritt tried on the one hand to sentimentalize Amy's profession, and on the other to denigrate it.[140]

Perhaps the *Washington Post*'s allusion to "Marty movies," was more than just a passing reference. The individualist, loner, down-and-outer, underdog, and crusader for social justice—all of whom tended to be alienated from the society in which they lived—were the hallmarks of Martin Ritt's movies. Though he continued to deny the auteurist label, it was possible for sophisticated film critics to see one of his movies without knowing it was his, and guess very quickly who made it.

He sometimes tended to make movies in "batches"; that is, dealing with a specific subject. With the black experience, one could list Ritt's films of *The Great White Hope, Sounder,* and *Conrack*—all made within a short time of each other. With women's liberation, one could cite *Norma Rae, Back Roads,* and *Cross Creek* (discussed below in chapter 9) as a cluster. These groupings, however, never dominated his career. He continued to do films that in his opinion would entertain first and enlighten second.

That is why he (and Adele) continued to read scripts even during the busiest of times. He thought reading *The Dollmaker* by Harriette Arnow was a "rich experience," and that it might become an "extraordinary film,"[141] although he did not offer to make it himself. Shiloh Productions sent him a script, "Angel City," saying that it compared favorably to *Conrack*. Ritt evinced no interest in it. He still heard from people who wanted jobs with his movies. One wanted to analyze literary properties for him, and assist in the development of films made from them. Ritt did not have an organization for such people; he went from one film to another and hired people "specifically for each project." Ritt and Adele tried to answer each query they received, time-consuming and mentally and physically demanding jobs. He was now 67 years old, and *Back Roads* was the 22nd film, excluding stage and television productions that he had directed and played in. Even before *Back Roads* was completed, he had begun negotiations for another movie to be called *No Small Affair.* He was physically exhausted, he had developed diabetes, and his physicians had told him that his heart was not the best in the world. All his life he had struggled with a weight problem, going to "fat farms," as he called them, losing weight slowly, and then gaining it back quickly.

He decided to take a year's sabbatical in April 1981. Thus he had to cancel any participation in *No Small Affair.* He also had to turn down an invitation to go to an international film festival at Prague and be a member of its jury. He spent the rest of 1981 quietly, at least by comparison to the pace he had set before. He still attended the races, watched sports events, read, and even played a bit of poker.

It was not until 1982 that he felt well enough to take on another movie. This was *Cross Creek*, a film that logically was an extension of his two previous productions, *Back Roads* and *Norma Rae*. All three of these movies, in a way, were glorifications of the liberated woman.

In the early 1980s Ritt's name was synonymous with movies that had socially driven themes. He was primarily interested in contemporary matters; he wanted to delineate problems faced by modern society. Even in movies that dealt with the past, reviewers and critics very quickly noticed modern themes to which they could be compared. The previous decade, the 1970s, had perhaps been Ritt's most profound period of moviemaking (although it would be hard to surpass the contemporary social themes of movies like *Hud, The Spy Who Came In From the Cold*, and *The Molly Maguires*, all made in the 1960s). He continued his social consciousness on into the eighties, but not quite with the fervor of times past.

Chapter 9

◆ ◆ ◆

"Marty Movies"

Martin Ritt waited for an impulse to strike him for the movies he made. His first consideration about a projected movie was not commercialism, but whether it suited his artistic and historical interests. If he could not make a film that in some way or other reflected his own temperament and philosophy of life, he would have nothing to do with the project. This stance repeatedly led him into socially conscious films that ranged from the black experiences in America to the plight of working women. *Norma Rae*, his first major depiction of a working woman, was followed quickly by the less successful *Back Roads*. "I make films about the underprivileged," he told a reporter from *Horizon*, "and women have been underprivileged for two thousand years."[1] After his illness of the early 80s, he once again tended to concentrate on movies that described strong-minded women, and the first of these was *Cross Creek*, a film based on the autobiography of famed novelist Marjorie Kinnan Rawlings.

During the 1980s Ritt used the 1920s to depict a woman —doing her own thing in her own way—who could easily have belonged to the 1990s. He went back to the past to make a film about the future.

In the movie, Marjorie Kinnan Rawlings is so determined to become a writer that she divorces her husband, buys an orange grove in Florida, driving alone all the way from Long Island to Cross Creek,[2] seeking the right kind of isolation in which to pursue her work. She wants to write a "Gothic" romance novel, much in vogue in the 1920s. Famed editor Maxwell Perkins (Malcolm McDowell) keeps telling her that her letters to him describing the terrain and residents of Cross Creek are infinitely more interesting than the "English tea parties" and lords and ladies she keeps pursuing, but "knew nothing about." Her subjects are all around her, and it takes her some time to realize it. When she writes *Jacob's Ladder*, a novel about some of her friends in Cross Creek, Perkins quickly accepts it for publication.

Rawlings's closest friend in Cross Creek is Norton Baskin (Peter Coyote) whom she eventually marries. Her nearest neighbor is Marsh Turner (Rip Torn) whose daughter, Ellie (Dana Hill), has a pet deer, Flag, that, as it grows to maturity, keeps jumping its fence and eating up the crops. The father ultimately shoots the deer, causing his daughter to become estranged from him. These people and these events, of course, are later the subject of Rawlings's much proclaimed novel, and then movie, *The Yearling*.

Ritt had read some of Rawlings's works, and "was not set on fire" by her.[3] He cared, however, for the land and the community she wrote about; thus, Cross Creek and its people were more Ritt's subject than Marjorie Kinnan Rawlings's career. He admired her fortitude, because it took a "modern" woman to do what she did: leave the comforts of urban life, and start on her "road to maturity" at age 30. Not many women, or men either, in the 1920s, 1980s, or 1990s, would attempt such a feat. He told a reporter that he wanted to let the world know what an extraordinary lady Rawlings was, "at a time when women were not functioning on that level at all."[4]

To play the role of Marjorie Kinnan Rawlings, Ritt contracted noted leading and character actress Mary Steenburgen. Steenburgen's career had been started by Jack Nicholson, who contacted Ritt in 1978 to see if he would cast her in the role of Norma Rae. Ritt telephoned Steenburgen to tell her that Sally Field had just accepted the part, and that "he'd get back in touch with me."[5] "Like everything else he said," noted Steenburgen, "he meant it."[6] Ritt made an interesting contrast between Sally Field and Mary Steenburgen. He needed a "kind of mutt to play Norma Rae,"[7] and he needed a "lady" for *Cross Creek*.[8] He was complimenting both actresses with these remarks. Steenburgen, he said, was "Middle American, and all the things that are good about it she has." She had a "kind of strength, stubbornness, and graciousness";[9] I knew right away there could be no other Marjorie."[10]

Except for a brief sequence in Long Island, *Cross Creek* was shot entirely in Florida, making it the third picture in a row filmed in the South. The weather was reminiscent of Louisiana a few years back when he shot *Sounder*. The temperature was 95 to 100 degrees every day, with a humidity to match. The mosquitoes were vicious, and there was an extreme amount of rain. During one two-day period, Ritt reported, it rained eighteen inches.[11] He and his crew rehearsed the movie for nine days, and everyone got a feel for the time and place. One reason why he liked to work on location was that the movie's ambience could be recaptured more quickly after a break than if he were working on a sound stage. As in so many of Ritt's previous movies, John Alonzo was the chief photographer in *Cross Creek*, beautifully capturing the Spanish moss and waterways in their colors at different times of day; Ritt's old friend Robert Radnitz was, along with Ritt, the movie's co-producer, Leonard Rosenman wrote the music, which was conducted by Lionel Newman, and the script was prepared by Dalene Young from Rawlings's autobiographical volume.

The critics were generally kind to Ritt and his colleagues for *Cross Creek*. Even *The New York Times* let him get away with shifting the story from Rawlings' creative process to the community itself. Ritt told Stephen Farber it was the land that ultimately inspired Rawlings and gave her a chance to fulfill herself.[12] Fortunately, Steenburgen felt comfortable in an "ensemble" situation. The story itself, she said, was the star. Cross Creek, both the place and the story, she felt, is "about the earth and the continuity of a place beyond the presence of its inhabitants."[13]

Janet Maslin, of *The Times*, believed the movie had little to do with rural life as it actually existed in the United States. The characters in *Cross Creek*, she believed, had bucolic fantasies that, in the hands of a less competent director, would have degenerated to pure hokum.[14] (One of Ritt's biggest fears about *Cross Creek* was that it would be compared with the brash sentimentalism of a popular TV show of the 1970s, with numerous reruns in the 1980s, *The Waltons*.) While Ritt did not bring anything like realism to *Cross Creek*, Maslin believed, he still endowed it "with passion and sincerity."[15] Gene Shalit of NBC thought *Cross Creek* was "beautifully made and truly told."[16] Gene Siskel of the *Chicago Tribune* observed that Ritt always made films with a strong sense of place,[17] while Roger Ebert of the *Sun-*

Times complimented Ritt for creating such an "offbeat heroine."[18]

English newspapers gave the movie mixed reviews. *The Guardian* said *Cross Creek* wore its lack of cynicism "like a badge advertising its honourable intentions."[19] Ritt, however, "wore his heart on his sleeve" in *Cross Creek*, and made a "liberal Hollywood movie that looks and tastes like fudge."[20] *The Financial Times*, writing as though it knew anything about movies, said that Steenburgen became a "silly prig" as the film progressed.[21] Both the *Daily Mail* and the *Sunday Telegraph* spoke about the "narrowness" of Ritt's subject in *Cross Creek*, in which "pockets of life" were delineated.[22] *The Observer* thought the movie a bit "smooth,"[23] but the *Sunday Express* found *Cross Creek* filled with a "lush, soothing old time charm."[24]

Universal Studios produced *Cross Creek* and reportedly some of its executives would have been happy just to break even on the venture, fearing it would be lost completely on the younger generation of moviegoers. (*Cross Creek* did earn back the investment, but it was not a profit maker). They were surprised when Ritt's movie received a nomination from the National Board of Review of Motion Pictures. It came in ninth (*Betrayal* and *Terms of Endearment* tied for first).[25] Also *Cross Creek* gained quite a bit of attention—some positive, some negative—at the annual Cannes Film Festival, where its world premiere was screened in 1983.

According to some critics, the movie tried to make a statement about women's equality, but was incomplete, because it dealt only with literature and not with politics and the larger society. At Cannes, *Observer* reporter Philip French called *Cross Creek* "limp," "sentimental," and even "meretricious."[26] Observers at Cannes grumbled at what they perceived to be the general lack of quality of all the films shown at the festival. To some, *Cross Creek* was a bit of a respite. "A little cheerfulness" broke in with *Cross Creek*, exulted the reporter for *The Daily Telegraph*.[27] It was also one of the few movies at Cannes in 1983 that received a standing ovation at its conclusion.[28]

Cross Creek was primarily a "Marty movie," in that it depicted the themes of individualism, the outsider, and the underdog fighting against formidable odds. Marjorie, however, unlike many of Ritt's previous subjects, is not a loner. She desires the company of other people, frequently having Norton over for supper, and going to the numerous "pound" (where everybody had to bring a pound of food) parties in her neighborhood. Neither does she remain an outsider (at least in the sense of *Hud* so many years before). She is not only accepted by the community but looked upon by it as a savant, someone who can help them solve their own problems. Even Ellie's excoriation at the end of the movie, when distraught at the death of her father, telling Marjorie to leave Cross Creek "because you don't belong here," is temporary. It becomes increasingly clear in the movie that Marjorie Kinnan Rawlings in Florida with her novels, neighbors, and orange groves, is exactly in this world where she is supposed to be.

Directly after the shooting of *Cross Creek* Ritt made his way back to California, where, primarily, he rested for the next several months. There were numerous movie offers waiting for him on his return home, even one, *Roadshows*, from Jack Nicholson. He turned them all down because his physicians had once again ordered a "go-slow." (He turned 70 on 2 March 1984.) He suffered from diabetes, and in a checkup it was learned that years before he had sustained a "silent" heart attack. Then, too, there was the constant weight problem. He checked into another "fat farm" for a time and temporarily lost a bit of poundage.

Ritt, however, was not the kind of individual to sit still too long. Even while his activities were restricted, he managed to do a number of things related to movies. For one thing, he became a consultant for Ray Stark's film company, Rastar. He said on the occasion of his appointment that he liked the trend toward independent filmmaking and the loosening of the film industry's rating systems,[29] continuing an argument that he had long made that whether or not children saw certain films should primarily be up to their parents. The best "control" device, he believed, at the parents' disposal, was the "off" button on the television set. He received the Don Williams Film Impact Award from the University Film and Video Association, and the Film Teacher Association conferred their Renoir Award on him in early 1984. The reporters who covered the story of Ritt receiving the Renoir Award seemed to be intrigued that instead of his usual jumpsuit he wore a gray business suit for the occasion.[30] He attended a film symposium at Elon College, where the students were "shy" and "embarrassed" to ask questions that seemed to them "foolish" and "unsophisticated."[31] He told his audience that "to be a serious artist you have to write poems, paint pictures or write novels that are a true reflection of yourself."[32] And, of course, he made the track on a regular basis, and continued to watch ABC's *Monday Night Football* at the home of his old and dear friend Gene Kelly.

What to Ritt was inactivity would have been a full schedule for most people. He chafed under the restrictions of not working as much as he wanted to. Therefore, when he had a chance in early 1985—shortly after his 71st birthday— to participate in another movie, he jumped at it, despite his physicians' advice to the contrary. It had been about ten years since he played Inspector Baerlach in *End of the Game*. Now he was offered one of the leading roles in a movie made from what was sometimes called "cut-rate" Neil Simon. His play, and its subsequent movie, was entitled *The Slugger's Wife*. This was a double whammy for Simon. In the same week as *The Slugger's Wife* opened in New York cinemas, his play *Biloxi Blues* debuted on Broadway. Ritt plays Burly De Vito, who is, some critics maintained, a prototype for Los Angeles Dodgers skipper Tommy Lasorda. The team represented in the movie is the Atlanta Braves, and the hero is hard-hitter Daryl Palmer (Michael O'Keefe).

The movie has an old, yet timely theme: conflict between a husband's and wife's professional careers. Daryl Palmer's wife, Debbie (Rebecca de Mornay), does not want him to "own" her; she wants freedom to pursue a singing career in night clubs and on record albums. Yet Daryl cannot get a hit at any of the games unless he knows his wife is in the stands. When the season gets down to the crucial point and Daryl's wife has left him, De Vito pulls a trick on him by taking advantage of his poor eyesight after being hit by a ball in practice. He has another singer, who vaguely resembles Daryl's wife, dress as Debbie, come to the hospital room, and pretend to be Daryl's wife. The ruse works. Daryl has a great day at the bat. His teammates, however, are angry at De Vito for the deception. He asks the players, "Do you think I am a son-of-a-bitch for playing that trick on Daryl?" To a person they answer "yes." But then, his next question reveals a universality about the movie: "If the trick causes us to win the pennant, am I still a son-of-a-bitch?"

"No freaking way," his players chorus.

Daryl learns about the deception, however, and again goes into a batting slump. His teammates bring over three ladies of the night to Daryl's house to get him sexually satiated, so perhaps he will break out of it. One teammate, Moose (Randy Quaid), in a takeoff on a well-known phrase of sporting lore tells Daryl to "screw one for the Moose." He cannot, however, and the only thing that ultimately saves him (although the Braves lose the pennant) is Debbie's return.

Newspaper critics were bemused, even nonplussed by *The Slugger's Wife*. Neil Simon was mostly congratulated for spanning the generation gap,[33] as he wrote about two young lovers removed from his own age by decades. The movie also seemed to reflect current societal mores with women entering the work force in great numbers and trying to be both home-makers and professional careerists, with varying degrees of success. Definitely, too, it dealt with the maturing process for both young persons, especially the baseball player.

Though *The Slugger's Wife* may have been timely and replete with "universal" truths, it was still, to one reporter, a "shock to find Neil Simon's name attached to something" so "resoundingly unfunny."[34] Simon's "youth" movie, as it had been touted, meant only "noisy,"[35] as the rock scores overlapped with not only the baseball games but the bedroom scenes as well. Hal Ashby, according to Janet Maslin, "out-standingly misdirected"[36] the picture.

For his part, Ritt was glad to be in front of the cameras again instead of behind them. "There's no pressure," he asserted, "when you have no reputation as an actor."[37] The responsibility of a single role, he believed, was less than that of a director, who had to oversee the entire production. He had somewhat of a problem learning his lines, but he thought he was suited for the role of Burly De Vito. How-ever, he did tell a reporter that if he had been the director of *The Slugger's Wife*, he would have canned himself and hired Charles Durning for the part.[38]

He was picked for the role in large part, however, because Neil Simon wanted him. Simon had known Ritt since the filming of *The Spy Who Came In From the Cold*, when they both frequently participated in the Sunday morning baseball games at Hyde Park.[39] *The Slugger's Wife*, Simon said, was mostly a "lark," and he was not too pleased with its final production.[40] Obviously, Ritt enjoyed the role of Burly De Vito, so much so that he remarked, "I don't know that I want to direct many more movies. It's very tough work, and I'm not totally well."[41] This was one of the rare occasions when Ritt let it be known publicly that all was not right with his health.

Even as he spoke, however, even before the final cuts were made on *The Slugger's Wife*, he was busy with yet another movie, this time as director rather than actor. In a way it was *déjà vu* for Ritt, because his old and dear friends the Ravetches did the script for the movie. Loosely based on Max Schott's novella, it was titled *Murphy's Romance*, a "romantic comedy," described by one journal as "*Norma Rae* set on a dude ranch."[42] According to another critic, the script was intended "to exploit sentimentally the rustic pluckiness of Sally Field as developed in *Norma Rae* and *Places in the Heart* [for which Field won her second Oscar as best actress] and to link her grit with James Garner's fetching ease."[43]

Sally Field, the lead star in *Murphy's Romance*, had formed her own company, Fogwood Productions, and was the movie's executive producer. She plays Emma Moriarty, divorced, in her thirties, with a young son, Jake (Corey Haim), to support. She comes to Eunice, Arizona, to open a horse boarding and training center. Because she is a woman, she finds it difficult to borrow money from the local banks or —at least at first—be accepted by the community as a business person.

James Garner plays Murphy Jones, the local pharmacist, a middle-aged widower who buys a horse just so he can board it at Emma's place. (Ritt showed his love of horses in this movie. While they were not as central to the theme as they had been in *Casey's Shadow*, they nevertheless created the unity between Emma and Murphy.) As the movie progresses, Murphy becomes something of a fixture at the Moriarty household, running into trouble now and then with Emma's no-good, drifting ex-husband, Bobby Jack (Brian Kerwin), who shows up and expects permanent handouts. Finally, however, true love reigns supreme as one of Bobby Jack's lovers from Tulsa shows up with twins he did not even know existed. Their departure leaves Emma and Murphy alone. It turns out that Murphy is 60 years old, and Emma 33, but what the hell?

When *Murphy's Romance* was in its planning stages, some officials at Columbia Pictures did not want Garner for the part. He was too much identified with television, they felt, particularly with *The Rockford Files*, to attract cinema audiences.[44] Martin Ritt, however, insisted that he have Garner; he felt Garner had the right kind of wry humor necessary for the part. And, of course, Ritt usually got what he wanted with film executives, at least at this late stage of his career.[45] When it was all over Ritt was proven correct: Garner was nominated for an Academy Award as best actor, one of the few nominations the movie received.

Seventy-one-year-old Martin Ritt complained during the shooting of *Murphy's Romance* that he was "getting too old" for "this kind of work." He had begun to hate night shootings. He told a reporter: "Last night, I was dragging my butt. Fussed at extras driving cars down the street. Geeze, they drive almost as bad as I do."[46] As Ritt was preparing for a new scene, a young female assistant asked him if he would move a few feet down the street because he was obstructing the cameras' views. Ritt grumbled, and then complied with the request. He said, "Look, even the director has to take directions." Then he pointed out that the assistant was his daughter, Tina (frequently billed in his movies as Martina Ritt, assistant director). "It's O.K.," he told people around him. "That's my daughter. I do whatever she says—and fast."[47]

Many reviewers complimented Ritt for "knowing his subject." Though he came from New York City, the residents of Eunice, Arizona, were "his kind of people." "Martin Ritt," said one, "has a way with the outdoors" and an ability to turn his performers into "remarkably sincere and true to life people."[48] Another reviewer exclaimed that Ritt had a "better ability with small-town tempo than any other working director."[49] *Murphy's Romance* was full of "warmth and down-home charm,"[50] and contributed to the current waves of nostalgia by throwing into the movie "bingo games, dinners, card games and root beer floats."[51] Ritt may have come from the largest city in the United States, but he was identified—at least by the moviegoing public—as small town and rural. He said, "I may be 71, but when everything is going well, I feel good. I've still got the drive. They may have to wheel me out of here by the time this movie's over, but I still really enjoy the job."[52]

Ritt, well-known for his dislike of current Hollywood fare, injected some of it into *Murphy's Romance*. One night Emma, Murphy, Jake, and Bobby Jack go to a movie, a slasher film. Everyone except Bobby Jack, who loves the movie, get up and leave in disgust during one particularly horrible splatter scene. Their walkout is, as one journal put it, "an acid comment on Hollywood's incessant feeding of the slash-and-bash appetite."[53] Murphy explains to Jake that the blood and gore in the film are phony. "They fake everything out there in Hollywood."[54] Then Murphy takes Emma to a bingo game where she wins $200.

Murphy's Romance is also notable for its lack of violence. Even when Murphy and Bobby Jack are competing for Emma's affections, the threat of violence is more tacit than real. Ritt moves their argument from the kitchen to the living room, and finally to the front porch where Murphy tells Bobby Jack that he will "kick his ass" into the next county, "and I've got the boots to do it with." Rather than the usual Hollywood brawl at this point, Ritt has Bobby Jack simply walk off. Later, at a dance, when the two keep cutting in on each other, Emma angrily tells both of them to dance with themselves; which they do, much to the amusement of the audience.

The movie is also notable for its lack of nudity.[55] Even in the haystack scene when Emma and Bobby Jack kiss and look as though they are going to become lovers once more, not a strap of her clothing is touched. Who knows where the scene would have gone if it had run its natural course; Emma gets into a sneezing fit and has to leave the barn.

And, finally, one might say that in *Murphy's Romance*, age triumphs over youth; but love does not have to be limited by boundaries of age. Martin Ritt and co-scriptwriter, Irving Ravetch, both 71 when *Murphy's Romance* was made, were delighted to see the senior citizen walk off with the prize. Much was being made at the time in the United States—both by government and private institutions—about the "graying of America," and *Murphy's Romance* fit well into this motif. Understandably, the movie turned out to be more popular with the older generations than with the young.

There were enough positive reviews of *Murphy's Romance* to gladden all those connected with its making. Joe Leydon of the *Houston Post*, said that in his directing of

Murphy's Romance, Ritt was a "thoroughgoing professional,"[56] a stance that drew "superlative performances"[57] from the cast, and produced a memorable movie. The demanding film critic Rex Reed said that *Murphy's Romance* had been directed by "the great Martin Ritt";[58] he maintained, said a second critic, a "steady sensitivity and an even pace throughout,"[59] and a third said Ritt took a "mellow view" of the human condition.[60] *The New Jersey Herald* gave the movie an "A+ rating,"[61] and Philip Wuntch at *The Dallas Morning News*, said that "even in its weakest moments, this is the sort of film that makes you glad to go to the movies."[62] *Boxoffice* liked Ritt's delineation of "smalltown naturalism,"[63] the *Albuquerque Journal* admired the lack of tension,[64] and the *Muncie Evening Press* lauded Ritt's "no-frills approach to storytelling."[65] It was clear that small towns and rural America were paying attention to Martin Ritt. Perhaps Michael Burkett in *Westword* summed it up best:

There may be flashier directors. There may be directors who have won more awards, or who have better luck at the box office. But no American filmmaker is as consistently dependable as Martin Ritt. . . . He has specialized in pleasant surprises for 30 years. . . . He has proven over and over again that the most memorable movies are not high concept jobs favored by the latest superstar of the week, but simple, honest straightforward films that attempt to build bridges of understanding between human beings.[66]

Although they wrote admiringly of Ritt, most critics of *Murphy's Romance*, found at least one or two flaws in it. It was, to one, "extraordinarily one-dimensional and better suited for television."[67] For all the movie's homespun themes, Ritt never allowed his audiences to know the "whys and hows" leading up to such activities.[68] There is a hint of a dark side to Murphy; it is said that when his wife died he drank to excess and was not nice to his neighbors. *The Cincinnati Post* believed Ritt took his audiences on a trip "down memory lane," and enhanced the "nostalgic quality of his fantasy" by plunking them down in a small town, Eunice, Arizona, "that has escaped the ravages of time."[69] Robert Butler of *The Kansas City Star*, objected to the movie's predictability. It telegraphed its intentions "so far ahead that you could go out to dinner in the middle of it and still know what was going on when you returned."[70] The movie needed more "foul air" than it had, said Lawrence O'Toole of *Maclean's*, and that is why the role of Bobby Jack was the most interesting.[71] All the other roles were "squeaky clean." *Newsweek* argued that a "little of the movie's virtuous diffidence goes a long way."[72] And *Time* believed the film was "basically a bottle of January molasses, running slow."[73]

Murphy's Romance was quintessential Ritt, a movie where he meant to make a statement about conditions in the United States, and did. Women's rights groups liked his movie for its depiction of Emma's unfair treatment in not being able to participate in the business world because she did not have a husband. Various retirement groups, such as the American Association of Retired People lauded it for portraying vigor and strength in a person from the older generation. Strong-mindedness and individuality had marked most of Ritt's pictures in the past, and *Murphy's Romance* was no exception. Then, too, there was the jab at Hollywood, which many of the older generations appreciated.

It was not long after *Murphy's Romance* that Ritt became involved in still another movie that described current themes. A major social problem in America during the mid-eighties was child abuse, especially in the form of incest; and the battered-wife syndrome became a part of our daily vocabulary. Many victims sought psychological help to overcome their traumas, and some were even willing—years after the incidents—to identify their tormenters. Ritt became involved in these subjects when Barbra Streisand approached him to do a movie from one of Tom Toper's plays. It was *Nuts* and, despite the frivolous title, it dealt with a very serious matter indeed.

Streisand had formed her own production company, Barwood, and was not only the lead actress in *Nuts*, but was, along with Ritt, the co-producer. At the beginning of the movie a sign proclaimed that this was a "Barwood Film/ Martin Ritt Production." Such announcements were rare for Ritt, because he thought a good film was the result of collective activity rather than the achievements of just one or two persons. He and his colleague Sidney Lumet were alike in their disdain of the auteur system.

Streisand plays the role of Claudia Draper, a high-priced hooker. One of her clients one night does not want to leave and a fight ensues. She stabs him to death in her apartment, and is thus brought into court on a charge of first degree manslaughter. The question of the movie, however, is whether Claudia is competent to stand trial and to participate in her own defense. Her mother and father (Maureen Stapleton and Karl Malden), a prison psychologist (Eli Wallach), and an aggressive prosecutor (Robert Webber), try to persuade a judge (James Whitmore) that Claudia belongs in a mental ward. Her feisty attorney (Richard Dreyfuss) almost becomes a crusader ("I've got an aunt in Long Island who's crazier than Claudia," he said, "and she's a member of the PTA") for women's rights as the movie progresses.

In the riveting courtroom scenes there are flashbacks of Claudia's youth, and it becomes apparent that her stepfather abused her, paying her money and forcing her to have sex with him. When Claudia got married, her husband beat her on a regular basis. During her marriage, she became pregnant, but had an abortion. "I don't believe in childhood," she explains to the court. She divorced her husband, and became a high-priced ($500 an hour) prostitute. In the court she rails out against "assholes" with power, such as the prosecutor, the judge, and prison psychologist, who, no matter what transpires, will never believe that she is sane. At the movie's end, however, the judge rules in her favor, which is that she stand trial for first-degree manslaughter instead of being sent back to the mental ward. A final postscript on screen points out that Claudia was subsequently tried and acquitted. She killed her client while defending her own life.

Ritt told a reporter that *Nuts* was "the most commercial movie he ever made"[74] (apparently forgetting that long ago he had made *Five Branded Women*, as he said at the time, "purely for money"). Despite its aspects of commercialism, *Nuts* still hit upon serious social problems in the United States. Gene Shalit, on NBC's *Today* show hailed *Nuts*, believing that "if several academy award nominations didn't come out of *Nuts*, including ones for Streisand and Dreyfuss and for Director Martin Ritt, there is no justice." There was, of course, no "justice." *Nuts* did not receive any nominations in the best actor, actress, or director categories. Apparently Ritt believed the movie did have a chance. Shortly after he finished *Nuts* he and Adele invited Norman Jewison and his wife, Dixie, to dinner one night at a restaurant in Venice, California. Jewison reported, "It seemed to take him forever to get to the point of what he wanted to talk about and it ended up being what my opinion was regarding Streisand's chances of getting an Academy nomination."[75] This was the first time, according to Jewison, that Ritt had ever expressed to him any interest in Academy nominations or awards. Jewison, who had just produced *Moonstruck*, never got around to answering Ritt's questions.

From all accounts of *Nuts*, Streisand was not the easiest person in the world with whom to work. Some producers make the money available and then stand aside and let the director do his job. A few do not (David O. Selznick, for example), and Barbra Streisand was one of this type. She wanted ultimate control over every aspect of the movie. Two strong personalities, Martin Ritt and Barbra Streisand, confronted each other on *Nuts* as much as they cooperated. Ritt was known in some circles as an "Orson tamer," going back to the days when he and Orson Welles worked on *The Long Hot Summer*. He had also had his problems, but ultimately coped, with Richard Burton in *The Spy Who Came In From the Cold*. One source noted that Streisand was "rude," "loud," "uncouth," "overbearing," and then almost in understatement, "ill-mannered." Another simply referred to her as "that woman." Still another called her a "barracuda" consuming everything that came into her sight. The kindest thing said about her during the shooting of *Nuts* was that "she is a perfectionist."

Ritt got along just fine with all the other members of the cast. Eli Wallach wanted to leave for several days after he had done his shooting, but Ritt (and Streisand?) insisted that the entire cast stay on hand for unexpected changes. "Everytime I turn the camera on in any room," Ritt told Wallach, "I want to see you." Wallach, who played a psychiatrist, jokingly protested, "I've got to get away. I have a full case load of other patients, and they are waiting for me." Ritt looked him squarely in the face, smiled, and said "get your ass in there."[76] Maureen Stapleton remembered that Ritt "yelled a lot"[77] while directing *Nuts*.

Some reviews of *Nuts* complimented Streisand for the scenes where she "pitched a fit," but panned her "philosophical" performances in which she spoke of her earlier life and waxed idealistically concerning "who is fit in society and who is not." The reviewer for *Maclean's* summed it up this way: "When she is being sassy and abusive, and constantly getting on the nerves of her lawyer and the judge, she is marvellously vulgar."[78] Otherwise, however, "she is stiff, mannered, and given to fake tears."[79] (Even the most unsophisticated viewer would detect her phony tears.) "Her rage has real guts," said *Newsweek*, "her passion real fire, and when she talks dirty hooker talk you can see her delight in trashing her star image."[80] On the other hand, "one can't help but notice that even when she's down and out in the psycho ward, her makeup remains impeccable."[81]

For some, *Nuts* was a "no-risk" psychodrama[82] because the formula "is the old one of the bond between the star and the audience from Moment One."[83] The moviegoer knows instinctively that Claudia will win her case; thus, the telegraphing in *Nuts* is considerably more than in *Murphy's Romance*. It is, however, the unfolding reasons for her behavior and her present predicament that provide the drama in *Nuts*. Thus, audiences and even many reviewers "forgave" the movie's predictability.

To one reviewer the movie was a can of "mixed *Nuts*."[84] Janet Maslin of *The New York Times* panned Ritt's participation in the film: "Miss Streisand . . . didn't direct it. And Martin Ritt, who is the director of record, didn't either. The film is almost entirely adrift, with no momentum."[85] Another reviewer disagreed with Maslin's opinion, believing that Ritt made a wise decision to "cut away from the brown courtroom and the stark mental hospital to Claudia's apartment."[86] Ritt let his audiences know that the mental ward is infinitely worse than jail by expressing the "edgy, clangy, jittery claustrophobia of Claudia's cell."[87] Ritt was a director, said Noel Taylor of *The Ottawa Citizen*, "with the kind of mind that slices through the fat of dramatic trimmings to the lean meat of argument and interior emotion."[88] An example of what he meant was that the audience never gets even a glimpse of Claudia's lawyer at home. Obviously, Ritt felt that to bring in the lawyer's family and emotions would quite clearly be a distraction to the theme he was following. And Noel Gallagher of *The London Free Press* gave his opinion that Ritt's directing saved the movie, because he knew his "way around this no-

nonsense woman."[89] (Whether the "no-nonsense woman was Claudia Draper or Barbra Streisand, he did not say.)

Ritt was expert, Neil Hirsch of the *New York Law Journal* said, "in capturing the bustle of a busy Manhattan criminal court."[90] He went on, however, to complain about the flashbacks, especially those of Claudia as a teenager, a role Streisand simply could not fill.[91] Richard Blake of *America* magazine said that *Nuts* was a good example of Ritt's professionalism: "It's a nicely packaged classic courtroom melodrama that can be quite engrossing," even though so many clues were left so early in the movie that there was "little room for surprise."[92] Blake even made a connection between *Nuts* and the decade: "[Claudia's] impassioned justification of bad manners, self-centered posturing and amorality coupled with a smug moral superiority struck me as a manifesto dragged mouldy and shopworn from the rag and bone shop of the 1960's."[93] Though the play came to Broadway in 1980, its inception was in the 1970s when thoughts of the uproarious 1960s were uppermost in people's minds.[94]

From a technical view, some critics believed *Nuts* was better suited for the small screen than large cinematic expanses. Its subject matter was suitable for the intimacy of a TV screen in a den or living room. Andrzej Bartkowiak was the chief photographer, and his shots complemented the story line. For example, Ritt directed him to shoot the judge's decision from behind the judge's bench, "looking down over his shoulder at Streisand and Dreyfuss at their table. It puts the scene in its complete judicial frame while it gives the point of perspective to the two individuals most concerned."[95]

In writing about Streisand's movie, prominent screen reviewer Stanley Kauffmann said, "Martin Ritt likes to direct. I don't suppose that he would do any script at all, but I'm glad he's not too choosy or he might not have done *Nuts*."[96] His observation brings up the question, Why did Martin Ritt choose to direct this movie? First and foremost he felt that the subject matter was important, interesting, and compelling, because it dealt with a very serious social problem in the United States. Perhaps the superstar status of Streisand (who had converted a lot of critics with her acting abilities in *Yentl*) and Dreyfuss attracted him to the movie. (Or, perhaps, one might say that Ritt attracted Streisand;

two of his actresses, Patricia Neal and Sally Field, had won Oscars as best actresses.) Again, he had been relatively inactive for several months before the movie started. It would have been totally uncharacteristic of him to do a movie specifically with any kind of award in mind, but he did yield to some of Streisand's bidding, because he had never been egocentric or dictatorial, and he had a broad capacity to accommodate as long as the integrity of the material was not compromised. For example, Ritt wanted his old friend and standby John Alonzo to do the camera work. Streisand did interview him, but turned him down in favor of Bartkowiak. Ritt felt that Streisand's choice of cinematographer would have no impact on the quality of the script; with Ritt camera work was always subordinate to the story line. And finally, it must have crossed his mind that with a cast that included Dreyfuss, Malden, Stapleton, Webber, and Whitmore, even if the plot were not everything it should have been, the acting would be absolutely superb. He loved directing, and he loved actresses and actors—always being known as the "actor's director"—so why shouldn't he become involved in *Nuts*?

After the completion of *Nuts*, Ritt again went on the "inactive" list (though he did teach a short seminar at UCLA). It was not until early 1989 that he found a project that greatly piqued his interest.

As he had shown in most of his movies, particularly his last two, *Nuts* and *Murphy's Romance*, he was vitally interested in the problems facing America in the 1980s. A major problem—in fact, a national emergency—that had developed was that of illiteracy. Ritt believed illiteracy was the gravest threat to our democracy; as Thomas Jefferson had said many years before, you cannot have a democracy in an illiterate society. Thus, Ritt made *Stanley & Iris*, a film about a diamond in the rough whose only failing was that he could not read or write. As it turned out, *Stanley & Iris* was to be Martin Ritt's last movie.

Stanley Cox (Robert De Niro) works in the cafeteria of a bakery where Iris King (Jane Fonda), a widow, is employed. When the manager finds out that Stanley cannot read, he fires him; it would be too easy for him to mistake a box of roach powder for baking soda. The only thing left to Stanley is menial work; cleaning out toilets and digging ditches. In one particularly dramatic part of the movie during a thunderstorm, Stanley asks Iris to teach him to read, and thus De Niro becomes "Eliza Doolittle" to Fonda's "Professor Higgins." It seems that Stanley is a genius in every respect except reading and writing. For example, he knows the names of every tree he sees, not just their common names, but their scientific names as well. He is an inventor, tinkering away at several gadgets in his garage apartment; one of his creations is a "cake cooler." After a few bumbles here and there, Stanley learns to read, and afterwards the world is his. There is really nothing he cannot do. He is even offered a job in Detroit. He flies off and comes back a few months later driving a brand new car, sporting a credit card, and offering marriage to Iris, and a happy home for her children, and grandchild. "It seems the only acceptable ending to a movie about the working class is to get out of it."[97] If ever there had been a "Martin Ritt happy ending," this was it. But, then, as one newspaper said, a Martin Ritt happy ending "isn't that a poor person becomes rich";[98] it is that poor people *become enriched.*[99]

Stanley & Iris, however, goes far beyond illiteracy for its subject matter. Again there is the problem of aging. Because he cannot read, Stanley cannot hold a job. Because he cannot hold a job, he cannot support his father, Leonides (Feodor Chaliapin), at home. Therefore, in tears, he admits his father into a state-run rest home, only to have him die within a matter of weeks. "When they come into a place like this, they go downhill fast," are the only comforting words the rest home superintendent can offer.

There is also domestic upheaval and violence. Because of hard economic times, two families have to live in Iris's house. Iris's brother-in-law (Jamey Sheridan) violently slaps her sister (Swoosie Kurtz) during an argument over the purchase of a six-pack of beer. There is teen-aged pregnancy and Iris slaps her daughter, Kelly (Martha Plimpton, who had done so many teenage rebellious roles that one reporter thought Ritt should not have signed her for the part),[100] when she learns about it. Iris's daughter quits school and goes to work in the bakery, despite Iris telling her that "this line doesn't go anywhere." (The despair of the workers is summed up when someone asks a black worker, "Where's your husband, Bertha?" She answers, "Doing time, just like me.")

It was as though Ritt sensed this was his last movie, and wanted to include every social problem he and scriptwriters Irving Ravetch and Harriet Frank, Jr., could possibly think of. The movie was loosely based on Pat Barker's novel, *Union Street*, but included themes and events that were not elucidated by the book.

The movie's setting, captured photographically by Donald McAlpine, was New England. It was shot in Waterbury, Connecticut, and Toronto, Canada. Fonda took a break in the shooting and visited Chicopee, Massachusetts, for a few days, where she was demonstrated against by various veterans' groups and right-wing organizations.[101] She was still widely known as "Hanoi Jane," for her anti-Vietnamese War stance during the sixties and seventies.

One of the problems with *Stanley & Iris* is Jane Fonda herself. No matter how much she tries to be an assembly line worker in a bakery, she cannot, as one reviewer put it, get rid of her "golden brown hair," and "California tan."[102] *Newsweek* reported that Fonda looks like a "princess improbably misplaced on a working-class doorstep,"[103] while another critic referred to her as the "svelte Workout Queen" trying to be "average and overweight."[104] *Variety* said that her voice and carriage belong to a person of "far more ability" than she portrays in the movie.[105] If she does not look like a New England factory worker, she said, it is "my failure."[106] Ritt had wanted in *Stanley & Iris* a co-star who was feminine, but at the same time strong.[107] Perhaps remembering Fonda's role in *The Dollmaker*, which had won her an Emmy, and which Ritt had liked when he read it, caused him to seek Fonda for the role in *Stanley & Iris*.

Calling a movie "important" almost always detracts from its box-office appeal, but Bill Hagan, reporting for the *San Diego Tribune* felt compelled to use that adjective.[108] Ritt was a "talented champion" of the "little people" in America,[109] who should have received better treatment at the hands of the Hollywood assessors than he ever did. "Committed film making" had been out of favor in recent years, said Vincent Canby of *The New York Times*.[110] Ritt, however, now "almost stands alone as an unembarrassed social realist and movie maker of conscience."[111] After *Nuts*, said one reviewer, Martin Ritt might have been ready for "the home," and then sarcastically added, "although working with Barbra Streisand, almost anybody would be."[112] He rescued himself with *Stanly & Iris*, by quietly outlining the problems faced by those people who cannot read and write. Ritt had a "fine eye" for "local color" and a "finely tuned" ear for humor, said one reviewer,[113] when he placed some important scenes in a library, a "secular cathedral."[114]

First Lady Barbara Bush made literacy her number one program, and praised *Stanley & Iris* as a "fine film."[115] The spokespeople for the estimated 27 million English-illiterate Americans saw *Stanley & Iris* as *their* film.[116] To be a "free" man, Stanley Cox must sacrifice his pride and ask someone to teach him to read and write,[117] a stance that causes the whole film to be "awash" in "positive thinking." By sacrificing "pride," however, he holds onto and even enhances his "dignity."[118] The "shame" of the movie is not in Stanley's illiteracy; on the contrary, the "glory" of the movie is that he seeks help and changes the situation.

After the final shootings of *Stanley & Iris*, Ritt returned to California, ill and exhausted, suffering from diabetes and heart trouble. He did very little during the next several months except watch sports on television and occasionally go to the track. He and Adele had already severed ties with their longstanding legal representatives, Cohn, Glickstein, and Lurie in New York. She believed that it would be better in the future to deal with attorneys on a project-by-project basis, "using individuals of particular expertise for each given problem."[119] All the mortgages and major debts had been paid off, and Ritt was unable seriously to consider any more movie possibilities. He realized his situation; nevertheless, the combination of illness and a sense of semi-retirement was hard on him.[120] It was frightening to his friends to see his body "deserting" him,[121] particularly because he had always been such a "tough guy."[122] Though he was becoming physically weak, his mental capacities remained powerful. Ritt's old friend Paul Newman apparently felt neglected because of long periods of noncommunication, and wrote to Ritt that he felt Ritt was for some reason or other "pissed off at me."[123] Ritt was "truly startled" at Newman's letter. "In spite of the fact that we don't see each other very often, I consider you one of my dearest friends."[124]

On into the fall of 1990 Ritt grew increasingly weak. In December he was hospitalized for a failing heart. He died on

8 December 1990, at a hospital in Santa Monica. Word of his death spread rapidly throughout the country and world, and he was hailed as being America's greatest maker of social films. He was cremated, and Adele put his ashes in a trophy that one of his favorite horses, Pampered Star, won on 21 July 1990, the Monmouth Park Oaks. The trophy rested on the mantle shelf in the Ritts' living room at their home in Pacific Palisades for several months after his death.

Following Ritt's death, a memorial service was held for him at the Directors Guild of America. A number of friends, associates, and stars from his movies gave tributes to his life and career. Arthur Hiller had always thought that "if anyone wouldn't die," it would be Martin Ritt. Irving Ravetch noted that there had been a "couple of messengers" before, but Ritt had always told them to "get the hell back." When he did get to The Gate, said Ravetch, one of his first questions was "Is there a union here?"

"Marty is *us*," said Norman Jewison, and Karl Malden reminisced about his long friendship with Ritt. "We were hired together and we were fired together," Malden told the audience; Ritt, always sympathetic to actors "made them better than they were." Ritt's films were not always pretty, said Robert Radnitz, or commercially tasteful, but they were always full of "people with whom we can sympathize." An emotional Sally Field said in this tribute that before she met Ritt she was an "aimless child." She remembered Ritt dancing in the streets of Opelika, Alabama, during the filming of *Norma Rae*, and "giggling" with his daughter, Tina, at the back of the sets. To Field, Ritt was "fearless, funny, and ferocious," and his passing left "a hole in the world." David Grinfels and Sidney Levin spoke of Ritt's winsome ways with children, while John Alonzo, at first overcome with emotion, told his audience exactly what Ritt would tell him: "Get a hold of yourself, kid!"

Mary Steenburgen gave Walter Matthau a "million dollar opening"[125] as she told the audience that when filming *Cross Creek* she woke up one morning in a sweat, having had "a sexy dream about Marty." She later wondered why she would have such a dream about a 69-year-old man in a dirty jumpsuit. But, "he was the youngest person I knew. The most passionate." Ritt did not sit on chairs the way most directors did; he directed under the cameras, with "his fist in your mouth." The only person who would tell you the truth, "in a town where people don't tell the truth," was Martin Ritt.

Matthau followed Steenburgen to the podium and he said "I dreamt about Marty, too—last night." But Matthau's dream had to do with holding a winning hand in poker against Ritt, which, because of Ritt's fierce poker-playing skills, was indeed a dream. He remembered some difficulties in making *Pete 'n Tillie*. Ritt cleared "the goddamned sets" and "then made us do the love scene."

Walter Bernstein said Ritt always remained "a man of the left."[126] Ritt was angry, rather than bitter, at social injustices. "The triumph of the powerful over the powerless left him enraged."[127] Anger, Bernstein said in the tribute, drew Ritt to the left; love kept him there. He was not blacklisted for nothing, said Bernstein; Ritt firmly believed in those things for which he was blacklisted in the first place.[128] The final speaker at the DGA tribute was Jane Fonda, who expressed her "jealousy" at Sally Field for having had the privilege of making so many films with Martin Ritt.

Ritt would probably have guffawed at all the kind things being said about him—and then found a quiet corner somewhere and smiled with pleasure; not particularly about his own accomplishments, but for those of his actors and actresses who had outlined and delineated the human experience for so many years. He was, first and foremost, a person who wanted to fight against what he perceived to be injustices; the medium of his fight was the cinema. More could be accomplished, he believed, through movies than through novels and history books.

Of course, his passing brought up this question: Are there any more socially conscious movie directors around? Are there any more coming up through the ranks? Generally, the people asking those questions came up with resounding negatives. A few, however, mentioned Sidney Lumet, and some spoke of Spike Lee. The latter was countered as a "social" filmmaker because of the anger and the unremitting violence that always seemed to show up in his movies. The truth is that Martin Ritt was the long-time leader of a movie genre which, for all practical purposes in the 1990s no longer exists. We do, of course, have tender dramas today, at least from time to time, depicting battered women, orphans, homelife, and racial prejudices (that is, *content* over senseless killings, car chases and the like), but the fact remains that the director of one such film is rarely the director of the next such film. There is no single director today who has made movies in a sequence in the way, for example, Martin Ritt made *The Great White Hope, Sounder,* and *Conrack.* And this point could also apply to such sequential movies as *Norma Rae, Back Roads, Cross Creek,* and *Murphy's Romance.* And there are numerous other examples as well.

Martin Ritt's movies were of loners, individualists, outsiders, underdogs, and underprivileged, and no thinking person ever walked away from one of his films without having gained or augmented a perception of justice. Such a perception was right at the heart of the social experience of America. Martin Ritt fit very well into this perception, and in more ways than one, raised it to new levels.

Chapter 10

◆ ◆ ◆

Martin Ritt:
An Assessment

Martin Ritt was fond of saying, "If you have any talent, start at the top; there's plenty of room there." In a less accomplished person such a statement might have been taken as frivolity or even condescension. With Ritt, however, it was the expression of a pragmatic principle. The best way to become a director, he felt, was to have both academic training and experience for it. If, however, one had to make a choice between the two, he would take experience any day. He emphasized to many an audience that there were directors long before colleges and universities added cinema studies to their curricula. He was not denigrating the intellectual route; he was simply avowing that it was not "the only way to heaven." Success in directing, he felt, was about 60 percent "gift," and 40 percent "being able to take care of yourself in a street fight."[1]

Perhaps because of his theatrical roots, Ritt always accepted the ensemble approach to making movies. He strongly believed a film was made through the efforts of many persons, exemplifying the idea that people can go far when egos are left behind. He had some problems in this respect with Orson Welles, Richard Burton, and Barbra Streisand, but for the most part, he had his way in cooperative moviemaking. Nevertheless, he would not accept the proposition that directing is democratic. "You can't throw decisions up for grabs," he said; everyone making a decision is tantamount to no one making a decision. "You absolutely need the team but you have to be a boss, and they [the cast] expect it, they need it."[2] The director has to do his job, and if the actor has "any sense at all" he understands that the director can help him in a way that nobody else can. Everybody on a movie set must have a strong sense of professionalism; otherwise, nothing would ever get done. Thus, unless an actor is "a fool," or "egomaniacal to the point of stupidity," he will recognize the help of other professionals around him, and be grateful. Performers, Ritt said, do not always get that kind of help from producers and directors; chances are, therefore, that when they do get it, they respect it. Ritt happily exclaimed, "I've had no trouble during my career with actors."[3] (Perhaps forgetting for the moment Orson Welles, Richard Burton, and Barbra Streisand?)

He was Jewish, and his membership in a minority, he agreed, influenced his movies—in fairly much the same way as being black had influenced the films of the numerous black directors of the day. "I think the fact that I grew up as a Jew in itself has influenced the content of my films. I think this would be true of any young man from any minority group. I don't think any Negro director of films growing up in this period of history could be unaffected by being a Negro."[4] He never made a film about Jews (though he did consider for a time Bernard Malamud's *The Assistant*). He felt that most Jewish films were "do-goodish" or sentimental, or both, and he did not wish to pursue those lines in any picture he made.[5]

"I am not a genius," he once told a reporter, "but I am a professional."[6] He liked to tell people that Johann Wolfgang von Goethe always claimed to be a genius because he knew exactly what he looked like at the moment of orgasm; "now that's being objective," Ritt said; "he [Goethe] had that kind of objectivity."[7]

Ritt was a professional with a reputation of being the greatest social filmmaker in America, if not the world. Ritt objected to the general practice of classifying social films as leftist. In fact, he argued, the very first social films were conservative. Edwin S. Porter's *The Great Train Robbery*, he believed, had scenes of social import; definitely this was true of D.W. Griffith's *Birth of a Nation*, and Cecil B. DeMille's *The Squaw Man* and *The Ten Commandments*.[8] In the 1930s, Ritt believed, social films *were* liberally oriented, but they were also "anguished outcries" for a better social justice system than was practiced at the time. He mentioned movies like *The Crowd, Hallelujah,* and *Fugitive from a Chain Gang*, as points in reference. Contemporary makers of social film (and Ritt included Frank Capra in this category) try to "focus the contradictions in our social values, using irony as the lens."[9] The first function of a social film, he argued, was not to "convert, to convince or proselytize."[10] It was to entertain. If an audience knew they would not enjoy a film, they would not come to see it; enjoyment first, enlightenment second, were the propellers of Ritt's movie philosophy.

At either end of the political spectrum, there can be social films. Those of Sergei M. Eisenstein, and others from the idealistic communism of the early Soviet cinema, for example, had great social impact. Some audiences watching *Potemkin* literally "ran from the theatre in terror."[11] To the far right were the "social" films of Leni Riefenstahl, whose *Triumph of the Will*, and others, were "triumphs of infusion of social views in film making."[12]

All of these descriptions of various filmmakers bring up the question, Where do social films end and propaganda films begin? Ritt would have explained the difference according to freedom and independence. If a person made a "social" film only at the behest of a dictator (such as Lenin with Eisenstein and Hitler with Riefenstahl), and if that film glorified the dictator in question, then it would be propaganda. If, on the other hand, a person voluntarily and through the dictates of his or her own conscience, made a film about injustices—either by government or private individuals —there would be nothing propagandist about it.

Ritt started out in movies as a director—and only a director. As time progressed, however, he got into producing, though he never produced a movie that he did not also direct. For some, the producer's job was explained through the "Charles DeGaulle theory"[13]—you make people treat you the way you want to be treated. The producer was responsible for the entirety of the picture: getting studio approval, finding funds, hiring a scriptwriter and determining the direction of a developing screenplay, hiring a director, and in conjunction with him or her, deciding who would be cast in the movie. (Sometimes Ritt was asked why he did not become his own writer. He felt that writing, producing, and acting were three different entities that had to be brought together by the director. "I've written enough to know I don't do it well enough to please even myself," he said.[14] Writing, he believed, was a matter of talent, not intelligence or even brilliance.)

The creative force of a movie is its director, and this force included not only the work on the sets but the script from which that work was performed. He opposed actor approval for the script (if every star had to approve, nothing would ever get done) and, for that matter, once the final draft was written, studio approval also.

It became the general consensus in Hollywood that by the 1980s and 1990s, the producer's authority had been eroded, and in large part assumed by the director, because, presumably, the director was more visible to the moviegoing public than the producer, and supposedly was most knowledgeable about what movies would be box-office attractions. Generally, if a movie became a hit, it would be emulated by other studios. Thus, the style of a movie ensured that a director would be more apt to appear on television talk shows than a producer, and be exposed to millions of viewers. A producer could not stand up to this kind of competition; he had to grin and bear it, and produce the money for movies for which the directors would become famous.

Ritt saw movies change tremendously during his lifetime and career. The "star system" steadily vanished, and he thought this was good. In the past studios sold stars and actors, not the films in which they acted,[15] a practice that could and did lead to studio unconcern about thematic development and substance. The old objective was to turn out a number of "products" per year, knowing that no matter how fatuous some might be, if they had certain stars, they would find a patronizing public. The big studios and star system began to disintegrate after World War II, due to a new wave of liberalism washing the country, and the arrival of a number of new, young directors, including Martin Ritt, who thought substance was more important than form. Also integration and new expectations by blacks helped to bring about a moviemaking that was not "business as usual," as it had been in the 1920s, 1930s, and 1940s.[16] The day of the independent filmmaker arrived in the 1960s, an arrival that pleased Ritt, for it meant, among other things, a greater spectrum of movies, and a continued assault on the power of studio moguls.

In themes, however, Ritt remained old-fashioned; in fact, he was sometimes called "Old Hollywood,"[17] because he remained faithful to substance and thematic development, and because some of his films, such as *Norma Rae* and *The Molly Maguires* could well have been documentaries. Then, the baby-boomers of World War II grew to their majority in the 1960s, and, as in so many other things, they changed the movies.

People who truly appreciated Ritt's films were also likely to be readers—not necessarily avid ones, but enough to go through the daily newspapers, weekly news magazines, and enough books to know the situation of the world around them. Many critics say it was television that led so many people away from the printed page in the 1960s, 1970s, and 1980s. Whatever caused it, the practice of not reading can perhaps also be connected to making movies in which little or no thought had to be expended by the viewer. Many movies became totally escapist. Ritt despised the Rambo movies (although, according to one account, *First Blood*, which Ritt was supposed to make in the early 1980s, before he fell ill, was the film that evolved into the *Rambo* series). "I hate, as an American, to think that those films are viewed by the rest of the world as simple-minded . . . re-writing of history. That's exactly what it is. It is so simple-minded that, unfortunately, our President [Ronald Reagan] is in that camp."[18] *Rambo* gave a lot of viewers a sense of glory, otherwise missing from the Vietnam fiasco.[19] As noted in an earlier chapter, he also detested *The Exorcist* films, and refused to have anything to do with proposals sent to him for slashers, supernaturals, or those that dealt with subjects like child abuse (although *Nuts* to some extent was an exception), or serial killers.

Martin Ritt did not like the acting of Cary Grant; he thought he was too suave and "sophisticated" for any kind of sustained substance. Of Grant, he said ambiguously, "It's sufficient to be Beethoven; you don't have to be Mozart, too."[20] He liked to tell friends that in his earlier days he thought his physical appearance dictated against his becoming an actor, and, indeed, that fact was one big reason why he went into directing. He believed, however, if he had known that someone like Dustin Hoffman could be a success in acting, he would have remained in front of the camera. He did not like Peter Sellers, thinking he was overrated, and basically not a very funny man. (He did admit, however, to having seen every film Sellers made.) On the other hand, he did like Buddy Hackett, and Warren Beatty, for *Reds*, if for nothing else. "When I saw *Reds* I sat down. I loved the first half of the picture. Imagine the balls of a kid to get that picture on."[21] And he liked very much the music of Frank Sinatra.

The baby-boomers, Ritt believed, became the most conservative people in the United States. He discovered what every college professor knew in the 1970s and 1980s: average college students were primarily interested in getting degrees that would enable them to obtain good jobs at high wages, without in many instances, working their way to the top. They wanted to *start* at the top. Any program that would not facilitate their progress, they rejected. Therefore, the real liberals of the late-twentieth century were those of the older generations. Ritt spoke pointedly about American youth of the 1980s: "The younger people are . . . for suburbia, that's it. They want that $250,000 house, that steady job. The kids. It's tough to say, but they ain't worth a shit."[22] Of course, the "kids" retaliated by not going to see very many of Martin Ritt's later movies. *Hud* was probably the high watermark for Ritt's movies with the country's young people.

The 1970s and 1980s were also years when the study of American history and literature hit all-time lows, and liberal arts in general came under attack. Certainly, this situation explained a great deal of why younger people did not patronize Ritt as much as other, more action-oriented, directors. In a way, most of Ritt's films had a distinct historical aspect. Even if one did not, its theme usually evoked a piece of history with which his viewers were familiar. He was never exactly satisfied with his efforts at historical drama: "There's a lot I want to say before I turn in my spikes."[23] He wanted to express what he felt; but, of course, to do that, he had to be entertaining. A movie without entertainment would fail, and then "very few people would ever get to see the 'message' or have an opportunity to know what it is and consider its value."[24] He knew that the audiences he did attract would be historically minded. "There's always the risk of being accused of revising American history. But that's one of the best things about film. You can be provocative—not ordinary and predictable."[25]

Sometimes he took the seminar-lecture circuit to explain to students why he made the kind of films he did and how.

Even here, he usually wound up more disappointed than otherwise. As noted earlier, when he tried to explain *The Front* to student audiences at Stanford University, a majority in the class had never even heard of Joseph McCarthy. He was offered many academic positions—jobs that went beyond a single lecture or seminar, for entire terms. For example, in the spring of 1986 he became UCLA's first Distinguished Director in Residence, working with six film and video students in the graduate school. At the many places he lectured, such as Brigham Young, Eastern Illinois University, and the University of Kansas, he was constantly asked to become a permanent member of the faculty. Just four days before his death he was offered the professorship of the newly endowed chair of Motion Picture Directing/ Producing at the Ohio University School of Film. He would have received a salary and benefits amounting to about $100,000 a year.[26] The only reason Ritt was ever tempted to teach at a university full time was so that perhaps someone would tell him that what he had to say was important. Unfortunately, he rarely heard such a statement. "Film students today," he complained, "are totally preoccupied with form. Content doesn't exist."[27] The students—at least in the lectures and seminars he presented—did not say anything. "They're only interested in making money. They voted for Reagan."[28] Conversely, they were always nice and courteous to Ritt, very careful not to offend him, because someday "they might be coming looking for a job."[29] A cynic might have accused Ritt of sour grapes with these statements. In his defense, however, one might be reminded that Ritt's career had now spanned more than half a century, and he had not varied throughout all those years on what he thought constituted good art, either in the theater or cinema.

Even as he excoriated film and writing students in his lectures, seminars, and classes, he still offered at least a modicum of hope for numerous other scholars who wanted to get into the movie business. These were usually university students in fields other than cinematic studies, and most were about halfway through their university careers. One young man—a telecommunications major—from the University of Georgia, had spent his fourth summer in a row as a projectionist for a local cinema while trying to find funding to make films. He wanted Ritt to give him a job; if he couldn't, he would be grateful "if you just answered this letter and at least offered a few tips on how to get started in this industry."[30] Ritt had always made it a point to answer most, if not all, of the letters he received. He was not sure what to tell the young man, especially since he got "20 or so such letters" every year. These letters depressed Ritt, for he knew the frustrations "of not being able to express oneself as a filmmaker."[31] He wanted the Georgian to get in touch with him if he ever made another movie "in your neck of the woods."

Even older students could get bitten by the movie bug. A second-year resident in ophthalmology at Yale University wrote to Ritt that he had "decided to leave medicine in order to pursue a career in the entertainment industry, and particularly the film industry."[32] The desire was so "intense and irrevocable" that he had already announced to the authorities that he would leave the residency program at Yale at the end of the academic year. Ritt had never been "face to face" with such a dilemma; someone who was already a physician wanting to start out in an industry where any position he might gain would be "very minor" for years to come.[33] He told the internist that he would have to join a union before he could work, and that unions were difficult to get into. His best bet, Ritt felt, and this was a long shot, was to try his luck with companies like Lorimar or Rastar; that failing, he strongly hinted that the young man should stay in medicine.

With his own children, Ritt stayed neutral. He would neither encourage nor discourage them from show business, wanting them to make up their own minds about the matter. Both Tina and Michael, and very frequently Adele, accompanied Ritt to various locations around the country and world. Wherever the children went with Ritt on location, they were enrolled in a local school. At about the age of twelve, Tina let it be known that she wanted to "settle down" and have a "permanent" place for her schooling. Ritt acceded to her request. Tina, as noted previously, became Ritt's assistant director on several of his films, and Michael worked as a carpenter on sets such as *Sounder, Conrack, Casey's Shadow, Back Roads,* and others. (Today, Tina is a film producer in California, and Michael is a carpenter in Seattle.)

Ritt's family was extremely important to him, though he was away from them for extended periods. He was somewhat strict with Tina and Michael as they grew up. He once suspended Tina's car-driving privileges when she did not make the kind of grades in school of which he knew she was capable. He did not enter his children's world as much as they entered his.[34] He thought the "greatest thing" he could do for Tina was to have a "Father-Daughter" day, and take her to the racetrack at Santa Monica. On the way they would stop off at Uncle John's Pancake House and fortify themselves for the rigorous day ahead; at least rigorous for Tina. "All I did all day was get on my hands and knees and pick up the colored tickets. So I'd come home from the tracks with these stacks of green, blue, red, and pink tickets, filthy. I mean absolutely filthy. My mother would flip. 'What are you doing with this child?' And he would explain."[35]

During baseball and football seasons, the television sets in the house were generally "off limits" to everyone except Ritt himself. The TV in the den would have one football game going; the TV in the living room would have another. A radio upstairs might have a third. Ritt would walk from room to room, watch each game for a time, or listen, and then move on to another place in the house.[36] As stated earlier, it was the poetry of the games' movements that fascinated him so much. Tina frequently joined Ritt in his "athletic" parades throughout the Ritt household in Pacific Palisades.

Martin Ritt and Adele gave their children what all good parents want to give: the ability to be on their own. In 1982, 24-year-old Tina told her parents that she wanted to accomplish things in her life that "firstly I can be proud of, and secondly, that you can be proud of."[37] As she grew older, Tina increasingly looked upon her parents as role models: "You have shown me all the things I now look for in others I choose to bring into my life."[38] Such sentiments from their children made Martin and Adele successful in life quite apart from any movie or dancing career that either one followed.

Michael Ritt was not as interested in sports as Martin and Tina (though he did play chess and pool with his father), but he had a talent in building things, and that is why he showed up so often as a carpenter on the sets of one Ritt movie after another. He remembered that he once wanted to get out of high school and Ritt "hit the roof."[39] His father, he said, could get so absorbed in directing and watching a scene being filmed that he actually fell over things in his way—he was completely obsessed by the project at hand. "He knew what he wanted; he was a real professional."[40] Whenever Michael and Martin had disagreements with one another, the elder Ritt would say, "What can we work out between us to solve this problem?"[41] Martin told Michael to be the "best you can be," and "I'll get you your first day of work, and then it's up to you."[42]

Both Tina and Michael today are married and have children. Martin Ritt kept asking Tina when she was going to make him a grandfather. He never saw any of his grandchildren, but he knew Tina's was on the way when he died.

The greatest personal mainstay in Martin Ritt's life was Adele. Blue-eyed, blonde, with a well-defined profile, "like a face on a coin,"[43] Adele was married to Martin Ritt for 50 years. As a dancer, Adele helped to hone Martin's own considerable talents on the dance floor. As one author put it, "Much of Ritt's stubborn refusal to suborn his conscience during the tough times came from an absolute knowledge that Adele was willing to do whatever she had to, to keep their mutual pride in themselves intact."[44] Today (1994) Adele lives in Montecito, California.

What then does a director like Martin Ritt say to film viewers and students in the closing years of the twentieth century? Certainly, one message that comes through is that socially oriented films can be successfully made, even today. Perhaps one should say, especially today, in the conservative milieu in which most Americans live. Movies don't always have to have slasher scenes, car chases, sexual orgies, and victory in Vietnam. It takes a director, however, who does not automatically always go for the blockbuster, who is willing to make a decent profit on his endeavors, and not always expect to win prizes. Beyond those points, however, it probably would take a director who is keenly aware of social injustices and who can only be so because he or she has suffered some of them. With the exception of *Five Branded Women*, Ritt never made a film in which he did not believe.[45] With or without monetary profits, directors would have to possess this kind of commitment to the contents of any film they might make. Without the commitment, they could not be socially conscious picturemakers.

Perhaps Ritt's style today would fit the television screens better than those in large cinemas. When audiences stay home and watch network television, or basic cable, they do seem to be more amenable to programs that elicit nostalgia. One thinks of series such as *Evening Shade*, *The Wonder Years*, *The Homefront*, and the syndication of *Mayberry RFD*, *Bonanza*, and *Gunsmoke*. And, of course, there is the continuing popularity of the Disney channel. Audiences for these types of programs and movies never did go away; it was only the directors and studios who decided that these were too simplistic for them to handle. Ritt himself would not have made some of the pictures listed above, on the grounds that they were too sentimental. He disliked sentimentalism; he liked sentiment, and there was a world of difference between the two. But Ritt tended to like the same characters and many of the same themes that these presentations encompassed. The *human* value was what he was after; and he got it in more instances than not. And in getting it, he showed many of his audiences people they had known all their lives. It is not the strange that audiences go to see; it is the familiar, and one could walk away from a Ritt movie with the thought that "Gee, didn't old so and so remind you of Grandpa?" and so on. Thus, remembrance, nostalgia, humanism and the human condition, simple (as opposed to simplistic) times compared to our own, and a sincerity that always seemed to come through in his movies are all Ritt qualities that we could very well use today.

Some film scholars talk about "noise" in a movie. If a movie is "noisy," one can sometimes detect the influence, if not the presence of the director. In a "noiseless" movie, the viewers forget all about the director; they rarely even think of the director after the initial flashing of the name at the beginning of the movie. Though Martin Ritt shouted and swore at a lot of people while his movies were in progress, he was a "noiseless" director. He could detect what the performers needed, and they could detect what he wanted, and this symbiosis did indeed produce some memorable movies for our time. Right to the end of his life he remained an "actor's director," someone always in their corner, to instruct, cajole, and teach them in the proper ways of depicting important forms of human life. He "picked up the tab" here more than once, and in the process gave everyone interested in movies an unforgettable gift.

Appendix A

Martin Ritt in the Theater

As actor in:

Golden Boy (also Assistant Stage Manager)
Plant of the Sun
The Gentle People
Two on an Island
They Should Have Stood in Bed
The Eve of St. Mark
Winged Victory
Men of Distinction
Maya
The Flowering Peach
Born Yesterday

As director of:

Mr. Peebles and Mr. Hooker
Yellow Jack
The Big People
Set My People Free
The Man
Cry of the Peacock
Golden Boy
Boy Meets Girl
The Front Page
A Memory of Two Mondays
A View from the Bridge
A Very Special Baby

Appendix B

Martin Ritt in Films

As player in:

Winged Victory, Twentieth Century Fox, 1944.
The End of the Game, Twentieth Century Fox, 1976.
Hollywood on Trial, Lumiere, 1977.
The Slugger's Wife, Columbia, 1985.
The Group Theatre, PBS, 1985.
Fifty Years of Action, Directors Guild of America Golden Jubilee Committee, 1986

As director of:

Edge of the City (also known as *A Man Is Ten Feet Tall*) MGM, 1957
No Down Payment, Twentieth Century Fox, 1957
The Long Hot Summer, Twentieth Century Fox, 1958
The Black Orchid, Paramount, 1959
The Sound and the Fury, Twentieth Century Fox, 1959
Five Branded Women, Paramount, 1960
Paris Blues, United Artists, 1961
Adventures of a Young Man (also known as *Hemingway's Adventures of a Young Man*, Twentieth Century Fox, 1962
Hud, Paramount, 1963
The Outrage, MGM, 1964
The Spy Who Came In From the Cold, Paramount, 1965
Hombre, Twentieth Century Fox, 1967
The Brotherhood, Paramount, 1968
The Great White Hope, Twentieth Century Fox, 1970
The Molly Maguires, Paramount, 1970
Pete 'n Tillie, Universal, 1972
Sounder, Twentieth Century Fox, 1972
Conrack, Twentieth Century Fox, 1974
The Front, Columbia, 1976
Casey's Shadow, Columbia, 1978

Norma Rae, Twentieth Century Fox, 1979
Back Roads, Warner Brothers, 1981
Cross Creek, Universal, 1983
Murphy's Romance, Columbia, 1985
Nuts, Warner Brothers, 1987
Stanley & Iris, MGM, 1990

Notes

Chapter 1

[1]Martin Ritt, letter to Ivan, 17 Oct. 1968, Herrick Library, Beverly Hills, CA. Hereafter referred to as Herrick Library.

[2]Harriett Frank, Jr., interview, Los Angeles, 11 May 1991.

[3]Paul Newman, interview, Westport, CT, 3 June 1991.

[4]Harriett Frank, Jr., and Irving Ravetch, interview, 11 May 1991; Karl Malden, interview, 16 May 1991; Newman, interview, 3 June 1991.

[5]Malden, interview.

[6]Sally Field, telephone interview, Oct. 1991.

[7]Charles J. Maland, *Frank Capra* (Boston: Twayne, 1980) 20. Some other fairly recent books that touch upon the subject of the social film are Tom O'Brien, *The Screening of America* (New York: Continuum, 1990); Lea Jacobs, *The Wages of Sin: Censorship and The Fallen Woman Film 1928-1942* (Madison: University of Wisconsin Press, 1991); Les and Barbara Keyser, *Hollywood and The Catholic Church: The Image of Roman Catholicism in American Movies* (Chicago: Loyola University Press, 1984); Christopher Sharrett, ed., *Crisis Cinema: The Apocalyptic Idea and Postmodern Narrative Film* (Washington, DC: Maisonneuve Press, 1993); Paul Monaco, *Ribbons in Time: Movies and Society Since 1945* (Bloomington and Indianapolis: Indiana University Press, 1988); and Hal Erickson, *Baseball in the Movies: A Comprehensive Reference 1915-1991* (Jefferson, NC: McFarland & Co., 1992).

[8]Carrie Rickey, "The Long, Hot Career," *Fame* Winter 1990: 36.

[9]*The New York Times* 2 Mar. 1914.

[10]Of course, there was no Poland as such in 1892. That ancient country had been partitioned by its neighbors, Prussia, Austria, and Russia. It was not until the immediate post-World War I period that Poland was resurrected. The restoration of Poland was a part of President Woodrow Wilson's Fourteen Points.

[11]Jerome J. Arnowitz, letter to the author, 11 June 1991.

[12]Ibid.

[13]Ibid.

[14]Jerome Arnowitz, letter to Martin Ritt, 26 Feb. 1979, Academy of Motion Picture Arts and Sciences, Herrick Library.

[15]Rickey 36.

[16]Jerome J. Arnowitz, letter to the author, 11 June 1991.

[17]Ibid.

[18]Adele Ritt, interview, Pacific Palisades, CA, 8 May 1991.

241

[19]New York *Sunday News*, Wanda Hale interview, 26 Nov. 1972.

[20]Walter "Firpo" Latham, telephone interview, 21 Aug. 1991.

[21]Burlington (NC) *Daily Times*, 18 July 1966.

[22]Jack Hirschberg interview of Martin Ritt, unpublished, Sept. 1969. A copy of this interview can be found at the Ritt home in Pacific Palisades, CA.

[23]Rickey 36.

[24]Latham, interview.

[25]Adele Ritt, letter to the author, undated, 1992.

[26]Rickey 36.

[27]Telephone interview, Charles and Edith Holmes (both former classmates of Ritt at Elon College), 18 Apr. 1994.

[28]Hirschberg, interview of Martin Ritt.

[29]Ibid.

[30]Ibid.

[31]Rickey 36.

[32]Jay Williams, interview of Martin Ritt, Boston University Archives, date unknown. Used with the permission of Mrs. Barbara Williams.

[33]Adele Ritt, interview.

[34]Williams, interview.

[35]Ibid.

[36]Adele Ritt, interview.

[37]Gene Kelly, letter to the author, 4 Apr. 1991.

[38]Ibid.

[39]"American Masters Broadway Dreamers: The Legacy of the Group Theatre," PBS Documentary, New York: WNET, 18 Jan. 1989, Joan Kramer, director. Lee Strasberg, director of many plays for the Group Theatre, used the "naturalistic" method of acting. Some other people instrumental in making the Group Theatre a success were Ruth Nelson, Eunice Stoddard, Stella Adler, Margaret Barker, Morris Carnovsky, and Phoebe Brand. Katharine Hepburn would not join the Group Theatre because she did not want to share her talent in an ensemble performance. She wanted to be a star. See also Harold Clurman, *The Fervent Years* (New York: Hill and Wang, 1957) 196.

[40]Ibid.

[41]Ibid.

[42]Williams, interview.

[43]Martin Ritt, interview by Jack Hirschberg, Sept. 1969.

[44]Martin Ritt, interview by Ralph Hicklin, *The Toronto Globe and Mail* 30 Mar. 1967. Qtd. in *Current Biography*, 1979: 309.

[45]Karl Malden, interview.

[46]Julian Claman, untitled article on Martin Ritt, Ritt household, Pacific Palisades, CA, undated.

[47]Ibid.

[48]Martin Ritt, letter to Jack Garfein, 11 Apr. 1979, Herrick Library.

[49]Williams, interview.

[50]Roberto Ellero, "Martin Ritt," *Castoro Cinema, La Nouva Italia* Mar.-Apr. 1989: 12.

[51]Adele Ritt, interview.

[52]Karl Malden, interview.

[53]*Variety* 17 Oct. 1944.

[54]Hirschberg, interview.

[55]Adele Ritt, interview.

[56]Claman article.

[57]Ibid.

Chapter 2

[1]Brooks Atkinson gave *Mr. Peebles and Mr. Hooker* a fairly good review in the *The New York Times* 11 Oct. 1946.

[2]*Yellow Jack* received a quite favorable review by Brooks Atkinson in *The New York Times* 28 Feb. 1947.

[3]Brooks Atkinson, *The New York Times* 28 Feb. 1947.

[4]Brooks Atkinson, review of *The Man, The New York Times* 20 Jan. 1950.

[5]*The American Film Institute Seminar, Part I; The New York Times Oral History Program*, (Glen Rock, NJ: Microfilming Corporation of America, 1977) 40.

[6]Hamilton Morgan letter to Mr. Harrison, 16 Apr. 1980, Herrick Library.

[7]Jack Hirschberg, interview of Martin Ritt, Ritt residence, Sept. 1969.

[8]Ibid.

[9]Ibid.

[10]Maeve Southgate letter to Martin Ritt, 21 Nov. 1951, Herrick Library.

[11]Sally Malin letter to Martin Ritt, undated, Herrick Library.

[12]*Red Channels* 215.

[13]*Counterattack* 6.21 (23 May 1952): n.p.

[14]"Martin Ritt," *Current Biography* 1979: 310.

[15]*Counterattack* 6.39 (26 Sept. 1952): 1.

[16]*Red Channels: The Report of Communist Influence in Radio and Television* (New York: Counterattack, The Newsletter of Facts to Combat Communism, 1950) 9.

[17]Ibid.

[18]*Red Channels* 11.

[19]Ibid. 12.

[20]Ibid. 17-18.

[21]Ibid. 31, 37, 43, 58, 110-11, 120-21, 130, 134-35, 155-57.

[22]Martin Ritt, interview by Rex Reed, New York *Sunday News* 10 Oct. 1976. Qtd. in *Current Biography* 1979: 310.

[23]Clamen, *"Martin Ritt."*

[24]Carrie Rickey, *Fame* Winter 1990: 36.

[25]Adele Ritt, interview.

[26]FBI report on Martin Ritt, 2 Dec. 1964.

[27]Ibid.

[28]Adele Ritt, interview.

[29]*Current Biography* 1979: 310.

[30]Roberto Ellero, "Martin Ritt," *Castoro Cinema, La Nuova Italia,* Mar.-Apr. 1989: 13.

[31]House Un-American Activities *Report* No. 2516; 82nd Cong., 2nd sess., 3 Jan. 1952. For general information about the HUAC, see Cedric Belfrage, *The American Inquisition 1945-1960* (Indianapolis: Bobbs-Merrill, 1973); Eric Bentley, ed., *Thirty Years of Treason: Excerpts from Hearings Before the House Committee on Un-American Activities, 1938-1968* (New York: Viking, 1971); David Coute, *The Great Fear: The Anti-Communist Purge Under Truman and Eisenhower* (New York: Simon and Schuster, 1971); and Richard M. Fried, *Nightmare in Red: The McCarthy Period in Perspective* (New York: Oxford University Press, 1990).

[32]Vincent W. Hartnett, "Rascalry on the Air Waves," *Catholic World* 171 (July 1950): 166.

[33]Ibid. 169.

[34]In 1977 John Huston narrated a documentary, *Hollywood on Trial.* Martin Ritt made a brief appearance in this film, speaking about the "nature of the beast" in reference to the blacklist era. One of the ironies Huston pointed out in this movie was that the first chairman of HUAC, J. Parnell Thomas of New Jersey, was convicted in 1951 of padding his congressional payroll, and had to spend some time in jail with Dalton Trumbo and other members of the "Hollywood Ten," whom Thomas had earlier indicted!

[35]Martin Ritt, quoted in Carrie Rickey, "The Long Hot Career," *Fame* Winter 1990: 38. In 1952 Merle Miller wrote a book about *Red Channels* entitled *The Judges and the Judged* (Doubleday). Francis Biddle reviewed Miller's book in the *Saturday Review* 12 Apr. 1952. "The sponsors, the advertisers," he said, "determine the type of entertainment or instruction that shall be permitted to the public by considering the political ideologies of the writers and artists. . . . Until public opinion is shocked into revolting against this dark surrender of our freedoms to the exhortation of fear we shall, I am afraid, continue to drift towards acceptance of the new controls."

[36]Cloris Leachman, telephone interview, 13 Apr. 1991.

[37]Claman article.

[38]Ibid.

[39]Ibid.

[40]Cloris Leachman, interview.

[41]Joanne Woodward, interview, 3 June 1991, Westport, CT.

[42]Jack Hirschberg, interview of Martin Ritt, Sept. 1969, Ritt household. The principal founder of the Group Theatre, Harold Clurman, said about the Actors Studio: "Some of the spark of that enthusiasm whch emanated from the Group Theatre and kindred organizations has been transmitted to young people of today through the conversations and group scene study of the Actors Studio . . . but though it serves a praiseworthy purpose one wishes that general understanding of it would not be limited to a publicity which has willy-nilly been incorporated into the glamour-fetishes of the Broadway assembly line." Harold Clurman, *The Fervent Years: The Story of the Group Theatre and the Thirties* (New York: Hill & Wang, 1957) 291.

[43]Curt Conway letter to Martin Ritt, 6 Aug. 1957, Martin Ritt to Curt Conway, 9 Aug. 1957, Herrick Library.

[44]Herbert Rubensohn, interview, New York, 26 May 1992.

[45]Rickey 40. Walter Matthau, telephone interview, 13 Nov. 1991.

[46]Claman article.

[47]Rickey 38.

[48]Tina Ritt, interview, Pacific Palisades, CA, 15 May 1991.

[49]Elia Kazan, letter to the author, 19 Nov. 1991.

[50]Elia Kazan, "Where I Stand," *Reader's Digest* 61 (July 1952): 45-46.

[51]Elia Kazan, *A Life* (New York: Alfred A. Knopf, 1988) 455.

[52]Ibid. 457, 458.

[53]Ibid. 459.

[54]Kenneth R. Hey, "Ambivalence as a Theme in *On the Waterfront* (1954): An Interdisciplinary Approach to Film Study" in *Hollywood as Historian,* ed. Peter C. Rollins (Lexington: University Press of Kentucky, 1983) 163.

[55]Ibid. 166.

[56]Adele Ritt, interview.

[57]FBI report on Martin Ritt, 6 Nov. 1951, Ritt household, Pacific Palisades, CA.

[58]Ibid.

[59]Ibid. 26 Oct. 1959.

[60]FBI report on Martin Ritt, 11, 16 Feb. 1952; 8 Mar. 1952, Ritt household, Pacific Palisades, CA.

[61]Adele Ritt, interview.

[62]FBI report on Martin Ritt, 20 Oct. 1953, Ritt household, Pacific Palisades, CA.

[63]Ibid.

[64]Ibid.

[65]Ibid.

[66]*Martin Ritt: An American Film Seminar on His Work. New York Times Oral History Program* (Glen Rock, NJ: Microfiliming Corporation of America, 1977) 6.

[67]Arthur Miller, letter to the author, undated, 1991.

[68]Ibid.

[69]Ibid.

[70]Ibid.

[71]Ibid.

[72]Ibid.

[73]Ibid. Miller also discussed James Dean in *Timebends*, his autobiography.

[74]Ibid.

[75]Ibid. Miller closed his letter to the author by saying: "All this is nearly thirty-five years ago, incredibly enough. I still have my original affection for Marty Ritt; there was an appealingly idealistic kid inside that bulk he carried around."

[76]See Sheila Whitaker, *The Films of Martin Ritt* (London: British Film Institute, Oct. 1972) for full discussions of Ritt's pursuit of the "outsider" or "loner."

[77]Ruby Dee, letter to the author, 5 June 1991. She continued in her letter: "Now when trying to reach young actors in some of the work I do, I remember vividly Marty's trust in the process and I become calm, more capable of creative patience. Part of Marty, I believe, lives in me, the performer."

[78]Hirschberg, interview of Martin Ritt, Ritt household, Sept. 1969.

[79]*Sunday Times* (London) 24 Mar. 1957. For an additional discussion of Ritt's direction of *Edge of the City*, see Colin Young, "The Hollywood War of Independence," *Film Quarterly* Spring 1959: 4-22. Also, Lindsay Anderson, "Ten Feet Tall," *Sight & Sound* 27 (Summer 1957): 34-37; and Lionel Godfrey, "TALL When They're Small," *Films and Filming* 14.11 (Aug. 1968): 42-48.

[80]Hirschberg, interview, Sept. 1969.

[81]Kermit Bloomgarden, letter to Martin Ritt, 30 July 1956, Herrick Library.

[82]Martin Ritt, letter to Kermit Bloomgarden, 4 Aug. 1956, Herrick Library.

[83]Bloomgarden to Ritt, 8 Aug. 1956, Herrick Library.

[84]Colin Young, "The Hollywood War of Independence," *Film Quarterly* 7 (Spring 1959).

[85]Lionel Godfrey, "TALL When They're Small," *Films and Filming* 14.11 (Aug. 1968): 43.

[86]Joanne Woodward, interview.

[87]Jerry Wald, letter to Helen Turpin, 23 Apr. 1957, Herrick Library.

[88]Frank McCarthy, letter to Jerry Wald, 18 June 1957, Herrick Library.

[89]Jerry Wald, letter to Martin Ritt, 14 June 1957, Herrick Library.

[90]Robert Radnitz, telephone interview, Sept. 1991.

[91]Adele Ritt, interview.

[92]Adele Ritt, letter to the author, undated, 1992.

[93]Claman article.

[94]Ibid.

[95]Adele Ritt, interview.

[96]Ibid.

[97]Walter Bernstein, tribute to Martin Ritt, American Film Institute, Dec. 1990.

[98]Ibid.

[99]Ibid.

[100]Ibid.

[101]Adele Ritt, interview.

Chapter 3

[1]Robert Hughes and Peretz Johnnes, letter to Martin Ritt, 1 Aug. 1957, Herrick Library.

[2]Ibid.

[3]Ibid.

[4]Gideon Bachmann, letter to Martin Ritt, 18 July 1957, Herrick Library.

[5]Martin Ritt, letter to Gideon Bachmann, 9 Aug. 1957, Herrick Library.

[6]Martin Ritt, letter to Audrey Wood, 19 Sept. 1957, Herrick Library.

[7]A. Ronald Lubin, letter to Martin Ritt, 5 Sept. 1957, Herrick Library.

[8]Lewis Allen, letter to Martin Ritt, 20 Nov. 1957, Herrick Library.

[9]Lewis Allen, letter to Martin Ritt, 26 Nov. 1957, Herrick Library.

[10]Yul Brynner, letter to Martin Ritt, 24 May 1958, Herrick Library.

[11]Ibid.

[12]Ibid.

[13]L.D., letter to Martin Ritt, 9 Aug. 1957, Herrick Library.

[14]Martin Ritt, interview with Aljanmar Metz, *The New York Times* 25 Feb. 1979.

[15]Roberto Ellero, "Martin Ritt," *Castoro Cinema La Nuova Italia*, Mar.-Apr. 1989: 23.

[16]Michael Adams, "How Come Everybody Down Here Has Three Names?": Martin Ritt's Southern Films," *Southern Quarterly* 19.3-4 (Spring-Summer 1981): 144.

[17]Frank Brady, *Citizen Welles: A Biography of Orson Welles* (New York: Charles Scribners' Sons, 1989) 494.

[18]Joe Hyams, *New York Herald Tribune* 1 Apr. 1958.

[19]Douglas McVay, "The Best and Worst of Martin Ritt," *Films and Filming* Dec. 1964: 44. Also *Current Biography* 310.

[20]Bosley Crowther, review of *The Long Hot Summer*, *The New York Times* 4 Apr. 1958. See also *Current Biography* 1979: 310.

[21]Brady, *Citizen Welles* 494.

[22]Interview, Lee Remick, Los Angeles, CA, 16 May 1991. The author wishes to note the graciousness of Miss Remick in granting an interview at a time when she was seriously ill. She was so charming and polite and beautiful. I will always treasure her kindness to me.

[23]Ibid.

[24]Joanne Woodward, interview, Westport, CT, 3 June 1991.

[25]Ibid.

[26]Ibid.

[27]Ibid.

[28]Bob Ellison, *Toronto Daily Star* 11 Dec. 1965.

[29]Ibid.

[30]Orson Welles, letter to Martin Ritt, 12 Mar. 1958, Herrick Library.

[31]Ibid.

[32]Ibid.

[33]Ibid.

[34]Ibid.

[35]Ibid.

[36]Ibid.

[37]Ibid.

[38]Ibid.

[39]Ibid.

[40]Martin Ritt, letter to Orson Welles, 24 Mar. 1958, Herrick Library.

[41]Ibid.

[42]Ibid.

[43]Ibid.

[44]Ibid.

[45]Joe Hyams, *New York Herald Tribune* 1 Apr. 1958.

[46]Ibid.

[47]*Courier Express* (Buffalo, NY) 4 Mar. 1979.

[48]Richard Cuskelly, *Los Angeles Herald Examiner* 23 May 1976.

[49]McVay 44.

[50]Review, 22 Jan. 1959.

[51]Cuskelly, *Los Angeles Herald Examiner* 23 May 1976.

[52]*Saturday Review* 15 May 1976.

[53]Several attempts by the author to contact Ernest Borgnine, who played the title role in *Marty*, have been futile. It is likely that Borgnine was not privy to behind-the-scenes discussions about who was considered for the roles in the movie. The truth of the matter probably died with Paddy Chayevsky several years ago.

[54]Martin Ritt, interview, by Walter Burrell, 12 June 1973, unpublished manuscript, Ritt household, Pacific Palisades, CA.

[55]Ibid.

[56]Bosley Crowther, *The New York Times* 13 Feb. 1959.

[57]Ibid.

[58]Ibid.

[59]Jean Negulesco, letter to Martin Ritt, 4 Mar. 1958, Herrick Library.

[60]Burrell, interview.

[61]Ibid.

[62]Anthony Quinn, letter to the author, 11 Oct. 1991.

[63]Ibid.

[64]Ibid. Also years later, Quinn said, Ritt called him about a script that would also include Paul Newman in the movie. Newman, however, wanted to give Quinn's part to someone else. As a result, Ritt said, according to Quinn, "I promised Tony the part, and I see Tony in the part better than [anyone else] . . . Paul didn't agree with him, so Marty did not direct the picture. I thought that was so wonderful of Marty, and I've always loved him for that—his word was his word."

[65]See Adams, "How Come" 145.

[66]Woodward, interview.

[67]Ibid.

[68]Berry Reece, *Jackson* (MS) *Daily News* 5 Mar. 1959.

[69]Archer Winsten, *New York Post* 29 Mar. 1959. Also *Current Biography* 1979: 311.

[70]*New York World Telegram and Sun* 28 Mar. 1959.

[71]New York *Daily News* 28 Mar. 1959.

[72]*Time* 16 Mar. 1959.

[73]*Variety* 4 Mar. 1959. *Variety* 17 Mar. 1959 also stated that Ritt's direction of *The Sound and the Fury* is "sure and vigorous." The magazine referred to him as an "uncommonly good director."

[74]Jane Petty, *State Times* (Jackson, MS) 4 Mar. 1959.

[75]Martin Ritt, interview by Lyn Goldfarb and Anatoli Ilyashove, Burbank, CA, 11 Sept. 1985.

[76]*Los Angeles Times* 5 Jan. 1973.

[77]Hirshberg, interview.

[78]Ibid.

[79]*Los Angeles Times* 11 Oct. 1967.

[80]Pat Aufderheide, "A Mensch for All Seasons," *In These Times*, 16-20 Apr. 1980.

[81]Martin Ritt, letter to Alvin H. Marill, Glen Rock, NJ, 30 June 1976, Herrick Library.

[82]Burrell, interview.

[83]Lee Remick, interview.

[84]*Chicago Tribune* 2 Sept. 1973.

[85]Ibid.

[86]Ibid.

[87]*Current Biography* 1979: 311.

[88]Ibid.

[89]Douglas McVay, "The Best and Worst of Martin Ritt," *Films and Filming* Dec. 1964: 44.

[90]Dora Jane Hamblin, letter to Martin Ritt, 5 Mar. 1960, Herrick Library.

[91]Ibid.

[92]*Variety* 6 Apr. 1960.

[93]Ibid.

[94]Ibid.

[95]It is still shown rather frequently in the 1990s on the Arts and Entertainment Channel.

[96]McVay 45.

[97]Ritt's use of music in his movies is briefly discussed in Sheila Whitaker, *The Films of Martin Ritt* (London: British Film Institute, Oct. 1972) 18.

[98]McVay 46.

[99]*Newsweek* 2 Oct. 1961: 86-87.

[100]Ibid.

[101]Ibid.

[102]*Variety* 26 Sept. 1961.

[103]Eli Wallach, interview, New York, 29 May 1992.

[104]Lionel Godfrey, "The Films of Martin Ritt as seen by Lionel Godfrey," *Films and Filming* 14.11 (Aug. 1968): 44.

[105]Ibid.

[106]Tina Ritt, interview, Pacific Palisades, CA, 16 May 1991.

[107]Ted Sherdeman, letter to Ned Brown, 17 July 1961, Herrick Library.

[108]Martin Ritt, letter to Martin Baum, 7 July 1961, Herrick Library.

[109]Ibid.

[110]William Bradford Huie to Ned Brown, 2 Apr. 1961, Herrick Library.

Chapter 4

[1]See *Los Angeles Times* 11 Oct. 1964.

[2]See Sheila Whitaker, *The Films of Martin Ritt* (London: British Film Institute, Oct. 1972) for an overly esoteric explanation of Ritt's "outsiders."

[3]Qtd. in Lionel Godfrey, "TALL When They're Small: The Films of Martin Ritt as seen by Lionel Godfrey," *Films and Filming* 14.11 (Aug. 1968): 46.

[4]Ibid.

[5]Sydney Field, "Outrage: A Print 'Documentary' on Hollywood Film-Making," *Film Quarterly* 18.3 (Spring 1965): 38.

[6]"Martin Ritt: Conversation," *Action* (1 Mar./Apr 1971): 28.

[7]Godfrey 46.

[8]C.L. Sonnichsen, *From Hopalong to Hud: Thoughts on Western Fiction* (College Station: Texas A & M Press, 1978) 126.

[9]Godfrey 46.

[10]Judith Crist, *Herald Tribune* 29 May 1963.

[11]"Dialogue on Film: Martin Ritt," *American Film* 7 (Nov. 1981): 20.

[12]Bosley Crowther, *The New York Times* 29 May 1963.

[13]Archer Winsten, *New York Post* 29 May 1963.

[14]Pauline Kael, "The Current Cinema," *New Yorker* 39.166 (8 June 1963).

[15]Justin Gilbert, *New York Mirror* 29 May 1963.

[16]*Saturday Review* 25 May 1963.

[17]Ibid.

[18]*The Sunday Express* 1 June 1963.

[19]*The Southern Jewish Weekly* 7 June 1963.

[20]Several years after *Hud*, Ritt was still corresponding with some of the citizens of Claude, Texas. William Dunn, a pharmacist, wrote in 1966 that "we are still the same kind of people you visited and worked with while you were here. Not much news from this area as things are just about the same most of the time." William Dunn, letter to Martin Ritt, 15 Aug. 1966, Herrick Library. Ritt replied, 22 Aug., that he "remembered all the people in Claude with great affection."

[21]Irving Ravetch, undated note, *Hud* files, Herrick Library.

[22]Wayne Warga, "Ritt a Tough Director Who Melted with 'Sounder,'" *The Los Angeles Times* 15 Oct. 1972. Also Russel J. Light, *Iconoclast* 5-12 Apr. 1974.

[23]"Cross Creek, Martin Ritt's New Film, is in some ways a Quintessential Ritt Picture," *American Film* Nov. 1983: 20.

[24]Paul Newman, interview, Westport, CT, 3 June 1991.

[25]Ibid.

[26]Field 35.

[27]Ibid.

[28]*Newsweek* 64 (26 Oct. 1964): 118.

[29]Field 25-26.

[30]Ibid.

[31]Warga.

[32]Field 27.

[33]Ibid. 28.

[34]Ibid.

[35]Ibid. 31.

[36]Ibid. 32-33.

[37]Henry Mancini, telephone interview, 27 Jan. 1992.

[38]Field 38.

[39]*America* 111.533 (31 Oct. 1964): 533.

[40]Godfrey 46.

[41]Ibid.

[42]Archer Winsten, *New York Post* 8 Oct. 1964.

[43]Philip T. Hartung, *The Commonweal* 81 (23 Oct. 1964): 136.

[44]Ibid.

[45]*Newsweek* 64 (26 Oct. 1964): 118.

[46]A.H. Weiler, "The Screen: An American 'Rashomon': Paul Newman Starred in 'The Outrage,' *The New York Times* 8 Oct. 1964.

[47]Ibid.

[48]At least by 1992, *The Outrage* had not been released on videotape.

[49]Frank R. Cunningham, *Sidney Lumet: Film and Literary Vision* (Lexington: The University Press of Kentucky, 1992) 236.

[50]Ray Olson, *Minnesota Daily* 27 Oct. 1972.

[51]James Proctor, letter to Martin Ritt, 20 Sept. 1966, Herrick Library.

[52]Richard Shepherd, letter to Martin Ritt, 12 Dec. 1963, Herrick Library.

[53]Ibid.

[54]Billy Rose, letter to Martin Ritt, 20 July 1965, Herrick Library.

[55]Martin Ritt, letter to Brendan Gill, 11 Jan. 1966, Herrick Library.

[56]Carl Seith, letter to Martin Ritt, 2 Dec. 1966, Herrick Library.

[57]*The Daily Worker* 8 Mar. 1966.

[58]*Current Biography* 311.

[59]Dilys Powell, *The Sunday Times* (London) 16 Jan. 1966.

[60]Claman article, Ritt household, Pacific Palisades, CA.

[61]Ibid.

[62]Ibid.

[63]Patricia Neal, letter to the author, Fall 1991.

[64]Roald Dahl, letter to Martin Ritt, n.d. 1965, Herrick Library.

[65]*The New York Times* 2 Jan. 1966.

[66]James Wong Howe, letter to Martin Ritt, 25 Sept. 1964, Herrick Library.

[67]*Toronto Daily Star* 11 Dec. 1965.

[68]For more on Ritt's relationship with Richard Burton, and how Ritt successfully transformed le Carré's novel into a film, see

Karen M. Radell, "The Triumph of Realism Over Glamour: Martin Ritt's Realization of Le Carre's *The Spy Who Came In From the Cold, Proceedings of the Fifth Annual Conference on Films, Kent State University,* 7-8 Apr. 1987: 192-97.

[69]Claman article.

[70]Ibid.

[71]Ibid.

[72]*New York Herald Tribune* 10 Mar. 1965.

[73]John le Carré, letter to the author, 20 Mar. 1991.

[74]Ibid.

[75]According to Cynthia Grenier, *New York Herald Tribune* 9 Mar. 1965, Ritt paid $38,000 for the film rights to *The Spy Who Came In From the Cold.*

[76]le Carré to the author, 20 Mar. 1991.

[77]*The New York Herald Tribune* 9 Mar. 1965.

[78]Claman article.

[79]Neil Simon, telephone interview, 17 Sept. 1991.

[80]Jerry Bresler, letter to Martin Ritt, n.d. 1965, Herrick Library.

[81]Verne Llewellyn, letter to Martin Ritt, n.d. 1965, Herrick Library.

[82]Ritt folder on *The Spy Who Came In From the Cold,* Herrick Library.

[83]Annette Savory, letter to Martin Ritt, 14 Jan. 1966, Herrick Library.

[84]John Carlino, letter to Martin Ritt, 30 Dec. 1965, Herrick Library.

[85]Kim del Conte, letter to Martin Ritt, 9 Feb. 1966, Herrick Library.

[86]Martin Ritt, letter to Oskar Werner, 31 Dec. 1965, Herrick Library.

[87]Dilys Powell, *The Sunday Times* (London) 16 Jan. 1966.

[88]Alta Maloney, *The Boston Traveler* 24 Dec. 1965.

[89]Peter Bart, *The New York Times* 2 Jan. 1966.

[90]*News and Observer* (Raleigh, NC) 11 Apr. 1966.

[91]Stanley Kauffmann, *The New Republic* 1 Jan. 1966. On 21 Jan. 1991, a little over a month after Ritt's death, Kauffmann paid this tribute to Ritt and *Spy:* "He . . . made the best film version of a le Carré novel (Yes, I've seen *The Russia House*). If you want to see an exceptionally fine film this evening, rent the tape of *The Spy Who Came In From the Cold.*

[92]*Washington Post* 15 Dec. 1965.

[93]*The Christian Science Monitor* 2 Jan. 1965.

[94]Richard Roud, *The Guardian* 14 Jan. 1966.

[95]Jeff Millar, *Houston Chronicle* 30 Dec. 1965.

[96]Blume, letter to Martin Ritt, 8 Apr. 1966, Herrick Library.

[97]Cynthia Grenier, *New York Herald Tribune* 9 Mar. 1965.

Chapter 5

[1]Paul Newman, interview, Westport, CT, 3 June 1991.

[2]For Zane Grey's views of the desert, see Carlton Jackson, *Zane Grey* (Boston: Twayne, 1973; rev. ed. 1989).

[3]Joe Morella and Edward Z. Epstein, *Paul & Joanne: A Biography of Paul Newman and Joanne Woodward* (New York: Delacorte Press, 1988) 116.

[4]Ibid.

[5]Ralph Hicklin, *The Globe and Mail* 30 Mar. 1967.

[6]Marjory Adams, *The Boston Sunday Globe*, 2 Apr. 1967.

[7]Adele Ritt, letter to Sigmund M. Hyman, 15 Aug. 1966, Herrick Library.

[8]Claman article, Ritt household, Pacific Palisades, CA.

[9]Michaela Williams, *Chicago Daily News* 31 Mar. 1967.

[10]Owen McClean, letter to Louis F. Goldman, 15 July 1966, Herrick Library.

[11]American Humane Society, letter to Martin Ritt, 24 Jan. 1966, Herrick Library.

[12]Frank Ferguson, letter to Martin Ritt, 19 Jan. 1966, Herrick Library.

[13]G.C. Chapman, *The Daily Reflector* (Greenville, NC), 5 May 1966. See also *Bethel* (NC) *Herald* about the Lathams, visiting *Hombre* sets as guests of Martin Ritt.

[14]Latham diary, 1966.

[15]Ibid.

[16]Ibid.

[17]Seymour Poe, letter to Irving Ravetch, 8 Feb. 1967, Herrick Library.

[18]Irving Ravetch, letter to Seymour Poe, 3 Feb. 1967, Herrick Library.

[19]Ibid.

[20]Sydney Field, letter to Martin Ritt, 13 Apr. 1967, Herrick Library.

[21]Sidney Cosson, letter to Martin Ritt, undated, *Hombre* files, Herrick Library.

[22]Henry Rogers, letter to Martin Ritt, 1 Mar. 1967, Herrick Library.

[23]Richard Guttman, letter to Martin Ritt, 28 Feb. 1968, Herrick Library.

[24]Stanley Meyer, letter to Martin Ritt, 28 Feb. 1967, Herrick Library.

[25]Julio Mario Ronco, letter to Martin Ritt, Feb. 1966, Herrick Library.

[26]*The New Statesman* 14 Apr. 1967.

[27]Bosley Crowther, *The New York Times* 22 Mar. 1967.

[28]*Los Angeles Times* 26 Apr. 1966.

[29]*Chicago Tribune* 16 Apr. 1967.

[30]Arthur Groman, letter to Kirk Douglas, 6 Feb. 1967, Herrick Library.

[31]Ibid.

[32]Efforts by the author to contact Kirk Douglas on this and other matters have been futile.

[33]Maurizio Lodi-fe, letter to Martin Ritt, 5 Aug. 1967, Herrick Library.

[34]Kirk Douglas, letter to Martin Ritt, 4 Aug. 1967, Herrick Library.

[35]Douglas to Ritt, 24 June 1967, Herrick Library.

[36]Douglas, letter to Charles Boasberg (of Paramount Studios), 20 Aug. 1968, Herrick Library.

[37]Henry Rogers, letter to Martin Ritt, 18 Dec. 1968, Herrick Library.

[38]Robert Evans, letter to Martin Ritt, undated, 1968, Herrick Library.

[39]Don Safran, *Dallas Times Herald* 1 Jan. 1969.

[40]John Neville, *The Dallas Morning News* 2 Jan.1969.

[41]Ted Mahar, *The Oregonian* 1 Jan. 1969.

[42]E.B. Radcliffe, *Cincinnati Enquirer* 6 Dec. 1968.

[43]*Boston Record-American* 21 Dec. 1968.

[44]Vincent Canby, *The New York Times* 17 Jan. 1969.

[45]Pauline Kael, *The New Yorker* 44.95 (25 Jan. 1969): 97.

[46]Joseph Jordon, letter to Martin Ritt, 30 Dec. 1968, Herrick Library.

[47]Ibid.

[48]Ibid.

[49]Godfrey Smith, letter to Martin Ritt, 24 May 1967, Herrick Library.

[50]Ibid.

[51]Martin Ritt, letter to Arthur Miller, 4 Nov. 1968, Herrick Library.

[52]Howard Kane, letter to Martin Ritt, 1 Mar. 1968, Herrick Library.

[53]*Sunday Times* (London) 2 June 1968.

[54]See Joseph P. Rayback, *A History of American Labor* (New York: The Free Press, 1966) 132-33.

[55]Ibid. 133.

[56]Ibid.

[57]Martin Ritt, letter to Walter F. Kraus, Jr., 19 Feb. 1968, Herrick Library.

[58]Wayne G. Broehl, Jr., *The Molly Maguires* (Cambridge: Harvard University Press, 1964).

[59]Frederic M. Philips, letter to Martin Ritt, 25 Sept. 1968, Herrick Library.

[60]Allan Pinkerton was a native of Glascow, Scotland, born 25 Aug. 1819. In 1842 he married Joan Carfrae, and immigrated to the United States. In 1850 he established his detective agency, and 1850-51 was the first detective on the Chicago police force. In 1860 he established Pinkerton's Preventive Watch, and the next year, organized the first secret service division of the U.S. Army. From 1861 to 1862, he was the first chief of the U.S. secret service. He died on 1 July 1884 in Chicago.

The papers of Pinkerton's National Detective Agency were given to the Library of Congress in 1956 by Robert A. Pinkerton, and the Library purchased supplementary material in 1972. The agency's literary rights in these papers were "dedicated to the public," except that until 1 July 1980, researchers wanting to use the material had to gain the permission of the managers of the agency or Robert Pinkerton himself. For the past dozen years or so, the restrictions that operated against Broehl and Lewis, and indeed the makers of *The Molly Maguires,* have not been applicable.

The Molly Maguires was the last case Allan Pinkerton personally handled. A report of 24 Jan. 1875 by Benjamin Franklin, superintendent of Pinkerton's Philadelphia branch, recounted the movements and statements of James McParlan, the operative "who infiltrated the Molly Maguires." Report, Library of Congress Manuscript Division, "The Papers of Pinkerton's National Detective Agency."

[61]See the *Pottsville* (PA) *Republican* 8 Apr. 1968.

[62]See Carlton Jackson, *The Dreadful Month* (Bowling Green, OH: Bowling Green State University Popular Press, 1982) for detail on mine conditions in the United States.

[63]Netti Postupack, letter to Martin Ritt, 21 July 1968, Herrick Library.

[64]J.P., letter to Martin Ritt, n.d., 1968, Herrick Library.

[65]Martin Ritt, in a questionnaire from "Ivan," Watford, Hertfordshire, England, 17 Oct. 1968.

[66]Henry Mancini, telephone interview, 28 Jan. 1992.

[67]Bobbi Ann Warren, letter to Martin Ritt, 27 May 1968, Herrick Library.

[68]Senior Class, Wyoming Valley West High School, letter to Martin Ritt, May 1968, Herrick Library.

[69]Kathleen Reimold, letter to Martin Ritt, 28 May 1968, Herrick Library.

[70]Richard Tomasko, letter to Martin Ritt, 19 May 1968, Herrick Library.

[71]Anthony Reznak, Jr., letter to Martin Ritt, 20 May 1968, Herrick Library.

[72]Clem McGinley, letter to Martin Ritt, 7 May 1968, Herrick Library.

[73]Fred Henry, letter to Martin Ritt, 16 Aug. 1968, Herrick Library.

[74]Bernardine Logo, letter to Martin Ritt, 28 May 1968, Herrick Library.

[75]Andra K. Brandt, letter to Martin Ritt, 6 May 1968, Herrick Library.

[76]Martin Ritt, letter to Beatrice Straight, 28 Mar. 1968, Herrick Library.

[77]Joseph F. Clark, *Congressional Record* 90th Cong., 2nd sess. (18 Apr. 1968): 10015.

[78]Joe F. Sloan, letter to Martin Ritt, 24 May 1968, Herrick Library.

[79]Bradner Petersen, letter to Martin Ritt, 25 Jan. 1968, Herrick Library.

[80]Ibid.

[81]Bradner Petersen, letter to E. Compton Timberlake, 25 Jan. 1968, Herrick Library.

[82]Ibid.

[83]Law firm of Royal Koegel, Rogers, and Wells, letter to Paramount Pictures, 19 Apr. 1968, Herrick Library.

[84]Ralph Kamon, letter to Martin Ritt, 9 Aug. 1968, Herrick Library.

[85]Ibid.

[86]Herbert C. Earnshaw, letter to E. Compton Timberlake, 12 Sept. 1968, Herrick Library.

[87]Ibid.

[88]Pauline Kael, review of *The Molly Maguires, The New Yorker* 45.91 (7 Feb. 1970).

[89]Philip Bonosky, review of *The Molly Maguires, The Daily World* (New York) 11 Feb. 1970.

[90]*Boston Herald-Traveler* 13 Feb, 1970.

[91]Thomas Blakley, *Pittsburgh Press* 11 Feb. 1970.

[92]Ruth Melhado, letter to Martin Ritt, 30 Jan. 1970, Herrick Library.

[93]Pat Aufderheide, "A Mensch for All Seasons," *In These Times* 1980: 16-22.

[94]Martin Ritt, letter to Pierre Rissient, 6 July 1970, Herrick Library.

[95]*Christian Science Monitor* 11 Feb. 1970.

[96]*San Francisco Chronicle* 20 Feb. 1970.

[97]Lyn Goldfarb and Anatoli Michael Ilyashov, interview of Martin Ritt, Ritt household, Pacific Palisades, CA, 1990.

[98]Ibid.

[99]In August 1969 Ritt sent Bernstein a birthday greeting. "Just in case you should be startled by the fact that I know your birth date," Ritt told his friend, "be aware that your lovely wife informed

me. As we both know, there are informers and informers." Martin
Ritt, letter to Walter Bernstein, 11 Aug. 1969, Herrick Library.

[100]Roger Ebert, review of *The Molly Maguires*, *Chicago Sun
Times* 20 Nov. 1970.

[101]Ibid.

[102]Gene Siskel, review of *The Molly Maguires*, *Chicago Tribune*
25 Nov. 1970.

[103]Ibid.

Chapter 6

[1]Carlton Moss, "The Great White Hope," *Freedomways* 2nd qtr.
1969: 128.

[2]Ibid.

[3]Martin Ritt, interview with Jack Hirschberg, Ritt household,
Pacific Palisades, CA, Sept. 1969.

[4]Ibid.

[5]Martin Ritt, letter to Flora Roberts, 6 Feb. 1969, Herrick
Library.

[6]Production notes on *The Great White Hope*, Herrick Library.

[7]Ibid.

[8]Ibid.

[9]Ibid.

[10]Ibid.

[11]Neill Ross, *Today's Cinema* 6 Jan. 1970.

[12]*Variety* 9 Oct. 1970.

[13]*San Francisco Chronicle* 24 Oct. 1970.

[14]*Time* 19 Oct. 1970.

[15]*The Boston Herald Traveler* 21 Dec. 1970.

[16]William Collins, *The Philadelphia Inquirer* 24 Dec. 1970.

[17]Ibid.

[18]Pauline Kael, *The New Yorker* 17 Oct. 1970.

[19]Ibid.

[20]*San Francisco Examiner* 25 Dec. 1970.

[21]Carrie Rickey, "The Long Hot Career," *Fame* Winter 1990:
40.

[22]Ibid.

[23]*Memphis Press-Scimitar* 29 Mar. 1974.

[24]Ibid.

[25]Ibid.

[26]Martin Ritt, *New York Times* Oral History Program, The
American Film Institute Seminars, Part I (Glen Rock, NJ:
Microfilming Corporation of America, 1977) 38.

[27]Gary Arnold, *The Arizona Republic* 7 Jan. 1973.

[28]Arthur Knight, *Salt Lake City Tribune* 29 Sept. 1972.

[29]Roger Greenspun, *The New York Times* 25 Sept. 1972.

[30]John A. Alonzo, interview, Los Angeles, 9 May 1991. Also Robert Radnitz, telephone interview, 20 Nov. 1991.

[31]Ellen Holly, *The New York Times* 15 Oct. 1972.

[32]Ibid.

[33]Ray Olson, *Minnesota Daily* 27 Oct. 1972.

[34]Will Jones, *Minneapolis Tribune* 23 Sept. 1972.

[35]Alonzo, interview.

[36]Ibid.

[37]Radnitz, interview, 20 Nov. 1991.

[38]Will Jones, *Minneapolis Tribune* 23 Sept. 1973.

[39]David Whitman, "The Great Sharecropper Success Story," *The Public Interest* 104 (Summer 1991): 3-19.

[40]Ross Martin, letter to Martin Ritt, 9 Jan. 1973, Herrick Library.

[41]Delbert Mann, letter to Martin Ritt, 13 Mar. 1973, Herrick Library.

[42]Susan Hamner, letter to Martin Ritt, 28 Sept. 1972, Herrick Library.

[43]Julian Lewis, letter to Martin Ritt, 13 Oct. 1972, Herrick Library.

[44]Ossie Davis, letter to Michael Wright, 12 Dec. 1972, Herrick Library.

[45]Raymond Schiff, letter to Martin Ritt, 3 Apr. 1973, Herrick Library.

[46]David Niven, letter to Martin Ritt, 12 Nov. 1972, Herrick Library.

[47]Ibid.

[48]Jack Lemmon, letter to Martin Ritt, 31 Oct. 1972, Herrick Library.

[49]Ibid.

[50]Joel Fluellen, letter to Martin Ritt, 17 Oct. 1972, Herrick Library. The author wishes to pay a tribute to Joel Fluellen. When I was working on a previous book, *Hattie: The Life of Hattie McDaniel*, Mr. Fluellen granted me several interviews, telephoned me on occasion with information about his friend Hattie McDaniel, and in many other ways directed me away from error in my treatment of the star who was the first black ever to win an Oscar—for her supporting role as "Mammy" in *Gone With the Wind*. Mr. Fluellen died in 1990.

[51]Martin Ritt, letter to Joel Fluellen, 24 Oct. 1972, Herrick Library.

[52]Mrs. Perrye Lewis, letter to Martin Ritt, 4 Oct. 1971, Herrick Library.

[53]Martin Ritt, letter to Perrye Lewis, 22 Oct. 1971, Herrick Library.

[54]*Congressional Record* 92nd Cong., 2nd sess. (16-18 Oct. 1972): 37,628.

[55]Ibid. 37,629.

[56]*Congressional Record* 93rd Cong., 1st sess. (15-22 Mar. 1973): 8,020.

[57]*Congressional Record* 93rd Cong., 1st sess. (7-14 Mar. 1973) 6,904.

[58]Ibid.

[59]Ibid.

[60]Wayne Warga, "Ritt a Tough Director Who Melted with 'Sounder,'" *Los Angeles Times* 15 Oct. 1972.

[61]Ibid.

[62]Russell J. Light, *Iconoclast*, 5-12 Apr. 1974. Also *New York Times Oral History Program; The American Film Institute Seminars* (Glen Rock, NJ: Microfilming Corporation of America, 1977) 37.

[63]*Congressional Record* 92nd Cong., 2nd sess. (16-18 Oct. 1972): 37,629.

[64]*Philadelphia Daily Planet* 3-10 Oct. 1972.

[65]Martin Ritt, letter to Seymour Peck, 18 Oct. 1972, Herrick Library.

[66]Ibid.

[67]Ibid.

[68]For a full discussion of the "Hollywood Bureau," see Carlton Jackson, *Hattie: The Life of Hattie McDaniel* (Lanham, MD: Madison Books, 1990).

[69]Malcolm Boyd, *Los Angeles Times* 8 Oct. 1972.

[70]Warga, *Los Angeles Times* 15 Oct. 1972.

[71]ACLU, letter to Martin Ritt, Oct. 1972, Herrick Library.

[72]Pauline Kael, "The Current Cinema: Soul Food," *The New Yorker* 30 Sept. 1972: 109.

[73]Ibid.

[74]*Hollywood Reporter* 15 Aug. 1972.

[75]Donia Mills, *The Evening Star and Daily News* (Washington, DC) 20 Oct. 1972.

[76]Martin Knelman, *Toronto Globe and Mail* 23 Sept. 1972.

[77]Charles Champlin, *Los Angeles Times* 8 Oct. 1972.

[78]*The Christian Science Monitor* 25 Sept. 1972.

[79]Ibid.

[80]William B. Collins, *The Philadelphia Inquirer* 19 Oct. 1972.

[81]Joe Baltake, *Philadelphia Daily News* 18 Oct. 1972.

[82]Vincent Canby, *The New York Times* 12 Nov. 1972.

[83]*The New York Times* 26 Nov. 1972.

[84]Roger Greenspun, *The New York Times* 25 Sept. 1972.

[85]Ibid.

[86]Ellen Holly, *The New York Times* 15 Oct. 1972.

[87]*Time* 9 Oct. 1972.

[88]*Newsweek* 2 Oct. 1972.

[89]*Show Film Reviews* Nov. 1972.

[90]Lillian Warren, *Twin Cities Courier* 22 Sept. 1972.

[91]Bruce Cook, *The National Observer* 21 Oct. 1972.

[92]Irwin Silber, *The Guardian* 11 Oct. 1972.

[93]Ibid.

[94]Patrick Gibbs, *The Daily Telegraph* 16 Feb. 1973.

[95]Alexander Walker, *The Evening Standard* 15 Feb. 1972.

[96]*The Daily Mirror* 16 Feb. 1973.

[97]Ralph Nelson, letter to Martin Ritt, 20 Feb. 1973, Herrick Library.

[98]Richard Morris, telegram to Martin Ritt, Mar. 1973, Herrick Library.

[99]Charles LaTorre, letter to Martin Ritt, Mar. 1973, Herrick Library.

[100]Ibid.

[101]Carl Foreman, telegram to Martin Ritt, 11 Mar. 1973, Herrick Library.

[102]Martin Ritt, telegram to Carl Foreman, 12 Mar. 1973, Herrick Library.

[103]Martin Knelman, *Toronto Globe and Mail* 12 Oct. 1972.

[104]In 1976, *Sounder II* appeared, directed by William Graham. It was about David Lee trying to start a neighborhood school. Richard Eder, in *The New York Times*, 14 Oct. 1976, said the movie had "enough unleavened sentimentality to give a rhinoceros heartburn."

[105]John Alonzo, interview.

[106]Burrell, interview. Also, Jimmy Carter, letter to the author, June 1991. President Carter said further about Martin Ritt: "Later, on a visit to L.A. to attract other films, I visited M. Ritt in his home and he helped me make Georgia an attractive place to produce movies."

[107]*New York Times Oral History Program*: AFI, 50-51. Ritt complimented his chief photographer: "John Alonzo is a very good camaraman who has done a great many documentaries. He's a part of the team."

[108]Ibid.

[109]Burrell, interview.

[110]Alonzo, interview.

[111]*New York Times Oral History Project*, AFI 7.

[112]Ibid.

[113]*Chicago Tribune* 29 Mar. 1974.

[114]Ibid. 8.

[115]*Boston Sunday Globe*, 17 Mar. 1974.

[116]Jet Fore, letter to Martin Ritt, 27 Feb. 1974, Herrick Library.

[117]David Hartman, letter to Martin Ritt, 29 Sept. 1975, Herrick Library.

[118]Martin Ritt, letter to David Hartman, 20 Oct. 1975, Herrick Library.

[119]George Shdanoff, letter to Martin Ritt, 29 Jan. 1974, Herrick Library.

[120]Ibid.

[121]Ibid.

[122]Thomas Bass, letter to Martin Ritt, undated, 1974, Herrick Library.

[123]Hume Cronyn, letter to Martin Ritt, 13 June 1974, Herrick Library. One critic did not like Cronyn's performance as the school superintendent. He said that Cronyn's performance was disappointing. "In this part he acts instead of creating a new character." Shdanoff to Ritt, 29 Jan. 1974. Cronyn recently (1992) said of Ritt: "I knew Martin Ritt for over 40 years. I liked him, admired him, and considered him a militant friend." Hume Cronyn, letter to the author, n.d., 1992.

[124]Gordon Stulberg, letter to Martin Ritt, 4 Feb. 1974, Herrick Library.

[125]Chicago *Sun Times* 14 June 1974.

[126]Ibid.

[127]Ronnie Harris, letter to Martin Ritt, n.d., 1974, Herrick Library.

[128]Madge Sinclair, letter to Martin Ritt, 20 Mar. 1974, Herrick Library.

[129]Rebecca Cobb, letter to Martin Ritt, 16 Mar. 1974, Herrick Library.

[130]Martin Ritt, letter to Rebecca Cobb, 2 Apr. 1974, Herrick Library.

[131]Kathy Turner, letter to Martin Ritt, undated, 1974, Herrick Libary.

[132]Ibid.

[133]Martin Ritt, letter to Kathy Turner, 21 May 1974, Herrick Library.

[134]Pauline Kael, *The New Yorker* 11 Mar. 1974.

[135]Russell Light, *Iconoclast* 12 May 1974.

[136]A.R. Weiler, 8 Oct. 1972.

[137]Eugenia Collier, *The New York Times* 21 Apr. 1974.

[138]Ibid.

[139]Edwin Howard, *Memphis Press-Scimitar* 6 Apr. 1974.

[140]Martin Ritt, letter to Edwin Howard, 16 Apr. 1974, Herrick Library.

[141]Ibid.

[142]Jim Stingley, "Real 'Conrack': Evolution of a Country Boy," *Los Angeles Times* 12 Apr. 1974.

[143]Ibid.

[144]Ibid.

[145]Ibid.

[146]Ibid.

[147]Pat Conroy, telegram to Martin Ritt, 13 Apr. 1974, Herrick Library.

[148]Irving Ravetch and Harriet Frank, Jr., interview, Los Angeles, 11 May 1992.

[149]Pat Conroy, letter to Martin Ritt, Apr. 1974, Herrick Library.

[150]Ibid.

[151]Ibid.

[152]Pat Conroy, letter to Martin Ritt, Irving Ravetch, and Harriet Frank, Jr., 24 Apr. 1974, Herrick Library.

[153]Pat Conroy, letter to the *Los Angeles Times* 28 Apr. 1974.

[154]Ibid.

[155]Ibid.

[156]Martin Ritt, letter to Pat Conroy, 28 Apr. 1974, Herrick Library.

[157]Ibid. Apparently, Conroy does not wish today (early 1990s) to comment on these events, as several letters from the author to him have gone unanswered.

Chapter 7

[1]Stanley Eichelbaum, *San Francisco Sunday Examiner & Chronicle* 28 May 1972.

[2]Ibid.

[3]Joanne Woodward, letter to Martin Ritt, May 1972, Ritt household.

[4]Martin Ritt, letter to Joanne Woodward, 8 June 1972, Ritt household.

[5]David Elliott, *Chicago Daily News* 23 Dec. 1972.

[6]*Newsweek* 1 Jan. 1973.

[7]Rich Brough, *Daily Utah Chronicle* 22 Dec. 1972.

[8]Susan Stark, *Detroit Free Press* 23 Dec. 1972.

[9]*The Financial Times* 16 Mar. 1973.

[10]Richard Barkley, *Sunday Express* 18 Mar. 1973.

[11]*Daily Telegram* 16 Mar. 1973.

[12]Ian Christie, *Daily Express* 14 Mar. 1973.

[13]*Sunday Telegraph* 13 Mar. 1973.

[14]John Laycock, *Windsor Star* 28 Dec. 1972.

[15]Jane Fonda, telephone interview by the author, 29 May 1991.

[16]Ibid.

[17]Charles Champlin, *The Los Angeles Times* 17 Dec. 1972.

[18]Ibid.

[19]George McKinnon, *The Boston Globe* 23 Dec. 1972.

[20]*Herald Traveler and Boston Record American* 22 Dec. 1972.

[21]Rex Reed, *Sunday News* 22 Dec. 1972.

[22]*The New Yorker* 30 Dec. 1972.

[23]By 1992, for example, *Pete 'n Tillie* had not yet been issued on videotape for home viewing. Nor is it shown anymore in cinemas or late-night TV movies. The author saw *Pete 'n Tillie* at the Library of Congress in Washington, DC. The library has an entire inventory of Ritt's films, both the ones he directed and the one in which he acted.

[24]*Buffalo Courier-Express* 4 Mar. 1979.

[25]"Within Martin Ritt Lurks a Good Guy," *Biography News Washington Star-News* (Washington, DC) 26 Mar. 1974.

[26]Martin Ritt, letter to Sheila Whittaker, 26 Dec. 1973, Herrick Library.

[27]Edward Spivia, letter to Martin Ritt, 23 Aug. 1973, Herrick Library.

[28]Martin Ritt, letter to Victor Sherle and William Turner Levy, 20 Sept. 1974.

[29]Aljean Harmetz, *The New York Times* 25 Feb. 1979.

[30]Walter Matthau, telephone interview by Matthew Jackson (author's son), 11 Feb. 1992.

[31]Ibid.

[32]Ibid.

[33]Wanda Hale, *Sunday News* 26 Nov. 1972.

[34]*The New York Times* 25 Feb. 1979.

[35]Roald Dahl, letter to Martin Ritt, 28 Nov. 1974, Herrick Library.

[36]Martin Ritt, letter to Roald Dahl, 3 Feb. 1975.

[37]*The New York Times* 25 Feb. 1979.

[38]Herbert Rubensohn, interview, New York, 26 May 1992.

[39]Martin Ritt, letter to Marguerite Sausville, 20 Sept. 1974, Ritt household.

[40]*Buffalo Courier Express* 4 Mar. 1979.

[41]*Daily News* (New York) 13 May 1976.

[42]*Los Angeles Examiner* 23 May 1976.

[43]*Daily News* 5 May 1976.

[44]Richard Eder, *The New York Times* 13 May 1976.

[45]Richard Cuskelly, *Los Angeles Herald Examiner* 23 May 1976.

[46]Ibid.

[47]Richard Eder, *The New York Times* 13 May 1976.

[48]*Saturday Review* 15 May 1976.

[49]*Globe & Mail* 12 May 1976.

[50]Mary Steenburgen, telephone interview by the author, 11 June 1991.

[51]Harriet Conrad, letter to the author, 4 June 1991.

[52]Rubensohn, interview, 26 May 1992.

[53]Thomas Meehan, "Woody Allen in a Comedy About Black-listing? Don't Laugh," *The New York Times* 7 Dec. 1975.

[54]Walter Bernstein, interview, New York, 28 May 1992.

[55]Ibid.

[56]Pat McGilligan, "Ritt Large: Martin Ritt, interviewed," *Film Comment* 22 (Feb. 1986): 43.

[57]*The New York Times* 7 Dec. 1975.

[58]Martin Ritt, interview by Lyn Goldfarb and Anatoli Michael Ilyashov, Ritt household, 1990.

[59]Martin Ritt, letter to Robert D. Kasmire, 17 July 1975, Herrick Libary.

[60]*The New York Times* 7 Dec. 1975.

[61]Ibid.

[62]Hirschberg, interview, Ritt household, Sept. 1969.

[63]Goldbarb and Ilyashov, interview, Ritt household, 1990.

[64]Fort Worth *Star Telegram* 17 Oct. 1976.

[65]*The New York Times* 3 Oct. 1976.

[66]Martin Ritt, letter to Becky Wild, 6 Jan. 1976, Herrick Library.

[67]*Films Illustrated* (London) Jan. 1976: 187.

[68]Martin Ritt, letter to Leo Jaffe, 15 Jan. 1976.

[69]Fred Wellington, letter to Martin Ritt, 17 Feb. 1977.

[70]Ibid.

[71]Martin Ritt, letter to Fred Wellington, 7 Mar. 1977, Herrick Library.

[72]Perry Bruskin, letter to Martin Ritt, 15 Sept. 1977, Herrick Library.

[73]Ibid.

[74]Arthur Mayer, letter to Martin Ritt, 1 Feb. 1977, Herrick Library.

[75]Edward Eliscu, letter to Martin Ritt, 4 Nov. 1976, Herrick Library.

[76]Ibid.

[77]Shepard Traube, letter to Martin Ritt, 19 Oct. 1976, Herrick Library.

[78]Lee Steiner, letter to Alan Hirshfield, n.d., 1976, Herrick Library.

[79]Laura Bock, letter to Martin Ritt, 15 Nov. 1976, Herrick Library.

[80]Henry Hack, letter to Martin Ritt, 3 Nov. 1976, Herrick Library.

[81]Roger Woodis, letter to Martin Ritt, 25 Feb. 1977, Herrick Library.

[82]John P. McLaughlin, letter to Martin Ritt, 22 Nov. 1976, Herrick Library.

[83]Dino De Laurentiis, telegram to Martin Ritt, Oct. 1976, Herrick Library.

[84]*The New Yorker* 4 Oct. 1976.

[85]Ted Allen, letter to Martin Ritt, 24 Sept. 1976, Herrick Library.

[86]Frank Rich, *New York Post* 1 Oct. 1976.

[87]*Variety* 9 Sept. 1976.

[88]*The Boston Phoenix* 5 Oct. 1976.

[89]*The Christian Science Monitor* 1 Oct. 1976.

[90]Judith Crist, *Saturday Review* 2 Oct. 1976.

[91]*The Times Picayune* (New Orleans) 23 Oct. 1976.

[92]Vincent Canby, *The New York Times* 1 Oct. 1976.

[93]Bernstein, interview.

[94]Martin Ritt, letter to David Golding, 2 Nov. 1976.

[95]Martin Ritt, letter to Mr. and Mrs. David Shaw, 5 Nov. 1976, Herrick Library.

[96]Ibid.

[97]Martin Ritt, letter to Dagmar Hirtz, of Munich, Germany, 2 Feb. 1977, Herrick Library. Hilton Kramer, "The Blacklist and the Cold War," *The New York Times* 3 Oct. 1976.

[98]Martin Ritt, letter to Nancy Green, 16 Nov. 1976, Herrick Library.

[99]Ibid.

[100]Arthur Schlesinger, Jr., letter to the author, 8 July 1991.

[101]Ibid.

[102]Lillian Hellman, *Scoundrel Time* (Boston: Little Brown, 1976).

[103]Ibid. Arthur Schlesinger, letter to the editor, *The New York Times*, 17 Oct. 1976.

[104]Ibid. Schlesinger said: "Had I known that Kramer was (or was soon to become) an irritating rightwing ideologue, I doubt that I would have bothered to write; but I was only aware of him at that time as an art critic. I still think his slant on the 1940s was about right."

[105]Hilton Kramer, "The Blacklist and the Cold War," *The New York Times* 3 Oct. 1976.

[106]Schlesinger to the author, 8 July 1991. "I have met Kramer only once in my life," Schlesinger said, "and do not regard him as kind of ally or soulmate."

[107]Ibid. McCarthy attacked Schlesinger in a nationwide telecast in 1952.

[108]Ibid.

[109]James Quivey, letter to the author, 18 June 1991.

[110]Ibid.

[111]Ibid.

[112]Ibid.

[113]Ibid.

[114]Morella and Epstein, *Paul and Joanne* 57.

[115]Martin Ritt, letter to Rebecca Wild, 31 Mar. 1977, EIU English Department and Herrick Library.

[116]Martin Ritt, letter to James Quivey, 19 Apr. 1977, EIU English Department.

[117]*The New York Times* 1 Apr. 1978.

[118]David McClintick, *Indecent Exposure* (New York: William Morrow & Co., 1982) 199-200. McClintick's book on the Begelman affair remains the definitive work on the subject.

[119]Ibid.

[120]Ibid.

[121]Martin Ritt, letter to Robert Elias, 17 Jan. 1978, Herrick Library.

[122]"Ritt Large: Martin Ritt, interviewed by Pat McGilligan," *Film Content* 22 (Feb. 1986): 39.

[123]Martin Ritt, letter to Mike Wallace, 12 Jan. 1978, Herrick Library.

[124]McGilligan 39.

[125]Ibid.

[126]Mike Wallace, telephone interview by the author, 9 Dec. 1991.

[127]McClintick 200.

[128]According to some Hollywood gossip, Robertson's career suffered because he blew the whistle on Begelman.

[129]Jeanie Kasindorf, "The Incredible Past of David Begelman," *New West* 13 Feb. 1978.

[130]Ibid.

[131]Ibid.

[132]Ibid.

[133]Martin Ritt, letter to Jeanie Kasindorf, 21 Feb. 1978, Herrick Library.

[134]Ibid.

[135]Ibid.

[136]Martin Ritt, letter to Sid Luft, 2 Feb. 1978, Herrick Library.

[137]*Herald Tribune* (New York) 4 Apr. 1966.

[138]Martin Ritt, letter to Scott MacDonough, 1 Apr. 1977, Herrick Library.

[139]Dexter Masters, *The Accident* (London: Penquin, 1985) i.

[140]Ibid.

[141]Ibid.

[142]Dexter Masters, letter to Martin Ritt, 23 Mar. 1977, Herrick Library.

[143]Ibid.

[144]Martin Ritt, letter to Dexter Masters, 31 Mar. 1977, Herrick Library.

[145]Martin Ritt, letter to William Goldman, 8 Mar. 1977, Herrick Library.

[146]Martin Ritt, letter to Tim McDowell, 27 June 1977, Herrick Library.

Chapter 8

[1]Thomas W. Downer, letter to S. Lesser, 10 Aug. 1976, Herrick Library.

[2]Martin Ritt, letter to Ray Stark, 3 Jan. 1978, Herrick Library.

[3]Ibid.

[4]Ibid.

[5]Martin Ritt, letter to Bob Dudich, 10 Apr. 1978, Herrick Library.

[6]Ibid.

[7]Martin Ritt, letter to Ray Stark, 28 Mar. 1978, Herrick Library.

[8]David Sterritt, *The Christian Science Monitor* 10 Mar. 1978.

[9]G. William Jones, letter to Mary Kay Powell, 13 Mar. 1978, Herrick Library.

[10]*Los Angeles Times* 12 Mar. 1978.

[11]David Ansen, *Newsweek* 27 Mar. 1978.

[12]*The Christian Science Monitor* 10 Mar. 1978.

[13]*Playboy* Mar. 1978.

[14]Ibid.

[15]Vincent Canby, *The New York Times* 17 Mar. 1978.

[16]*Valley News* 17 Mar. 1978.

[17]Ibid.

[18]Goldfarb and Ilyashov, interview.

[19]*Herald Examiner* 8 Feb. 1981.

[20]*The New York Times* 25 Feb. 1979.

[21]*Washington* (DC) *Star* 7 Mar. 1979.

[22]*American Film* Nov. 1983.

[23]Tom Sweeten, *The Knoxville Journal* 9 Mar. 1979.

[24]Ibid.

[25]Ibid.

[26]*The Boston Globe* 13 Mar. 1979.

[27]Ibid.

[28]Field, interview.

[29]George Wallace, letter to the author, 11 Sept. 1991.

[30]Ibid.

[31]*Herald American* (Boston) 26 Jan. 1980.

[32]Bob Dingilian, *Martin Ritt, Director of "Norma Rae" Discusses Actors and Acting*, Twentieth Century Fox Publicity, n.d., 1979.

[33]Ibid.

[34]Ibid.

[35]"Cross Creek, Martin Ritt's New Film, is in some ways a Quintessential Ritt Picture," *American Film* Nov. 1983.

[36]Paul Wilner, *Herald Examiner* 8 Feb. 1981.

[37]Peter Gard Steven, *Hollywood's Depiction of the Working Class from 1970 to 1981*, Ph.D diss. (Evanston: Northwestern University, 1981) 209.

[38]Ibid.

[39]Crystal Lee Sutton, telephone interview, 21 June 1992.

[40]Goldfarb and Ilyashov, interview.

[41]Janis Cantwell, letter to Martin Ritt, 20 Apr. 1984, Herrick Library.

[42]Adams, "Ritt's Southern Films" 153.

[43]Ibid.

[44]Ibid.

[45]Gary P. Zieger and Robert H. Zieger, "Unions on the Silver Screen: A Review-Essay on F.I.S.T., Blue Collar, and Norma Rae, *Labor History* 23.1 (1982): 76.

[46]Ritt discusses this point, and others, in the interview he gave to Lyn Goldfarb and Anatoli Michael Ilyashov, a copy of which is at the Ritt household in Pacific Palisades, CA. Also, in reference to *Norma Rae*, he was again asked about his affinity to the South. He gave his usual answer that the essence of drama is change, and that the South was changing faster than the rest of the country. "The South still has remnants of feudal society. On a racial level though, I don't think it's any more bigoted than the North." The demarcations in reference to race were drawn more sharply in the South than in the North, but subtle racism—practiced widely in the North—was as abominable as racism in the South. See Paul Wilner, *The Herald Examiner* 8 Feb. 1981.

[47]Amalgamated Clothing and Textile Workers Union, letter to Martin Ritt, 7 Apr. 1980, Ritt household.

[48]International Union of United Auto, Aerospace and Agricultural Implements Workers of America, letter to Martin Ritt, 27 Mar. 1979, Herrick Library.

[49]Carolina Brown Lung Association, letter to Martin Ritt, 9 May 1979.

[50]Gene Mierzejwski, letter to Martin Ritt, 13 Apr. 1979, Herrick Library.

[51]Martin Ritt, letter to Gene Mierzejwski, 12 June 1979, Herrick Library.

[52]Judith Paget, letter to Martin Ritt, 16 May 1979, Herrick Library.

[53]Martin Ritt, letter to William H. Maness, 14 June 1979, Herrick Library.

[54]Martin Ritt, letter to William H. Maness, 23 July 1979, Herrick Library.

[55]*Variety* 18 Mar. 1980.

[56]Virginia Durr, letter to Martin Ritt, n.d., 1979, Herrick Library.

[57]Ibid. Durr told Ritt that she wished a movie could do for poor young blacks in the south what *Norma Rae* had done for poor young whites. There was, in 1979, a 60 percent unemployment rate among young blacks, and all Alabama could do was build more jails. "We are rotting from within and it is frightening to see a whole generation of young blacks destroyed and turned into criminals."

Ritt, who met Mrs. Durr while *Norma Rae* was being shot answered her on 10 Apr. 1979. "It is astonishing," he said, "to find a woman like you in Wetumpka, Alabama, but that will teach Yankees like us not to be so snobbish about the rest of the country."

[58]James L. Vickery, letter to Martin Ritt, n.d., July 1978, Herrick Library.

[59]For years the University of Montevallo was a women's college. It went co-ed in the late 1950s, and its name became Alabama College at Montevallo. The author taught history there in 1959-60. Its name was changed to the University of Montevallo sometime in the 1970s.

[60]Martin Ritt, letter to James L. Vickery, 24 July 1978, Herrick Library.

[61]John Randolph, letter to Martin Ritt, 18 Apr. 1979, Herrick Library.

[62]Kirk Douglas, letter to Martin Ritt, 25 Apr. 1980, Herrick Library.

[63]David Brown, letter to Martin Ritt, 27 July 1979, Herrick Library.

[64]Alfons Sinneger, letter to Martin Ritt, 8 June 1979.

[65]Ted Z. Danielevsky, letter to Martin Ritt, n.d., 1979, Herrick Library.

[66]Albert Maltz, letter to Martin Ritt, 18 Feb. 1979, Herrick Library.

[67]Martin Ritt, letter to Albert Maltz, 13 Mar. 1979, Herrick Library.

[68]Albert Maltz, letter to Martin Ritt, 5 Apr. 1981, Herrick Library.

[69]Crystal Lee Sutton, telephone interview, 21 June 1992.

[70]Martin Ritt, letter to Sidney E. Kohn, 27 Feb. 1978, Herrick Library.

[71]*The New York Times* 28 Apr. 1980.

[72]Ibid.

[73]Pat Aufderheide, "A Mensch for All Seasons," *In These Times* 16-22 Apr. 1980.

[74]*Palm Beach Post* 18 Apr. 1980.

[75]Pamela Woywad, telephone interview, 18 June 1992.

[76]Crystal Lee Sutton, interview, 22 June 1992.

[77]Ibid.

[78]Ibid.

[79]Woywad, interview, 18 June 1992.

[80]Aufderheide, "Mensch for All Seasons."

[81]Adele Ritt, telephone interview, 8 June 1992.

[82]Sutton, interview, 21 June 1992.

[83]*The Boston Globe* 13 Mar. 1979.

[84]Ibid.

[85]*The Seattle Times* 14 Mar. 1979.

[86]Archer Winsten, *New York Post* 2 Mar. 1979.

[87]Aljean Harmetz, *The New York Times* 25 Feb. 1979.

[88]Vincent Canby, *The New York Times* 2 Mar. 1979.

[89]Ibid.

[90]Vincent Canby, "Sally Field's 'Norma Rae' is A Triumph," *The New York Times* 11 Mar. 1979.

[91]*The Boston Herald American* 9 Mar. 1979.

[92]The *Soho Weekly News* 11 Mar. 1979.

[93]*Palm Beach Post* 18 Apr. 1980.

[94]Sutton, interview, 21 June 1992.

[95]Carl Foreman, telegram to Martin Ritt, Feb. 1980, Herrick Library.

[96]Joel Fluellen, telegram to Martin Ritt, Feb. 1980, Herrick Library.

[97]Irving Ravetch and Harriet Frank, Jr., telegram to Martin Ritt, Feb. 1980, Herrick Library.

[98]David Chasman, telegram to Martin Ritt, Feb. 1980, Herrick Library.

[99]Kirk Douglas, letter to Martin Ritt, 25 Apr. 1980, Herrick Library.

[100]Eric Roth, letter to Martin Ritt, 7 Feb. 1980, Herrick Library.

[101]Robert Lewis, interview, New York, 29 May 1992.

[102]Eli Wallach, interview, New York, 30 May 1992.

[103]Ravetch, interview, May 1991.

[104]Barry Irwin, letter to Martin Ritt, 19 Sept. 1980, Ritt household.

[105]Ibid.

[106]Martin Ritt, letter to Barry Irwin, 23 Dec. 1980, Ritt household.

[107]Ibid.

[108]Sally Field, telephone interview, Oct. 1991.

[109]*Variety* 6 June 1980.

[110]*The New York Times* 25 May 1979.

[111]Janet Maslin, *The New York Times* 29 Dec. 1979.

[112]Maslin, *The New York Times* 20 Dec. 1979.

[113]*The Greensborough Record* 11 May 1980.

[114]*Herald Examiner* 5 Aug. 1980.

[115]*The New York Times* 12 Oct. 1980. Sally received $650,000 for *Back Roads*.

[116]Ibid.

[117]*The Film and Videotape Production Magazine* Aug. 1980: 108-09. Tommy Lee Jones received $375,000 for *Back Roads*.

[118]Seth Cagin, *Soho News* 11 Mar. 1981.

[119]*The New York Times* 12 Oct. 1980.

[120]*The Film and Videotape Production Magazine* Aug. 1980: 108.

[121]Ibid.

[122]Ibid.

[123]Ibid.

[124]Donald March, letter to Ronald Shedlo, undated, Herrick Library.

[125]March, letter to Martin Ritt, 8 Oct. 1980, Herrick Library.

[126]Ibid.

[127]*St. Louis Globe Democrat* 5 Mar. 1981.

[128]*Newsweek* 16 Mar. 1981.

[129]Allan Burns, letter to Martin Ritt, 2 Apr. 1981, Herrick Library.

[130]Vincent Canby, *The New York Times* 13 Mar. 1980.

[131]Ibid.

[132]Elin Evans, *The New York Times* 24 May 1981.

[133]*Newsweek* 16 Mar. 1981.

[134]*Soho News* 11 Mar. 1981.

[135]Ibid.

[136]*Washington Post* 13 Mar. 1981.

[137]Ibid.

[138]Archer Winsten, *The New York Post* 13 Mar. 1981.

[139]Ibid.

[140]*Los Angeles Times* 13 Mar. 1981.

[141]Martin Ritt, letter to Joanna Crawford, 31 Mar. 1976, Herrick Library.

Chapter 9

[1]Dan Yakir, "A Special Way of Life," *Horizon* 26.7 (1983): 46.

[2]In a way Steenburgen's career as an actress had started the same way Rawlings's career as a novelist. She left her home in North Little Rock, Arkansas, at 19, headed for New York. Her leaving home "wasn't something I debated or talked to anybody about. I had to do it, so I did it" (Yakir, *Horizon* 46).

[3]*Los Angeles Times* 6 Oct. 1983.

[4]*Screen International* 16 May 1983.

[5]Mary Steenburgen, telephone interview, 11 June 1991. Another famous actress who corroborated Steenburgen's assessment of Ritt was Jane Fonda. She said that Martin Ritt "understood in

his guts the social factors that made people what they are. He had a broad understanding of people. He never played games. He always told you the truth. If he didn't like what you were doing, he said so straight out." Jane Fonda, telephone interview, 29 May 1991.

[6]Ibid.

[7]*Americana Film* 9 (Nov. 1983): 19.

[8]Ibid.

[9]Ibid.

[10]Yakir, *Horizon* 47.

[11]*Film Journal* 86.12 (28 Oct. 1983): 12.

[12]Stephen Farber, *The New York Times* 18 Sept. 1983.

[13]Yakir, *Horizon* 47.

[14]Janet Maslin, *The New York Times* 21 Sept. 1983.

[15]Ibid.

[16]Gene Shalit, NBC broadcast, 28 Sept. 1983.

[17]Gene Siskel, *The Chicago Tribune* 17 Apr. 1984.

[18]Roger Ebert, *The Chicago Sun Times* 17 Apr. 1984.

[19]*The Guardian* 10 May 1984.

[20]Ibid.

[21]*The Financial Times* 11 May 1984.

[22]*The Daily Mail* 11 May 1984, *Sunday Telegraph* 13 May 1984.

[23]*The Observer* 13 May 1984.

[24]Richard Barkley, *Sunday Express* 13 May 1984.

[25]Michael Ventura, *Los Angeles Weekly* 4-10 Nov. 1983. See also Judith Trojan, *Wilson Library Bulletin* Dec. 1983: 296.

[26]Philip French, *The Observer* 22 May 1983.

[27]*The Daily Telegraph* 18 May 1983.

[28]*The Hollywood Reporter* 14 June 1983.

[29]Dale Pollock, *The Atlanta Constitution* 7 Oct. 1983.

[30]*The Hollywood Reporter* 9 Mar. 1984.

[31]Marc Barnes, *Burlington* (NC) *Times-News* 3 May 1984.

[32]Ibid.

[33]See Nina Darnton, *The New York Times* 24 Mar. 1985. Also, see Hal Erickson, *Baseball in the Movies: A Comprehensive Reference 1915-1991* (Jefferson, NC: McFarland & Co., 1992) 271, 276.

[34]Janet Maslin, *The New York Times* 29 Mar. 1985.

[35]Ibid.

[36]Ibid.

[37]*People* 6 May 1985.

[38]Ibid.

[39]Neil Simon, telephone interview, 17 Sept. 1991.

[40]Ibid.

[41]*People* 6 May 1985.

[42]*Playboy* Mar. 1986.

[43]Stanley Kauffmann, *The New Republic* 194 (3 Mar. 1986): 9.

[44]See Thomas O'Connor, *The New York Times* 12 Jan. 1986.

[45]In Dec. 1990 a memorial service was held for Martin Ritt, where numerous of his friends and acquaintances eulogized him. James Garner said that he had known Ritt for over 30 years. Yet, he would not grant an interview to the author concerning Martin Ritt. He said through his agency, "I do not give quotes." He most assuredly does give quotes. See, for example, Ellen Hawkes, "Gentle Heart, Tough Guy," *Parade Magazine* 12 July 1992.

[46]Patrick Goldstein, *The Los Angeles Times* 25 Apr. 1985.

[47]Ibid.

[48]Don Stotter, *Miami Community Newspaper* 31 Jan. 1986.

[49]David Elliott, *The San Diego Union* 31 Jan. 1986.

[50]Marylynn Uricchio, *Pittsburgh Post Gazette* 31 Jan. 1986.

[51]Randy Myers, *The State Hornet* 29 Jan. 1986.

[52]Patrick Goldstein, *The Los Angeles Times* 25 Apr. 1985.

[53]Pat McGilligan, "Martin Ritt, interviewed," *Film Comment* 22 (Feb. 1986): 39.

[54]See Thomas O'Connor, "Martin Ritt: Human Relationships and Moral Choices Fuel His Movies," *The New York Times* 12 Jan. 1986. For further comments, also see Steve Johnson's article in *Entertainment* 29 Jan. 1986.

[55]No nudity was one of the movie's best features to *The Arkansas Democrat. Murphy's Romance*, it said, "accomplishes its task, without nudity, without gratuitous violence, and even without a villain." *The Arkansas Democrat* 31 Jan. 1986.

[56]Joe Leydon, *Houston Post* 31 Jan. 1986.

[57]*Calgary Sun* 31 Jan. 1986.

[58]*Entertainment Today* 24 Jan. 1986.

[59]Andrew Jefchak, *Grand Rapids Press* 31 Jan.1986.

[60]Bob Thomas, *The Press Democrat* 31 Jan. 1986.

[61]*The New Jersey Herald* 31 Jan. 1986.

[62]Philip Wuntch, *Dallas Morning News* 31 Jan. 1986.

[63]*Boxoffice Magazine* Feb. 1986.

[64]Paul Attanasio, *The Albuquerque Journal* 7 Feb. 1986.

[65]*The Muncie Evening Press* 6 Feb. 1986.

[66]Michael Burkett, *Westword* 29 Jan.-4 Feb. 1986.

[67]Marylynn Uricchio, *Pittsburgh Post Gazette* 31 Jan. 1986.

[68]Randy Myers, *The State Hornet* 29 Jan. 1986.

[69]Robert Denerstein, *The Cincinnati Post* 3 Feb. 1986.

[70]Robert W. Butler, *The Kansas City Star* 31 Jan. 1986.

[71]Lawrence O'Toole, *Maclean's* 30 Jan. 1986.

[72]David Ansen, *Newsweek* 27 Jan. 1986.

[73]Richard Schickel, *Time* 13 Jan. 1986.

[74]*Penthouse Magazine* 10 Nov. 1987. *Penthouse* referred to Ritt as "Marvin" Ritt.

[75]Norman Jewison, letter to the author, 7 Feb. 1992.

[76]Eli Wallach, interview, New York, 30 May 1992.

[77]Maureen Stapleton, telephone call to the author, Jan. 1992.

[78]*Maclean's* 100.48 (30 Nov. 1987): 66.

[79]Ibid.

[80]*Newsweek* 23 Nov. 1987.

[81]Ibid.

[82]Richard Corliss, *Time* 30 Nov. 1987.

[83]Stanley Kauffmann, *The New Republic* 197.24 (14 Dec. 1987): 23.

[84]Richard Corliss, *Time* 30 Nov. 1987.

[85]Janet Maslin, *The New York Times* 20 Nov. 1987.

[86]*Ft Lauderdale News/Sun Sentinel* 20 Nov. 1987.

[87]*Philadelphia Inquirer* 20 Nov. 1987.

[88]Noel Taylor, *The Ottawa Citizen* 20 Nov. 1987.

[89]Noel Gallagher, *The London Free Press* 24 Nov. 1987.

[90]Neil Hirsch, *New York Law Journal* 20 Nov. 1987.

[91]Ibid.

[92]Richard A. Blake, "Peanut," *America* 157.20 (26 Dec. 1987): 506.

[93]Ibid.

[94]Ibid.

[95]Stanley Kauffmann, *The New Republic* 197.24 (14 Dec. 1987): 24.

[96]Ibid.

[97]David Ansen, *Newsweek* 19 Feb. 1990.

[98]*Philadelphia Inquirer* 9 Feb. 1990.

[99]Ibid.

[100]Stanley Kauffmann, *The New Republic* 202.9 (26 Feb. 1990): 26-27.

[101]For details, see the *Union-News* (Springfield, MA) 8 Feb. 1988.

[102]Ralph Novak, *People's Weekly* 33 (19 Feb. 1990): 13.

[103]David Ansen, *Newsweek* 19 Feb. 1990.

[104]Peter Travers, "An All-Star Sermonette," *Rolling Stone* 22 Feb. 1990.

[105]*Variety* 31 Jan. 1990.

[106]Jane Fonda, telephone interview, 29 May 1991.

[107]Ibid.

[108]Bill Hagan, *San Diego Tribune* 9 Feb. 1990.

[109]Ibid.

[110]Vincent Canby, *The New York Times* 9 Feb. 1990.

[111]Ibid.

[112]Peter Goddard, *Toronto Star* 8 Feb. 1990.

[113]*Philadelphia Inquirer* 9 Feb. 1990.

[114]Ibid.

[115]Monte Williams, "'Stanley & Iris' Draws Attention to Plight of Illiterate," *The Hartford Courant* 16 Feb. 1990.

[116]Ibid.

[117]*New York Observer* 19 Feb. 1990.

[118]*New York* 19 Feb. 1990. Also, see Pamela Young, "The ABCs of Love," *Maclean's* 19 Feb. 1990.

[119]Adele Ritt, letter to Richard Glickstein, 25 July 1989, Ritt household.

[120]Ravetch, interview.

[121]Joanne Woodward, interview, 3 June 1991.

[122]Ibid.

[123]Paul Newman, letter to Martin Ritt, 12 Sept. 1990.

[124]Martin Ritt, letter to Paul Newman, 24 Sept. 1990, Ritt household.

[125]Mary Steenburgen, interview.

[126]Bernstein also wrote this opinion of Ritt in "Martin Ritt: A Remembrance," *DGA News* Mar.-Apr. 1991: 19.

[127]Ibid.

[128]Ibid.

Chapter 10

[1]*Chicago Tribune* 2 Sept. 1973.

[2]Jack Hirschberg, interview of Martin Ritt, Ritt residence, Sept. 1969.

[3]Martin Ritt, interview by Walter Burrell, Ritt household, 12 June 1973.

[4]Claude Gauterur, "Questionnaire for the Jewish Condition in the Cinema" 30 Dec. 1968.

[5]Ibid.

[6]*Chicago Tribune* 2 Sept. 1973.

[7]Ibid.

[8]*Los Angeles Times* 11 Oct. 1967.

[9]Ibid.

[10]Ibid.

[11]Ibid.

[12]Ibid.

[13]Hirschberg, interview.

[14]Ibid.

[15]Ibid.

[16]For more information on the declines of the star system and studios, see Carlton Jackson, *Hattie: The Life of Hattie McDaniel* (Madison Books: Lanham, MD, 1990).

[17]Peter Gard Steven, *Hollywood's Depiction of the Working-Class from 1970 to 1981: A Marxist Analysis*, Ph.D diss., Northwestern University, Aug. 1982.

[18]Hirschberg, interview.

[19]Lyn Goldfarb and Anatoli Ilyashov, interview of Martin Ritt, Ritt household, 11 Sept. 1985.

[20]Julian Claman, unpublished article, Ritt household.

[21]Ibid.

[22]Goldfarb and Ilyashov, interview.

[23]Hirschberg, interview.

[24]Ibid.

[25]Ibid.

[26]David O. Thomas, letter to Martin Ritt, 4 Dec. 1990, Ritt household.

[27]Goldfarb and Ilyashov, interview.

[28]Ibid.

[29]Ibid.

[30]G.R., letter to Martin Ritt, Sept. 1980, Ritt household.

[31]Martin Ritt, letter to G.R., 23 Sept. 1980, Ritt household.

[32]J.W.L., letter to Martin Ritt, 18 Mar. 1977, Ritt household.

[33]Martin Ritt, letter to J.W.L., 7 Apr. 1977, Ritt household.

[34]Tina Ritt, interview, Pacific Palisades, CA, 11 May 1991.

[35]Ibid.

[36]Ibid.

[37]Tina Ritt, letter to Martin and Adele Ritt, 27 Sept. 1982, Ritt household.

[38]Tina Ritt, letter to Martin and Adele Ritt, 1 Jan. 1989, Ritt household.

[39]Michael Ritt, telephone interview, 16 Aug. 1992.

[40]Ibid.

[41]Ibid.

[42]Ibid.

[43]Claman article.

[44]Ibid.

[45]Walter Bernstein, "Martin Ritt: A Remembrance," *DGA News* Mar.-Apr. 1991: 19.

Bibliography

Manuscripts

Latham, Walter, diary, 1966.

Ritt Collection, Margaret Herrick Library; Academy of Motion Picture Arts and Sciences, Beverly Hills, CA.

Ritt Collection, Ritt household, Pacific Palisades, CA.

Reports and Government Documents

Clark, Joseph F. *Congressional Record* 90th Cong., 2nd sess. (18 Apr. 1968): 10015.

Congressional Record 92nd Cong., 2nd sess. (16-18 Oct. 1972): 37,628.

____. 93rd Cong., 1st sess. (7-14 Mar. 1973): 6,904.

____. 93rd Cong., 1st sess. (15-22 Mar. 1973): 8,020.

Federal Bureau of Investigation Report on Martin Ritt, 6 Nov. 1952.

Federal Bureau of Investigation Report on Martin Ritt, 20 Oct. 1953.

Federal Bureau of Investigation Report on Martin Ritt, 2 Dec. 1964.

House Un-American Activities *Report* No. 2516, 82nd Cong., 2nd sess. (3 Jan. 1952).

Interviews

By the author

Alonzo, John A., Los Angeles, 9 May 1991.

Bernstein, Walter, New York, 28 May 1992.

Field, Sally, telephone, Oct. 1991.

Fonda, Jane, telephone, 29 May 1991.

Frank, Harriet, Jr., Los Angeles, 11 May 1991.

Holmes, Charles, and Edith Holmes, telephone, 18 Apr. 1994.

Latham, Walter "Firpo," telephone, 21 Aug. 1991.

Leachman, Cloris, telephone, 13 Apr. 1991.

Lewis, Robert, New York, 29 May 1992.

Malden, Karl, Beverly Hills, CA, 11 May 1991.

Mancini, Henry, telephone, 27 Jan. 1992.

Newman, Paul, Westport, CT, 3 June 1991.

Radnitz, Robert, telephone, Sept. 1991.

Ravetch, Irving, Los Angeles, CA, 11 May 1991.

Remick, Lee, Los Angeles, 16 May 1991.

Ritt, Adele, Pacific Palisades, 8 May 1991.
Ritt, Michael, telephone, 16 Aug. 1992.
Ritt, Tina, Pacific Palisades, CA, 11 May 1991.
Rubensohn, Herbert, New York, 26 May 1992.
Simon, Neil, telephone, 17 Sept. 1991.
Stapleton, Maureen, telephone, Jan. 1992.
Steenburgen, Mary, telephone, 11 June 1991.
Sutton, Crystal Lee, telephone, 21 June 1992.
Wallace, Mike, telephone, 9 Sept. 1991.
Wallach, Eli, New York, 30 May 1992.
Woodward, Joanne, Westport, CT, 3 June 1991.
Woywad, Pamela, telephone, 18 June 1992.

Other
Matthau, Walter, interview by Matthew Jackson, 11 Feb. 1992.
Ritt, Martin, interview by Walter Burrell, Ritt household, n.d.
Ritt, Martin, interview by Lyn Goldfarb and Anatoli Ilyashov, Burbank, CA, 11 Sept. 1985.
Ritt, Martin, interview by Jack Hirschberg, Ritt residence, Sept. 1969.
Ritt, Martin, interview by Jay Williams, Boston University Archives, n.d.

Letters to the author from:
Arnowitz, Jerome, Jr., 11 June 1991.
Carter, Jimmy, President, June 1991.
Cronyn, Hume, n.d., 1992.
Dee, Ruby, 5 June 1991.
Jewison, Norman, 7 Feb. 1992.
Le Carré, John, 20 Mar. 1991.
Miller, Arthur, n.d., 1991.
Neal, Patricia, Fall 1991.
Quinn, Anthony, 11 Oct. 1991.
Quivey, James, 18 June 1992.
Schlesinger, Arthur, Jr., 8 July 1991.
Wallace, George C., 11 Sept. 1991.

Radio and TV Programs
"American Masters, Broadway Dreamers; The Legacy of the Group Theater." New York: WNET, 18 Jan. 1989.
Hollywood on Trial. Film Documentary, 1977.

Books and Dissertations

The American Film Institute Seminar, Part I. The New York Times Oral History Program. Glen Rock, NJ: Microfilming Corporation of America, 1977.

Belfrage, Cedric. *The American Inquisition, 1945-1960.* Indianapolis: Bobbs-Merrill, 1973.

Bentley, Eric. *Thirty Years of Treason: Excerpts from Hearings Before the House Committee on Un-American Activities 1938-1968.* New York: Viking, 1971.

Brady, Frank. *Citizen Welles: A Biography of Orson Welles.* New York: Charles Scribners' Sons, 1989.

Broehl, Wayne, Jr. *The Molly Maguires.* Cambridge: Harvard UP, 1965.

Clurman, Harold. *The Fervent Years: The Story of the Group Theater and the Thirties.* New York: Hill and Wang, 1957.

Coute, David. *The Great Fear: The Anti-Communist Purge Under Truman and Eisenhower.* New York: Simon and Schuster, 1978.

Cunningham, Frank R. *Sidney Lumet: Film and Literary Vision.* Lexington: UP of Kentucky, 1992.

Current Biography. 1979.

Erickson, Hal. *Baseball in the Movies: A Comprehensive Reference 1915-1991.* Jefferson, NC: McFarland, 1992.

Fried, Richard M. *Nightmare in Red: The McCarthy Era in Perspective.* New York: Oxford UP, 1990.

Hellman, Lillian. *Scoundrel Time.* Boston: Little, Brown, 1976.

Jackson, Carlton. *The Dreadful Month.* Bowling Green, OH: Bowling Green State University Popular Press, 1982.

____. *Hattie: The Life of Hattie McDaniel.* Lanham, MD: Madison, 1990.

____. *Zane Grey.* 1973. Boston: Twayne, 1989.

Jacobs, Lea. *The Wages of Sin: Censorship and The Fallen Woman Film 1928-1942.* Madison: U of Wisconsin P, 1991.

Kazan, Elia. *A Life.* New York: Alfred A. Knopf, 1988.

Keyser, Les, and Barbara Keyser. *Hollywood and the Catholic Church: The Image of Roman Catholicism in American Movies.* Chicago: Loyola UP, 1984.

Leifermann, Henry P. *Crystal Lee, A Woman of Inheritance.* New York: Macmillan, 1975.

Maland, Charles J. *Frank Capra.* Boston: Twayne, 1980.

Masters, Dexter. *The Accident.* London: Penguin, 1985.

McClintick, David. *Indecent Exposure.* New York: William Morrow, 1982.

Miller, Merle. *The Judges and the Judged.* New York: Doubleday, 1952.

Monaco, Paul. *Ribbons in Time: Movies and Society Since 1945.* Bloomington and Indianapolis: Indiana UP, 1988.

Morella, Joe, and Edward Z. Epstein. *Paul and Joanne: A Biography of Paul Newman and Joanne Woodward.* New York: Delacorte, 1988.

O'Brien, Tom. *The Screening of America.* New York: Continuum, 1990.

Rayback, Joseph P. *A History of American Labor.* New York: Free Press, 1961.

Red Channels: The Report of Communist Influence in Radio and Television. New York: Counterattack, The Newsletter of Facts to Combat Communism, 1950.

Sharrett, Christopher, ed. *Crisis Cinema: The Apocalyptic Idea in Postmodern Narrative Film.* Washington, DC, Maisonneuve, 1993.

Sonnichen, C.L. *From Hopalong to Hud: Thoughts on Western Fiction.* College Station: Texas A & M, 1978.

Steven, Peter Gard. *Hollywood's Depiction of the Working Class From 1970 to 1981.* Ph.D diss., Northwestern U, 1987.

Whitaker, Sheila. *The Films of Martin Ritt.* London: British Film Institute, 1972.

Magazine and Periodical Articles

Action. "Martin Ritt: Conversation." 1 Mar./Apr. 1971: 28-29.

Adams, Michael. "How Come Everybody Down Here Has Three Names? Martin Ritt's Southern Films." *Southern Quarterly* 19.3-4 (Spring-Summer 1981): 143-55.

America 111.533 (Oct. 1964): 533-34.

American Film 7 (Nov. 1981): 20-22, 9 (Nov. 1983): 19-20.

Anderson, Lindsay. "Ten Feet Tall." *Sight and Sound* 22 (Summer 1957): 34-37.

Aufderheide, Pat. "A Mensch for All Seasons." *In These Times* Apr. 1980: 16-20.

Boxoffice Magazine Feb. 1986: 41.

Burkett, Michael. *Westword* 29 Jan.-4 Feb. 1986: 38.

DGA News Mar.-Apr. 1991: 19-20.

Ellero, Roberto. "Martin Ritt." *Castoro Cinema: La Nouva Italia* Marzo-Aprile 1989: 12, 25.

Field, Sydney, "Outrage: A Print 'Documentary' on Hollywood Film-Making." *Film Quarterly* 18.3 (Spring 1965): 38-50.

Film Journal 86.12 (28 Oct. 1983): 12.

The Film and Videotape Production Magazine Aug. 1980: 108-09.

Godfrey, Lionel, "TALL When They's Small: The Films of Martin Ritt As Seen by Lionel Godfrey *Films and Filming* 14.11 (Aug. 1968): 42-48.

Hartnett, Vincent, "Rascalry on the Airwaves." *Catholic World* 171 (July 1950): 166-80.

Hartung, Philip T. *The Commonweal* 81 (23 Oct. 1964): 136-45.

Hey, Kenneth R. "Ambivalence as a Theme in *On The Waterfront* (1954): An Interdisciplinary Approach to Film Study." *Hollywood As Historian: American Film in a Cultural Context.* Ed. Peter Rollins. Lexington: UP of Kentucky, 1983: 159-89.

Iconoclast 5-12 Apr. 1974: 30.

Kael, Pauline. "The Current Cinema." *The New Yorker* 8 June 1963: 8-9, 25 Jan. 1969: 97-98, 7 Feb. 1970: 99-100, 17 Oct. 1970: 109.

____. "Soul Food." *The New Yorker* 30 Sept. 1972: 109-11.

Kasindorf, Jeannie. "The Incredible Past of David Begelman." *New West* 13 Feb. 1978: 19-24.

Kauffmann, Stanley. *The New Republic* 3 Mar. 1986: 9-10, 14 Dec. 1987: 23-24, 26 Feb. 1990: 9-10.

Kazan, Elia. "Where I Stand." *Reader's Digest* 61 (July 1952): 45-46.

Macleans 30 Jan. 1986: 20, 19 Feb. 1990: 52.

McGilligan, Pat. "Ritt Large: Martin Ritt Interviewed." *Film Comment* 22 (Feb. 1986): 43, 45.

McVay, Douglas. "The Best and Worst of Martin Ritt." *Films and Filming* Dec. 1964: 44, 50.

Moss, Carlton. "The Great White Hope." *Freedomways* 2nd qtr. 1969: 128-35.

New York Law Journal 20 Nov. 1987: 51-70.

Newsweek 2 Oct. 1961, 2 Oct. 1972, 27 Mar. 1978, 16 Mar. 1981, 27 Jan. 1986, 19 Feb. 1990.

Penthouse Magazine 10 Nov. 1987: 48.

People 6 May 1985: 45.

People's Weekly 19 Feb. 1990: 20-25.

Playboy Mar. 1986: 52.

Rickey, Carrie. "The Long Hot Career." *Fame* Winter 1990: 34-38.

Rolling Stone 22 (Feb. 1990): 20-25.

Ross, Neil. *Today's Cinema* 6 Jan. 1970: 15.

The Saturday Review 25 May 1963, 15 May 1976, 2 Oct. 1976.

Short Film Reviews Nov. 1972: 10.

Time 16 Mar. 1959, 19 Oct. 1970, 13 Jan. 1986.

Variety 4 Mar. 1959, 6 Apr. 1960, 9 Oct. 1970, 9 Sept. 1976, 31 Jan. 1990.

Whitman, David, "The Great Sharecropping Success Story." *The Public Interest* 104 (Summer 1991): 3-19.

Yakir, Dan. "A Special Way of Life." *Horizon* 26.7 (1983): 46-60.

Young, Colin. "The Hollywood War of Independence." *Film Quarterly* Spring 1959: 4-22.

Zieger, Gay B., and Robert H. Zieger. "Unions on the Silver Screen: A Review-Essay on F.I.S.T., Blue Collar, and Norma Rae." *Labor History* 23.1 (1982): 67-78.

Newspapers

Albuquerque Journal 1986.
Arizona Republic 1973.
Arkansas Democrat 1986.
Atlanta Constitution 1983.
Bethel Herald (NC) 1966.
Boston Globe 1972, 1979.
Boston Herald-American 1979.
Boston Herald-Traveler 1970.
Boston Phoenix 1976.
Boston Record-American 1968.
Boston Sunday Globe 1967, 1974.
Boston Traveler 1965.
Buffalo Courier-Express 1979.
Burlington Daily Times (NC) 1966.
Burlington Times-News (NC) 1984.
Calgary Sun 1986.
Chicago Daily News 1967, 1972.
Chicago Sun-Times 1970, 1984.
Chicago Tribune 1967, 1970, 1973, 1974, 1984.
Christian Science Monitor 1966, 1970, 1972, 1976, 1978.
Cincinnati Enquirer 1968.
Cincinnati Post 1986.
Daily Express (England) 1973.
Daily Mail (London) 1984.
Daily Mirror (London) 1973.
Daily Reflector (Greenville, NC) 1966.
Daily Telegraph (London) 1973, 1984.
Daily Utah Chronicle 1972.
Daily Worker 1966.
Daily World (New York) 1970.
Dallas Morning News 1969, 1986.
Dallas Times Herald 1969.
Detroit Free Press 1972.
Entertainment Today 1986.
Evening Standard (London) 1972.
Evening Star and Daily News 1972.
Films Illustrated (London) 1976.
Financial Times (London) 1973, 1984.
Ft. Lauderdale News/Sentinel 1987.
Fort Worth Star Telegram 1976.
Globe and Mail (Canada) 1967.
Grand Rapids Press 1986.
Greensborough Record 1980.
Guardian (England) 1966, 1972, 1984.

Hartford Courant 1990.
Hollywood Reporter 1959, 1972.
Houston Chronicle 1965.
Houston Post 1986.
Jackson Daily News (MS) 1959.
Kansas City Star 1986.
Knoxville Journal 1979.
London Free Press 1987.
Los Angeles Herald Examiner 1967, 1973, 1976.
Los Angeles Times 1964, 1966, 1972, 1973, 1974, 1983, 1986.
Los Angeles Weekly 1983.
Memphis Press-Scimitar 1974.
Miami Community Newspaper 1986.
Minneapolis Tribune 1972.
Minnesota Daily 1972.
Muncie Evening Press (IN) 1986.
National Observer 1972, 1984.
New Jersey Herald 1986.
New Statesman 1967.
New York Daily News, 1959.
New York Herald-Examiner 1980, 1981.
New York Herald Tribune 1958, 1963, 1965.
New York Mirror 1963.
New York Observer 1990.
New York Post 1959, 1964, 1976, 1979.
New York Sunday News 1972, 1976.
New York Times 1914, 1946-47, 1950, 1958, 1964, 1966, 1969,
    1972, 1974, 1975, 1976, 1977, 1978, 1979, 1980-86.
New York World Telegram and Sun 1959.
News and Observer (Raleigh, NC) 1966.
Oregonian 1969.
Ottawa Citizen 1987.
Palm Beach Post 1980.
Philadelphia Daily News 1972.
Philadelphia Daily Planet 1972.
Philadelphia Inquirer 1970, 1972, 1987, 1990.
Pittsburgh Post-Gazette 1986.
Pittsburgh Press 1970.
Pottsville (PA) *Republican* 1968.
Press Democrat 1986.
St. Louis Globe-Democrat 1981.
Salt Lake City Tribune 1972.
San Diego Tribune 1990.
San Diego Union 1986.
San Francisco Chronicle 1970.

San Francisco Examiner 1970.
San Francisco Sunday Examiner and Chronicle 1972.
Seattle Times 1979.
Soho Weekly News 1979.
Southern Jewish Weekly 1963.
State Hornet 1986.
State Times (Jackson, MS) 1959.
Sunday Express (London) 1963, 1984.
Sunday News (London) 1972.
Sunday Times (London) 1957, 1966, 1968.
Times Picayune 1976.
Toronto Daily Star 1965.
Toronto Globe 1967.
Toronto Globe and Mail 1972.
Toronto Star 1990.
Twin City Courier 1972.
Union-News (Springfield, MA) 1988.
Washington Post 1965, 1981.
Washington Star 1979.
Washington Star-News 1974.
Wilson Library Bulletin 1983.
Windsor Star 1972.

Index